I0765175

THE LIMITS OF KNOWLEDGE

PAUL O'HARA

To order additional copies of this book, contact:
Xlibris
1-800-455-039
www.Xlibris.com.au
Orders@Xlibris.com.au
793198

Contents

Introduction

Since the dawn of time, philosophers have found themselves divided over the question concerning the source of our knowledge—is this something that springs from our senses or is this something that springs from our minds? Plato painted the picture of a supersensible world aloof from the shadowy quagmire of our everyday lives. Democritus, unlike Aristotle, believed that matter was composed of particles that he called atoms. For a whilst, and during the Middle Ages, it appeared that the Aristotelian approach had gained the upper hand. Scholars such as St Thomas Aquinas, Suarez and St Anselm rigorously debated the questions concerning 'accident' and 'essence', 'body' and 'soul' and 'quality' and 'quantity'. Due to the influence of thinkers such as Descartes however and the monumental achievements of Newton, by the eighteenth century and well and truly by the nineteenth century, there was a definite change in the air. Today, and in the twenty-first century, our world is dominated by the scientific point of view. *Design* has become a dirty word the *Critique of Judgement* has become an idle curiosity. But the question still remains—in what sense is knowledge the product of our minds just as much as it is of our ability to organize and regulate that world in which we live?

We begin our journey in an Aristotelian spirit by reaffirming some of the stock concepts that have become part of our everyday vocabulary: the relation between matter and form, actuality and potentiality, unity and multiplicity, but of course, also making them conformable to our present state of knowledge. The first five chapters are especially important, since they lay the groundwork for much that follows or at least underpin many of the topics later taken up for discussion. At this point however, a word of warning may be in order. Some of the terms that appear in these early chapters are not, it is true, the sorts of things you are likely to find in contemporary literature (viz. specific and numerical identity, immanent and final causality) that is, the stock in trade for medieval thinkers. The point however is that they can be very useful in providing the context or the setting from which our enquiries proceed, especially in the case of individuation. Philosophy it must be remembered was not invented yesterday (even if linguistic analysis was) and we need, to some extent, to acknowledge the achievements of those who have come before us.

Woven into this general fabric, there are discussions about more traditional problems, e.g. the problem of universals and something of more recent interest, the analytic-synthetic distinction. With respect to the latter, there are two issues we are concerned with: (*a*) whether this supports a kind of psychologism and (*b*) whether there is any genuine knowledge that could be described as synthetic *a priori*. So far as it concerns the first, a case could be made for saying that a judgement is not the same as a proposition, or at least that it is a mental construct, whereas a proposition is both a composite (in terms of nouns and verbs) and what is real (or at least what corresponds to what is real). With respect to the second, the question could be asked why there are not propositions both analytic and *a posteriori*, which tends to fuel our suspicion that this is not something genuine but rather spurious in and of itself.

A central issue that we need to address is what we mean by causality. With the rise of science our understanding of this has undergone a considerable change, partly because at the microcosmic level, it is clear how much is owed to chance and how little is owed to design. Even at the level of the macrocosmic, causality must be understood not in a way that makes it dynamic but rather in a way that makes it efficient. Compare and contrast how a scientist might regard this with Kant's quite casual approach in the *Critique of Judgement*. For instance, in what sense is the possible income to be derived from the rent on a house the cause of its construction in the first place? This is only to speculate on something and for which there is no clear evidence whatsoever. In the sense that one tree generates another does that mean it also generates it as a species, or that the species is responsible for the tree just as the tree is responsible for the species? It seems this is utterly preposterous, otherwise we would not be able to say that it is a seedling that is responsible for a tree.

As a general observation, the logical content of this work could be said to be something that spans a wide divide, but there is no suggestion that what we are doing here is in any way precise or methodological. (Or at least that is outside a broadly metaphysical approach) Certainly we deal at length with the basic laws of thought, but that it is only to indicate the kind of restraints that *must* be placed on the way we think and deliberate. Our treatment of the law of identity is perhaps a little novel—not being of a monistic cast of mind, I have opted for something called the 'identity of coefficients' to encapsulate the meaning of unity in the face of a world that is essentially quite diverse. For the most part however, we canvass the work of a wide variety of logicians without supporting any particular approach.

One of the chief characteristics that needs to be noted is the more dynamical approach that we taken to the question of space. In 'Homogeneity and Heterogeneity', it is important to note the way that space is conceived of is not as an addendum to matter, but rather as a substance in and of itself. I say 'substance', but what I really mean is something self-sustaining. This is reflected in the fact that we always treat space and matter as if what they embodied were reciprocal properties and, thus in a sense, are but one and the same. Of course, it is true that space and matter are not coordinated in the same way as are space and time, but the intuitive idea is that they should at least be some latitude in the way we might think of the former. Thus, material parts are conjunctive with cavernous parts; the puncturing of space is conjunctive with the puncturing of matter; a proper whole as a scattered whole is conjunctive with a proper part as a solid part, etc. And although this may seem a little odd, it does enable us to develop certain ideas in a way that is consonant with our overall aims. The way we treat the meaning of a 'proper whole' also has implications for the meaning of a part that is either exclusive or inclusive. Since the whole is not really an undifferentiated whole, there will be a double meaning for what is inclusive or exclusive in itself. That is, it will depend on whether we are talking about an inclusive or exclusive part of space (that is, the 'whole' of space or a hole in space) or an inclusive or exclusive part of matter (that is, the whole as the sum of its parts). Where space is concerned, what we start with is something necessarily *inclusive*. Where matter is concerned, what we start with is something necessarily *exclusive*. This needs to be kept in mind in our treatment, for instance, of a compound judgement.

Something else that we need to to address is the relation between organisms and mechanisms. Given that we are living in a post-Darwinian age, it behooves us to give a more credible account of the way the earth was formed, in both a geological and an ecological sense. Since earliest times, philosophers have been somewhat remiss in this regard, preferring a set of assumptions to any active or constant seeking after facts. Invariably this account begins with an 'act of God' or some 'creative essence' and then moves on to a description of man as the image or the embodiment of His Maker. This in turn leads on to a spurious kind of causality and the belief that in order to be vital something must also be the cause and effect of itself, hence both 'immanent' and 'final' causality. We have attempted to debunk this by suggesting that versatility concerns both the obsolescence of any part in relation to the durability of any whole and the obsolescence of any whole in relation to the durability of any part. And so, in our chapter on personal identity, we have endeavoured to make clear that the identity of any person is not the same as the identity of any particular thing. It has often been said that the identity of anything concerns its persistence throughout space and time and that if you can map the coordinates of an object as it moves from place to place, then undoubtedly you would have to consider it as what is one and the same. But there is a problem about this so far as it concerns the question of personal identity, since consciousness may sometimes be skewed in one direction and sometimes be skewed in another. So far as time is concerned, the impressions we form of ourselves may be altogether clear and distinct, our memories may well remind us of who we were and what we have become. But this may be altogether different so far as it concerns the space that we occupy, or at least, the particles of matter that through their movement coalesce to form us as we are. A cripple who is confined to a wheelchair would hardly be aware of how the parts were vitally connected to any singular whole. Hence his consciousness of what he is in one respect may well be very different from what it was in any other. He may indeed have an active and vibrant memory, but we would not say on that account he had an active and energetic life.

The chapter called 'Creation, Destruction and Formation' is an attempt to provide a reasonably cogent account, within limitations, of the relation between these primitive and primordial forces, paying particular attention to the way that destruction may be viewed in both a transitional and ultimate sense. Traditionally philosophers have been reluctant to deal with the issue of disorder and decay, largely because of their desire to keep the world in a tidy and manageable state, that is, as they would wish it to be but not as it really is. The idea that everything persists in its own being and that there can be no discernible conflict from without, is a common theme amongst seventeenth-century thinkers, and it appears that Darwin could see something in nature they were not the least bit aware of. This is especially so in the case of Spinoza, whose seamless system is completely impervious to any elements not in keeping with the general design. What I have attempted to do here, if only in a small way, is rectify this appalling omission.

The last chapter concerns one of the perennial questions of philosophy, the meaning of a universal soul or the meaning of a universal spirit. We take Leibniz' classic essay called 'Reflections on the Doctrine of a Single Universal Spirit' (1702) as our starting point and then incorporate within this a range of elements both ancient and modern (e.g. the

Platonic conception of a supersensible realm and the Jungian conception of a collective unconscious). For Leibniz although the soul is different from the body, it always retains within it certain material organs, which in turn supports its connection with what is preformed and what is post-formed, or what is dormant and yet not gone. The belief that physical existents are born and die is merely an illusion, since what we understand by birth is really only a kind of augmentation and what we understand by death is really only a kind of diminution. For our own part, we have taken the view that a universal spirit can only be conceived of as a certain kind of individuality and that what the 'self' is in its universal guise is ultimately only what the 'self' is in its more concrete expression.

Chapter 1

Matter and Form

In addressing the issue at hand, the relation between matter and form, we do not do so on the assumption they may be compared in any strict or unconditional way. Nor do we do so on the assumption of any gradation or hierarchy of being. What is, quite simply is, and what is not, quite simply is not. What we can discern through our senses exists in a purely concrete or corporeal way. What we can discern through the mind or imagination exists in a purely chimerical or incorporeal way. Thus, what we would suggest is that form may be prior to matter or that matter may be prior to form, but not that the one is conditional upon the other or the *cause* of the other in any way that is altogether fixed. Form appears in the absence of matter and matter appears in the absence of form, but also in the case of the latter, under the species of quality, quantity and kind. Thus, in absolute terms we might describe matter as what is determinate or indeterminate and form as what is embodied or disembodied, although of course we are more likely to connect what is concrete with what is determinate and what is ideal with that which is less so.

Let us consider in the first place what we might mean when we say it is form that is prior to matter. There is the kind of matter that may be impressed or imposed on, as for instance when a piece of wax becomes a seal, a piece of clay becomes a brick or a piece of bronze becomes a statue. These are good examples of what might be termed *ideal form*, because the matter is inert and different influences may be brought to bear to shape it from without. Such may also be described as a versatile whole, since we have a definite product, but in conjunction with a somewhat nebulous background or base. Another illustration is when we have what could be called an *elemental form*, when the form is derived exclusively from a part but expressed in the manner of what is whole. We might consider the properties of something such as fire or water, where there is a constant state of flux but some degree of cohesion nonetheless. What we mean by an *extensive* whole is something that can undergo a change in its parts, but which retains the same basic shape, as in the case of a river or a plastic cast. On the other hand, when we consider how or in what sense it is matter that supersedes form, then this occurs when there is more complexity in the relation between whole and part. That is, when the parts are articulated, when the parts can be separated, or when there is diversity in their function or use. If the parts can in any sense be said to be self-existent or if a whole can be assembled from them, then it is the whole that is possible and the parts that are real. We can see this in the case of both artificial and living things. Certainly a living thing does not have appendages which we can remove and replace (or at least not easily), nor can it ever be reconstituted as a whole, but there is nonetheless, a certain wherewithal in each of its parts, and this should not be confounded with the meaning of the whole or at least a whole that is dependent upon all its parts. Thus, what we have in both instances could be described as something heterogeneous in its kind.

So far however as it concerns the relation between any object and its motive force, of what is indispensable and what is not, then in no way would we consider that there is any strict precedence in respect to one another. Matter is neither indispensable to form nor form to matter, and there is no 'actuality' in the one or 'potentiality' in the other, if what this implies is that the one is only cognizable through and in conjunction with the other. Since, as we shall later argue, the basis for creation is inexplicable, there is no more a being as the cause of what-is than there is a being as the consequence of what-was. We can only conceive of potentiality in either of two respects: first, where it concerns a change in quality, quantity or relation, and secondly, where something has the potential to desist altogether, or at least, that what waxes and wanes, what grows and diminishes, must ultimately take leave of such changes as well. What we mean by actuality on the other hand, or the reality and necessity of being, requires a somewhat different approach, and this we might pursue in terms of the difference between essence and existence.

If you take the view that all the things that occupy a world must be altogether different, then what is adventitious in one respect may yet be quite essential in another. That is, if what we mean by a subject is just this particular set of attributes, then what is proper to the individual will be incidental to any species, and what is proper to any species will be incidental to any member. Here we can see that it is numerical identity that is subordinate to specific identity, since although the number of such things may be illimitable, the classes or groupings that divide them must remain constant throughout. On the other hand, we might take a different viewpoint to this and argue that it is really specific identity which is contingent upon numerical identity. To the extent that a class or a species is exclusive of any coordinate group, one might suppose that its members are too, and that for each type will there be just one member that is exclusive to that type. The implication here is that although all the attributes of a species are not common to the genus, separate species may yet be linked through their differentiae, so that where there is a greater diversity in number this will also be mirrored by a greater diversity in detail. On the other hand, what this assumes is that the differentiae can be added to the genus, which, if it were true, would enable us to generate different individuals merely through the discernment of some minimal difference in the kinds of things which they are.

The concept that we have of a living organism, or at least at the highest level, is that it is a composite of two things: what is purely physical on the one hand and what is purely mental on the other. What we mean by the mind is what is rudimentary in both its operation and its *esse*, and by the body, an empty vessel in the hands of such a power, what can be acted on but cannot be active in and of itself. The body, and the organs that belong to it, may respond to outside influences, but it is the mind that has its own source of change (the will) and its own source of identity (the imagination). And so, if there is a reflexive sense of who and what we are, there can also be a reflexive sense of what we can and cannot do, or at least, not only what exists apart from us but also what is *causative* in and of itself. Since we know who we are and are aware of our surroundings, then so also do we know when we are mobile, and that by a discernible change do we mean not just the interaction of purely physical things. What we mean by volition or the will is consistent with the view that our 'doing' must proceed from within, not without, and that we have just as keen an awareness of desire as we do something altogether requisite for the attainment of any end. We tend to think that a watch or a radio for instance, will continue to operate so long as there is a battery to sustain it, but that in living organisms what pervades them is both self-sustaining and self-restoring - that it does not arise from without, but rather from within. Thus, we tend to connect the idea of what *becomes* with the idea of what just *is*, and just as we connect the instrument with its maker so is it self-scrutiny on the one hand that mirrors our aspirations and ideals on the other.

In order to address the question then of how something may be regarded as a 'cause in itself', or the cause of its very most being, we need to distinguish between two very different kinds of causality: what on the one hand could be called *efficient* and what on the other hand could be called *immanent*. Where it concerns the idea of efficient causality, we need to consider the relation between an instrument and its end, that is, in what the act terminates but not necessarily from whence it proceeds. We need only know the basis for what does what to what, not the *reason* that something is done, or what directs the requisite means to such and such an end. An earthquake for instance may have devastating effects on a building or a bridge, a bush fire may rip through a log cabin and lay it to waste, but this is no different from the way that any means may conspire to any quite unintended end. Where it concerns immanent causality on the other hand, then there is something more to be discerned, and that is the ultimate source or the ultimate ground from which such action proceeds. What we are dealing with here is the question of both an origin and an end, or the initial conception of an end and its realization through such and such a set of means.

And in broad terms, there may be two ways this could be viewed. In the first place, when it is the intention or purpose behind the act that guides it in some significant way, and in the second, when the origin is reflected in the instrumental value of the end. Let us consider this in a little more detail. In taking up the habit of walking or jogging the reason a person may have is to overcome an injury or simply to improve his general state of health. At another level, we tend to see this in the purpose or the function of a thing. Why for instance does the builder construct a house? So that it may serve as a fit place for human habitation. Why does the engineer design and the workmen construct a bridge? So that it may obviate the problem when there is the need for a certain conveyance. Why does the potter work diligently to mould and shape a piece of clay? So that he may create a utensil that is fit for human use. And in the same way, we may consider the parts of an animal as pertaining to such and such a use, only here where there is a deeper and more radical connection between the parts and that end they are meant to sub serve. What therefore we understand by an immanent cause involves the connection between three basic ideas. Firstly, we have the conception of a thing or its essence and function; secondly, we have the realization of a thing or its production and means, and thirdly, we have the materials or ingredients from which such a thing may be made.

So far as it concerns the question of any general critique, then there are two basic issues we need to address: firstly, whether the relation between matter and form is such that the latter must always take precedence, and secondly, whether we are entitled to treat a *final cause* as commensurate with what is original or primordial in itself. In the first place, it should be clear that the relation between potentiality and actuality is such that it is not the former that is subordinate to the latter but that latter that is subordinate to the former. That is, "to be" means having the potential to change, but in order for that to occur must there also be something *from which* it is changing, that is, from potentially what is-not as well as what is (e.g. a bud is not only potentially a flower but also potentially not a bud). And so, what is in one state at one time may well be in another at some other, but that is not to say that what becomes is merely the realization of what was but is no more, and what is, is the realization of what must be but is not yet.

In the second place, what we mean by a 'final cause' is really only the loose description of an action or the intention behind the action, not something of a truly portentous or prevalent kind. We may in many instances provide a reason for the way we behave, but that is not the same as stating the *causes* for the way we behave. And in a similar vein, we may provide the definition of a thing or state the use and purpose of a thing, but we cannot say how something will be until it exists, until it becomes or is ready to hand. In what sense for instance could a house ever be occupied if it had not first come to be, or in what sense *must* it always be occupied rather than *potentially* only so? In what sense could there ever be the use of a cupboard or a wardrobe if there were not first the sawing of wood or the hammering of nails? Quiet clearly then, the existence of a thing must be deemed prior to the purpose of a thing, just as the purpose of a thing must be deemed prior to the definition of a thing, otherwise we could make things just by using the building blocks of our mind.

And the tenor of these remarks will apply equally when we consider what is the purpose or intention behind our acts—as if the body were merely the instrument of the will and yet had no efficiency in and of itself. Of course, it is true that our actions ought not be regarded as what is simply automatic, that we cannot be conscious of what we are doing before we have done it, or that the batting of an eyelid is no different from the aiming of a dart. On the other hand, it will make a considerable difference to a person's capacity if he suffers a spinal injury, since no matter what the strength of his spirit this will not allow him to raise his legs or walk about freely.

In terms of the relation between form and function, we might approach this in the following way: (*a*) where there is a perfect coincidence between the two and this is reflected by the relation between whole and part, (*b*) where there is a chance connection and this reflected in the meaning of contingent being and (*c*) where there is complete disjunction and this is reflected in the absence of any whole or the absence of all its parts. So far as it concerns the last of these, we have already discussed this in terms of what is artistic, ideal or elemental in its kind. As for the first two, we need to address this in conjunction with a comparison of living and inanimate things, or organisms and mechanisms as such. In comparing art or engineering to nature, we need to consider the degree of organization or utility exhibited in the former and compare this to the organization or utility exhibited in the latter. What we mean by the form or function of an artefact is something that results from a purely *extrinsic* connection between the parts, but beyond that only indistinctly as concerns the meaning of such a whole. Efficiency could be described as a quantum or a sum of diverse powers, but it is not the parts that are dependent upon the whole, rather it is the whole that is dependent upon the parts. A living organism however is not merely an aggregate of parts, it is also a unified whole, and to the degree this form cannot be qualified it pervades the whole of the body and resides in each and every part.

Or at least what we have stated here is certainly the traditional account—and yet might it not also be a controvertible one? Let us for instance consider the parts that comprise a combustible engine, say the pistons, the spark plugs, the valves—can there be any doubt that what these evince is the most sparing and thrifty arrangement as such. The same might be said for the components that make a bridge (the suspenders, the cables, the towers)—again, is there anything lacking or wasteful in this? Or more broadly consider the *purpose* of an engine or the *purpose* of a bridge. Is there anything more evident or apparent than what these are for? Hence what we have here is a unified whole just as much as there is a variety or diversity of parts. There may also be a sense in which the value of a part is reflective of the whole—that we cannot have a watch without a regulator, that we cannot have a globe without a filament, that we cannot have a shoe without a sole. Consider on the other hand how we might regard the purpose of an animal or a plant. Certainly, we may know what is the purpose of an eye or what is the purpose of a hand, but do we really know what is the purpose of the head and consequently, what is the purpose of the whole? We might for instance define 'man' as a rational animal that has knowledge and uses language, and we might regard the speakers and bearers of such knowledge as pertaining to just this species, but can we in the same way say what men are good for, or what end they must subserve? Hence it seems that what is fundamental to a part may yet be incidental to the whole, and that we should no more regard a tree as comprising the whole of a root than we should a leaf as comprising the whole of a branch. By a heterogeneous whole therefore, what we mean is that some parts may be useful in and of themselves (as the hand or the eye) whilst others may not (as the toes or the head).

And yet there is also another line of reasoning which would seem to support exactly the same conclusion. Where it concerns the parts of an artefact there are two aspects to be discerned: first, that we can remove and replace all the parts so that the object can be reproduced as a whole, and secondly, that we can remove and *rebuild* all the parts so that the object can be revitalized as a whole. Furthermore, we can devise a plan or a blueprint for the things we construct, we can use ceramics in the plastic arts, chromatics in the visual arts and choreography in the dramatic arts. Where on the other hand it concerns a living organism then there are many more restrictions to be discerned. It cannot be reconstructed as a whole or returned it to its original state, and we cannot reverse those processes that are necessarily developmental in their kind. Consequently if there is any plenitude in the whole this can only be through the *actual* capacity of all its parts, if there is any growth this can only be through the *irregularity* of some of its parts, and if there is versatility this can only be through the loss of some of its less indispensable parts.

Chapter 2
Actuality and Potentiality

With respect to the relation between actuality and potentiality, we need to consider this within a particular arrangement of things, that is, as we ascend In in the first place, where it concerns the idea of artistic design, then there is certainly a sense in which it is actuality that precedes potentiality, since the matter is entirely indifferent to anything that may be imposed or impressed on it. The artist has a particular objective which he hopes to body forth, and so there is a very real sense in which it is the materials that have the potential to-be, that is, to be this or that colour, to be this or that harmony, to be this or that shape. We can however discern something similar in the workings of nature, as for instance, in a hive or a web, only where the end or ideal is exhibited in a certain uniformity of parts and where both the making and shaping contribute to what is useful on the whole. The activity of a spider or a bee represents one kind of intelligence, the diligence of a sculptor or a painter quite another. In the case of the former there is a collecting or a garnering for the sake of something else, in the latter, only a shaping or a moulding, since here the materials have no real value in and of themselves.

When we say therefore, that matter has the potential to be shaped in such and such a way, what we are not saying is that it is potentiality per se, rather, that when it is differentiated it serves what is *made* and when it is undifferentiated it serves what can be *changed*. Where however it concerns the idea of productive form or the meaning of a specialized whole, then we might approach this in either of two ways. First, we have potentiality in the matter and actuality in the form *qua* the product of building, and secondly, potentiality in the matter and actuality in the form *qua* the knowledge of construction and design. Let us pursue this in a little more detail. So far it could be argued that the *parts* of a house are a precondition for the *making* of a house, then the potential to be must antecede to the completed product. Even if we have the bricks and mortar, the framework and the tiles, a house will not be built unless we have the requisite means as well. It requires the agency of a builder, someone to assemble all these parts, a mason to lay the foundations, a plasterer to seal the walls. On the other hand, what could also be argued is that knowledge or the art of building must always precede any actual design, just as the process of building must always precede any finished result. And since the architect has a broader knowledge than does the builder, it is the skill of the former that will be reflected in what it is that results, not just the prospect of a result that is reflected in the materials for bringing it about. We might accept that a bee could construct a hive, but we would not imagine it could construct a house—what it has is a certain kind of knowledge, but not what is more perfected or more complete.

In the case of organic form, then what we are dealing with is pure potentiality, the dynamism of a living thing in conjunction with its *actual use*, not the use of a thing in conjunction with any underlying aim. Certainly, an organ such as an eye or an ear has a function which is peculiarly its own, but that is not to say that the capacity of an eye precedes the use of an eye or that the capacity of an ear precedes the use of ear, rather, this is something that can only be approached in an heuristic way— it ought not be assumed that the capacity of the whole will supersede the capacity of all its parts. Of course, we do not say of a person that he is deaf when he is simply inattentive, or that he is blind if he has simply closed his eyes, but that is not because the capacity for sensing overrides the occasion for sensing, rather how we regard the parts in relation to how the whole may be disposed. So far as we say a person who is sleeping is not someone who is active, someone who is walking not someone who is running, then this is because the whole may be incidental to any particular part, not because the capacity of the whole *must* supersede the capacity of all the parts. Sleep is indispensable for the sake of both a healthy mind and body, it returns the self to the self, it replenishes the source of its being, it dusts it off and allows it to begin all over again. It should be clear therefore that what we are not saying is that the capacity or aptitude to do something precedes the very act itself, as if there were two selves and not the one, rather that there must be a threshold for the whole just as there is for any particular part, that what is blind could *potentially* be sighted, that what is sluggish could *potentially* be nimble, that what is impotent could *potentially* be virile. To have the full use of one's faculties may also be what it means to be actually sensing, but that does not mean there cannot be sensing without all of our faculties intact. Rather, we must allow that there may not be just a division of powers in the sense of a division of functions, but a division of powers in connection with a diversity of parts, so that the true capacity of the body is measured by the real utility of all the parts, not the real utility of the parts measured by their full potentiality as such.

Having addressed our subject in terms of a certain gradation or ordering of being, what we need to do now is consider actuality and potentiality as this might be viewed in and of itself. If potentiality and actuality are the *same*, then a condition can only be described in terms of its actual existence—so that to be-able-to-sit-or-stand becomes sitting or standing, and to-be-able-to-walk-or-run becomes walking or running. So far however as they are not the same, it is the potential to do something or the potential to be something that precedes the doing or the being itself. And this would seem to be reasonable enough where it concerns activities and events that are automatic or instinctive in their kind. There is the potential for a person to do something and there is the potential for certain events to occur, but that is not true in the sense that there may be waking or sleeping, choking or breathing, where the implication is that what one has is simply lacking in the other. But then we also need to address the question how the loss of something, or the loss of a skill, relates to its retention and the opportunity for its continual display? In this case it would seem that actuality precedes potentiality, or at least, that we can only lose a skill once we have acquired it, and not the other way around.

However, we might also need to qualify this to some degree, since it is clear that some skills can be lost whilst others quite clearly cannot. It is certainly true in the case of learning to speak or learning to walk, that these are the sorts of skills that will stay with us and for the duration of our lives. Once you have learnt the art of speaking, there is no chance you will ever return to babble, and once you have acquired the art of walking there is no chance you will ever return to crawling, but that is not to say there may not be exceptions to just such a rule. If you undertake learning a foreign language or the playing of a musical instrument, then these are the sorts of habits that may not be so easily retained, especially in the case of the former if you are reduced to practising on your own. In this instance it is not so much actuality that precedes any *possible* use, but a *possible* means that prevents the loss of what might otherwise be deemed desirable in and of itself. Without a cello or piano you may not be able to maintain your musical skills, just as, without a certain coterie you may not be able to maintain your linguistic skills. There are some things that require persistence and the application of a quite strenuous means, and there are others that can be acquired with very little difficulty, and yet remain with us till the end of our lives. Even however in the case of the latter, a person who has learnt to walk may not retain that skill if he is unfortunate enough to be involved in something like a motor or skiing accident.

If potentiality and actuality are so related that this could be said to constitute something in the order of a necessary nexus, then it is surely the former and not the latter that must be given our utmost regard. We cannot conceive of becoming otherwise than in terms of what-is, but more importantly, of what was other than in terms of what it has become. In general, we tend to think of what comes *from* or what comes out of, in terms of the development or the completion of a thing, as the cow is the development of a calf, a horse is the development of a colt, a tree is the development of a seed. Or we might consider something as issuing from a certain place, as thunder or rain from the sky, a tremor or geyser from the earth, a wave or a spray from the sea. Quite clearly therefore, there is something actual in both the origin and the end, but not the same thing when the action is deliberate and the action is unintended. Certainly, the wood that is used in the making of a cabinet is not the same as the function of a cabinet, just as, the rubber in a set of tyres is not the same as the function of any tyre. Nonetheless there is a very real sense in which it is both the parts and the purpose of a thing that determines what it is, whereas a *potential* use must always be subordinate to an *actual* use, just as a potential parasite must always be subordinate to a potential host.

In respect to the the relation between matter and form, then if actuality is prior to potentiality, then what this means is that the actuality of matter is prior to the potentiality of form, which becomes clear as we work our way through a gradation of being, from the artistic, to the artificial, to the organic. Where it concerns the artistic, there is little doubt that we would tend to regard the overarching power as what is formative rather than elemental. The clay for a sculpture must always conform to the skill of the artist in the realization of such and such an end, since here, there is no discrepancy between the conceiving of such an end and how this might actually be attained. Of course that is not to say there is not something with which the artist *must* work, and that it is always the form which in some sense delimits the matter, since we could just as well create a statue from a piece of bronze as we could from a piece of marble, and clearly, no one has the licence to change marble into bronze. So far however as there is a shaping and not a making, it is the hand or the eye that is our guide, not how a brush or a chisel demands that we should act.

Where it concerns the mechanical or artificial on the other hand, there is a certain equivocation in our approach, since in one respect it is actuality that precedes potentiality and in another, potentiality that precedes actuality. Certainly, it is the architect or engineer who in one sense precedes the organization or the act, but equally also the materials and the builder which in another sense, precedes the outcome or result. Thus, there is actuality so far as there is (*a*) the knowledge of construction and design and (*b*) the product of building itself, but equally also potentiality so far as there are the materials from which such a building can be made. There is a sense in which it is not only the materials that have been assembled which precede the object that has been made, but also the 'actuality' or 'end' of knowledge which will be achieved through the 'potentiality' for such and such a *use*.

Where it concerns the organic, there is a clearer indication how and why we would say it is matter that precedes form rather than form that precedes matter. We may pursue this through a discussion of the relation between efficiency and use. From a certain point of view, it could be argued that the capacity for building must always precede the act of building, since you can only embark upon a task once you have acquired a certain proficiency to begin with. It seems obvious that a person can only play the harp once he has learnt the art of harp playing, that he can only drive a car once he has learnt the art of driving, that he can only swim the length of a pool once he has learnt the art of swimming, etc. The question that remains however is whether this is true with respect to the *parts* of a living organism just as it is with respect to what we mean by the whole. Would one say, for example, that it is the capacity for seeing which precedes the act of seeing or that it is the capacity for hearing which precedes the act of hearing? Perhaps the following will demonstrate the difficulty in adopting just such approach. When we say that a person may acquire the art of building, the art of flying or the art of diving, then of course, this does not preclude him from acquiring skilfulness in any other field, since a builder may also be a diver and a diver may also be a pilot. Thus, just as a builder is someone who has learnt the art of construction, so might we regard a pilot as someone who has learnt the art of flying and a pearl fisherman as someone who has learnt the art of diving. But where it concerns an organ such as the eye or the ear, it is clear this does not have the capacity to do more than one thing, in the case of the former the capacity to see and in the case of the latter the capacity to hear. And so given this restriction, it makes no sense to compare the 'actuality' of seeing with the 'potentiality' for sight, as if the eye could potentially be seeing at the same time it was hearing. Rather, we should compare the potentiality for sight with the potentiality for its absence, just as we compare the 'sighted man' with the man who is blind and the 'virile man' with the man who is impotent. Since there can be no sight without the 'active eye' and no hearing without the 'active ear' it is the actuality of the organ that precedes the potentiality for its use, but by this it should be clear we do not mean something formative in and of itself. To be a builder is to have the capacity for building but not necessarily the right materials at hand. In the same way, to have the capacity for sight does not necessarily mean to have the faculty of sight, nor also, to be seeing at the same time one is hearing, or seeing at the same time one is tasting etc.

In terms of the general question of what is changeable or mutable as such, we might view this issue in either of two ways: (*a*) where what has changed is what is *actual* and what is changing is what is *potential* and (*b*) where there is a succession of states such that what is actual is what has undergone a change in either its quality, quantity or place. To address the latter, consider how running may be derived from walking, how health may be derived from sickness, how happiness may be derived from sorrow and how heat may be derived from what is freezing. What we might say is that something which is, is derived from something which is not, or that something which is not is the precondition for something which is. And this kind of change is also convertible, since what is running may become what is walking, what is cold may become what is hot and what is happy may become what is doleful. Where, however, we wish to relate this change to that which is not changing, or what it is that underlies such a change, the implication must surely be that it is the same person who is walking or running, the same face that is happy or sad, the same bathtub that is steamy or cold. What we are dealing with here is a change in the quality of a thing, but it might just as well be a change in its size, a change in its place, or a change in its shape.

There is however another kind of change we might wish to consider, and that is not what is unstable but rather something more contextual. In this regard, we might consider the relation between the real and the potential where there is a greater emphasis on the former. In terms of the viewpoint we have already outlined, it is easy enough to see how a tree could be healthy or ill, how an oven could be scorching or cold and how a face could be happy or sad, but it is quite another matter when the substratum is something of a more elusive or esoteric kind. If for instance you consider the process of condensation and its relation to evaporation, then surely what we have are two things but not necessarily something that is common to them both. That is, we would say it is the heating of water that causes it to evaporate and the cooling of water that causes it to condense. So far as there is one thing that is coming-to-be and another that is passing-away, then it is natural to regard such change as both conjunctive and disjunctive in its kind. In a similar vein, where it concerns the existence of a corporeal thing, it is natural to regard creation as the *possibility* of its coming-to-be and destruction as the *necessity* of its passing-away, since there is either a 'coming in' or a 'going out' but there cannot be anything that is common to them both. (Or at least so far as we assume no cyclical conjoining of ends)

And yet there are those of a different persuasion who would argue that we can also admit change of an 'irreversible' kind and that just as there is a coming to be and a passing away in purely phenomenal terms, so also might there be in a more transcendental sense. That is, it is not just ceasing to be which is conditional upon coming to be, but coming to be which is conditional upon ceasing to be, since that which underlies the process of passing-away is no different from that which underlies the process of coming-to-be, only it is not altogether clear how this must be so. The gist of this would seem to be that it is natural to regard what is formed as prior to what is formless, that the producer must always be prior to the product just as the whole must always be prior to the part. And since the real must always proceed from what *is* real, that a fish can only be generated by a fish and a tree can only be generated by a tree, then quite clearly it is the egg or the germ that brings out what was formless and unshapen to begin with. The living thing will therefore grow and reproduce itself both on account of itself and on account of its form; it will preserve itself both as such and such an entity and as such and such a type.

However, the question that could be raised about this is that although it seems to identify the growth of the species with the growth of the individual, we really have no more reason to suppose the durability of the one than we do the durability of the other. That is, since the number of species on the earth at any given time is altogether arbitrary, as are the number of individuals, we can put no more trust in the longevity of any species than we can in that of any member. Thus, the cogency of our argument will be undercut if there is no more a sense of the individual as *preserving* the species than there is of the species as continuous in itself. What this leaves us with is the wholly ambiguous idea that there may be two states, coming to be and passing away, such that they are incompatible where it concerns a purely involuntary means, and yet compatible where it concerns some more calculated or deliberative end.

Chapter 3
Unity and Multiplicity

What we mean by unity, and the relation between unity and multiplicity, can be understood in either of the following ways: (*a*) in the constitution of a thing there is no aspect to which multiplicity could be said to apply, so that the one is altogether outside and apart from the other or (*b*) in the constitution of a thing it is unified in one respect but diversified in another, so that the one can be brought within the extremities of the other. The first of these pertains to a distinction between the necessary and the contingent, and the second to a distinction between the essential and the adventitious or the particular and the universal. The reality of anything which exists is due to either (*a*) the necessity of its own nature or (*b*) the contingency of its own nature, in conjunction with the necessity of a cause that lies outside. The emptiness or vacuity of what is not in but rather outside existence is due to either (*a*) the impossibility of conceiving of such an object or any means by which it could exist or (*b*) the impossibility of conceiving of any synthesis or any means by which it could be produced. What exists of necessity, in and of itself, can neither be joined to any cause outside it, nor strictly speaking, to any kind of differentiation at all. Neither can it be said to imply any reciprocal movement, since if one thing is the cause of another then it must be *prior* to that other, and you cannot say in any strict sense that what is later in its becoming is also what is earlier in its being. (Mathematics may deal with the transposition of terms but that is only in the sense of what is tautological).

Furthermore, if two things are coequal but nonetheless different, then this must be on account of something that belongs to the one and yet not to the other. If this be a deficiency, then at least one of them cannot be perfect; if a perfection, then at least one of them must be deficient. Or if the first possesses necessity and the other only contingency, then the implication must surely be that the one is only possible through and in conjunction with the other. If that were so however, then they could not be coequal or have a relation, since the former could just as well exist in the absence of the latter as the latter could not without some determinate cause. Or if it is the case that one thing possesses necessity with respect to another but only possibility with respect to itself, then it follows that the other must be like or unlike this, that is, be either possible or necessary in itself. If the former, then what we are dealing with are two entirely accidental beings, since as the cause must be prior to the effect so can the essence be only conveyed and as part of such an end. If the latter, then necessity or existence comes to the one through and in conjunction with the other, but to one whose existence is already assumed; from which it follows there must be both priority and posteriority in what it is.

As we will later see (in the chapter called "Creation, Destruction and Formation") in the case of a necessary being it is impossible to distinguish between the idea and the reality of such a thing, but that is not the case where it concerns either universal or accidental being: existence is no more a precondition for the former than essence is a precondition for the latter. That is, even if we admit that there are two forms or two species separate from one another it is still an open question whether they are also separate from any mind or any subject. And this leads on to the question what is meant by the essential and the accidental, or what is undivided so far as we conceive of it as any whole and what is undivided so far as we conceive of it as any part. We might claim for example that 'Elephants and horse are one with respect to animality', 'Peter and Paul are one with respect to humanity', 'Honey and treacle are one with respect to viscosity'—and essentially these are all correct, although what is meant by a common element will depend on whether we are dealing with a genus, a species or an individual. What is divisible is divisible by virtue of not being undivided, but what is undivided may be undivided either essentially or accidentally, and so from either a qualitative or a quantitative point of view. No doubt it is true that the valuation of a thing may sometimes be more important than the thing to be divided, but that should not obscure the conventional nature of any means we might choose to employ. What for instance is a metre long could be divided into units of one quarter or one half, but we do not call the 'half metre' a unit of length in any strict sense of that word. Thus, although there may be conversion from one system to another, as for instance, from pounds to kilograms or even more loosely from metres to half metres, there is certainly no universal standard and to which all these systems must comply.

On the other hand, if we were to argue for the universality of all being, then what this implies is that the privation of being must have its origin in the completeness of being, that darkness for instance must have its basis in light and that infirmity must have its basis in good health. What follows is that unity could be matched by a certain diversity in its members but not also what was diverse in itself, rather, that these were just partial expressions of something that was *becoming* more complete. This also has implications for the question of numerical unity, and how, in this context, the relation between matter and form may be such as to support a gradation from the less to the more complete, rather than the more to the less complete. For number what this pertains to is a world that is stable and not one that is changeful, and that is why every whole number has a set of properties that are peculiarly its own. However so far as it concerns any broader outline, we would regard number not as replete but rather as empty of being, since there can only be a sense of unity if there is something to be unified, and this only be evinced through a transposition of the terms. When we say $6 \times 4 = 4 \times 6$ or the ratio 1:2 is the same as 2:4, then what this underscores is that two things may be compared or contrasted only when this is suitable to our intentions or our aims.

Where however it concerns the application of number to a world that is *not* stable but amenable to change, then in no way ought it to be regarded as a principal constituent or what was elemental in itself. Consider for instance a situation where the relation between matter and form was such that the one was indivisible and yet the other was not. A body made of fabric such as a flag, may comprise any number of constituents or any number of colours, and yet although we would say any colour must remain the same, we would not say that all the constituents must remain the same. That is, when we say that the French flag comprises exactly *three* colours, that a linesman's flag comprises exactly *two* colours or that the socialist flag comprises exactly *one* colour, this does not pertain to any actual division as what is essential to any such division, rather only to what is 'actual' is what is adventitious in itself. Certainly the colour red that appears on a matador's cape *may* be accidentally divided if the object itself is divided, just as certainly colours may be accidentally combined, but although the colours themselves may be different we would not say this of any number of colours, otherwise, how could the French flag be distinguished from the famous Stars and Stripes?

And this highlights the folly in supposing that it is specific identity that is contingent upon numerical identity, rather than numerical identity that is contingent upon specific identity. There is an important difference between the way that two things may be formally excluded from one another, or only materially so, since in the one case we are considering only a difference in number whereas in the other in their nature as well. Suppose we are given twelve marbles, half of which are red and half are green. Now we might divide these into two sets: on the one hand where it concerns only a question of quality and on the other hand where it concerns only a question of quantity. If for instance we place the six red in one pile and the six green in another pile, then what this demonstrates is that the two must be different in their character. On the other hand, if we mix three red with three green, then what we can see is that all these groups are numerically the same. However, if we were to add a marble (of the same colour) to the first grouping and subtract a marble (of either colour) from the second grouping, what difference would this make? Certainly in the first instance, we could not achieve anything new with respect to quality, since seven red and six green or six red and seven green would be essentially just the same. In the case of the second, a single marble would certainly produce a change in both quality and quantity, but that is because their *relation* would remain the same. That is, we would be no closer to knowing whether a change in quantity had induced a change in quality or a change in quality had induced a change in quantity.

So far as it concerns the general view that it is unity that underlies multiplicity and not multiplicity that underlies unity, we need to address this and along the following lines. There is a kind of argument that asserts that a diversity of powers must be supported by either a singular *cause*, as the instigator of any action, or a single entelechy as the instigator of any being. In order that there be efficiency in both the instrument or the source and the purpose or design, what is requisite is that there be efficiency in both the means of producing something and in bringing it to its full effect. But since our bodily organs are the product of a single entelechy that fits them to its various ends, so also is this entelechy both the object and originator of itself. The intellectual or volitional act however, although it be one in its import, is really quite diverse in its forms, and that is why there will always be a greater variety in the parts of an animal than there will be in the parts of a plant.

Or at least this is how the traditional argument runs. And of course, there is certainly some truth to it if we consider simple forms of life such as a mollusc or a worm, since no matter how much you divide or dissect it, each part will retain the same power that it had first of all. Even where it concerns diversification and specialization, it is quite clear that the removal of some parts may prove harmful or damaging to at least some degree. A tree for instance, may well be able to survive the loss of its leaves but not necessarily the loss of its roots. A fish may be able to survive the loss of a fin but not necessarily the loss of its heart. On the other hand, we should not be misled by all of this where it concerns the versatility of those things which are much more complex in their kind. In this case, to the degree that an organism may be able to survive the loss of one or several parts, there is surely a discernible difference between the broader purport of any part and what it is in and of itself. A person who is stone deaf is surely less able than someone who is simply hard of hearing, just as a person who has lost a hand is surely less able than someone who has lost a thumb. And so looked at in these terms, to the degree there is a threshold for the efficiency of any part, must there not also be a threshold for the efficiency of any whole?

What we understand by the latter therefore does not imply a certain ordering or hierarchy of parts but a certain versatility in the parts themselves —that given a certain set of priorities we will order the parts in such and such a way. If for instance, we suppose hearing to be more important than the use of a limb, then what we might infer is that the loss of the former will be more disabling than the loss of the latter. Or if we consider the faculty of sight to be more important than that of hearing, then what we might infer is that someone who is blind is less capable than someone would is simply hard of hearing. It would then be a moot point whether someone who had lost his hearing and the use of a hand was more or less able than someone who had lost his sight and the use of his fingers, given that we are more capable on the whole if we have all our organs intact rather than being reliant on just a few. Whatever our estimates, it should be clear there is no 'model' efficiency but only a total efficiency, depending on which parts we deem to be more or less important.

So far as it concerns the second of these points, we need to consider the difference between positing perfection as an end or working from the assumption that what is good is only what is politic or expedient in the main. As with the the Schoolmen, we might suggest that there is a certain natural order or hierarchy of being and that what is less perfect must serve the end of what is more perfect, until we reach a point where it is the whole of being which is perfected in and through itself. On the other hand, we might adopt a very different approach to this, not taking as the extremities what is the most perfected or what is the most corrupted, but rather, what is the most and least effective as a means. We might define a *consonant* whole as one in which there are enough or sufficient parts to ensure some practical or attainable goal. A good example of this would be something like the workings of an orchestra—in its most usual form what it connotes is neither the striking of all the instruments nor the striking of just one. What all the instruments have in common is that they are more or less 'useless' in one context and more or less 'useful' in another. Their usefulness concerns the quality that each has to be accommodating and relevant to what is piecemeal or to what is whole. The violin for instance has relevance not only to the strings but also to the whole, so far as it is *played* at the right time or it is *stayed* at the right time. Their inutility on the other hand, concerns the quality that each has to be distinctive and dissimilar from all the rest. That is, if we can distinguish between the sounds of a saxophone and a harp, then so also can we within a broader complex between something that has a harmonious sound and something that has a cacophonous sound. What this also does is add a certain shade of meaning to a versatile and not a monolithic whole. By the former what we mean is any whole that comprises at least one 'useless' or 'functionless' part and where the fruitfulness of the whole may be reflected in the capacity of just this part. By the latter what we mean is any whole in which there are enough or sufficient parts to achieve some desirable result, but not however, the use of all those parts that may *actually* be brought into play. It is important to be clear that what we mean by a 'functionless' part (or what is *modemic* in its character) is something necessarily *active* in itself, whereas what we mean by a 'functioning' part (or what is *monadic* in its character) may be either active or inactive in itself.[1]

Perhaps we can address this issue a little more clearly if we embark on a broader definition of the terms. (*a*) By a consonant whole what we mean is any whole in which there are enough or sufficient parts to achieve some practical or worthwhile goal. (*b*) By a functioning whole what we

---

1   The term "modeme" is derived from the word 'mode' in the classical Cartesian sense of an accident or an attribute. It is however a specific attribute that pertains to organic nature.

mean is any section or any portion that is in keeping with itself (as in this instance, the strings, the woodwind and the brass). (*c*) By a diversity of powers what we mean is the amplitude of the pieces understood as a collection of sounds, since in this case it is not the person who directs but the musicians who create what is total in its effect. (*d*) By a diversity of functions what we mean are the pieces themselves and the different roles that each must play, thus, as either a unique sound or the difference in skill of the players who produce them. And finally, (*e*) what we mean by efficiency depends on how we might construe the meaning of any part, whether it be something adequate to itself or whether it be something that suffices as a means. A part is both functioning and *functional* when it has the capacity to be played at the right time or stayed at the right time. A part is both functionless and *functional* when it has the capacity to be played at the right time (that is, to be worked into an orchestra) and in the right way (that is, through the skill of the craftsman but not necessarily the skill of a musician).

Chapter 4

Homogeneity and Heterogeneity

To begin our study of homogeneity and heterogeneity, we need to review what we have already said about the relation between matter and form. We have identified two important respects in which form may be said to be prior to matter and they are where it concerns (*a*) the *ideal* and (*b*) the *elemental.* By ideal form we mean that form which may be 'impressed' or 'imposed' on matter, thus by supposing it to be active and not rather passive. The imperial seal for instance may be impressed on a piece of wax, the figure of David may be impressed on a piece of marble and a postal mark may be impressed on a stamp. By elemental form we mean that form which may be exhibited in every one of the parts of an object, although here we would not say that there was anything active or inactive in itself. The whole of a flame may be exhibited in each part of a flame, the whole of a snowflake may be exhibited in each part of a snowflake and the whole of a dewpond may be exhibited in each droplet of water. And to these meanings might we add a third, when the form of a thing may be regarded as its sort or its type, so that the sum of its members may be synonymous with the whole of the species and the sum of it species with the whole of the genus.

On the flip side are the implications for matter just as equally clear. What we mean by matter is something that is altogether inactive in itself - it is 'featureless' or 'functionless' until it assumes some character and which is imposed from without. Thus, it may have the potential to body forth such and such a specific form, but what it cannot do is decide or predict just exactly what this will be. The different forms that a body assumes may indeed make for a wide display, but this is not any inherent capacity, since a further analysis may well reveal a more singular and fundamental ground. What proceeds from above and is a true reflection of the whole can never be displaced by what proceeds from below and is a true indication of the parts. To be versatile means to be in keeping with an end and to be dissoluble means to be in keeping with an origin.

What however we mean by the condition of being similar or the condition of being dissimilar, is not necessarily what we mean by the identity of a thing, or what it is that makes one thing different from any other, otherwise, all we would have is the relation between identity and diversity which we call 'being different', and that cannot be so, since as we will later argue a relation is at best ideal but in no sense real. When we say that the parts of a whole are alike or unlike, then this does not suppose any relation that *must* hold, only a comparison by some objective but nonetheless extrinsic means. It is what we observe to be different that ultimately marks the difference between similitude and dissimilitude as such. Hence the claim that 'everything is different from everything else' is not meant to override the claim that everything is the same as itself, but only, that no two things can be the same in each and every respect. Thus, it is not a question in what regard anything may be the same or different from what it is, but rather whether 'the essential' can be encompassed through the individual or only through some specific class or group. Of course, the relation between likeness and unlikeness is by no means an invariable one, as when we compare the individual to the species or the species to the genus. There are different degrees of similarity and dissimilarity, so that a point of convergence in one respect may constitute a point of separation in another, just as a point of distinction may also constitute a point of coexistence. What is different is only different by virtue of that information gleaned through our senses—we neither perceive the round to be what is angular nor the soft to be what is unyielding, but we may nonetheless have the impression of what is round and rigid as in the case of a cannonball, or what is flat and springy as in the case of a pillow. Hence, we might regard texture and shape as properties that are coincidently but not essentially the same. What on the other hand we mean by an implicit or essential difference, is what is evident in a state of simple juxtaposition, as the colour black is opposed to the colour white, the virtue of courage is opposed to the vice of cowardice, a state of opulence is opposed to a state of austerity.

In the present context therefore, we need to consider (*a*) the sense in which actuality is opposed to potentiality and (*b*) the sense in which unity is opposed to divisibility. When we say that actuality is prior to potentiality then what we mean is that being is prior to becoming, because being is always the *end* of becoming (or at least where this concerns a certain design). What has potential, has the potential to be what it presently is not, and so it is a certain incapacity that separates what cannot-be from what may-be, just as it separates the aimless or capricious from the regulated or designed. Potentiality lies at the heart of what is changeful but by no means what is permanent. It consists in the fact that something in a certain state may become something else in another state, that what is hot may become what is cold, that what is pale may become what is flushed and that what is active may become what is dormant. Thus, there are opposites that exist potentially and at exactly the same time, but that does not mean they are equally the embodiment of what is good or ideal. The oven would rather be hot than cold, the snail would rather be dormant than active, the bride would rather be blushing than pale, and so, these are the ends they are naturally inclined to.

As to the second of these points, unity is prior to divisibility in the sense that (*a*) what is undivided in the genus must be prior to what is divided in the species and (*b*) what is indistinguishable in any whole must be prior to what is distinguishable in any part. The genus we might say is purer than any species and the species we might say is purer than any individual. What we mean by this of course is purer in its ground, the idiosyncrasies at one level matching the differentiae at another.

But where it concerns the object as something with both a form and function, it is more aesthetically pleasing if the whole comprises parts exhibiting this whole rather than parts that are distinctive in and of themselves. A watch for instance may comprise all the parts necessary for its making, but to the untrained eye it would be impossible to say how these might be connected or arranged. Not only that, but since it can be constructed as a whole the implication must surely be that it can also be dismantled as a whole. Even a skyscraper that is assembled in such and such a way could also be dismantled in such and such a way, without it being at all obvious how this might actually proceed. (Of course, from the viewpoint of expediency it might be difficult to explain why a skyscraper, unlike a watch, should ever be dismantled and not simply destroyed or blown apart). On the other hand, where it concerns something that is made up of parts that are entirely uniform, we might regard this as what is unyielding rather than extinguishable in its kind. And that is why where it concerns the human body, although it might appear to be altogether heterogeneous, what we would like to think is that it is imbued with an indestructible part, what could be termed its 'eternal soul'.

Another way we might regard the question of 'good form' is through the connection we have to our environment, and how we arrange the elements of our everyday world so that we can achieve a sense of what is continuous, through the means of what is varied, and a sense of what is singular, through the means of what is complex. These convening influences and the outcomes they engender are evident in what we call *gestalten*. Thus, if you consider the elements that go into the arrangement of any perceptual whole, then a grouping may occur in terms of the general rule that (*a*) similarity, (*b*) proximity and (*c*) continuity will all support a joining of the parts. Where it concerns the relation between figure and ground or the organization of any continuous whole, then our perception will always be skewed towards what is *more* regular or what is *more* symmetrical. The way for example that we tend to 'see' any object as what is two or three dimensional (given the lack of shading or distortion) hinges very largely on the regularity or irregularity in the appearance or presentation of such an object. Something that is three dimensional we tend to regard as more complex or more convoluted than something that is two dimensional, thus what we 'see' as comprising more irregular parts we tend to classify as three dimensional and what we 'see' as comprising more regular parts we tend to classify as two dimensional. This applies also to the amount of information that needs to be processed; what is 'less' will always be what is more preferable and what is 'more' will always be what is less preferable.

Having now addressed the question of what is simple and what is diverse, we might pursue our enquiries through a comparison of (*a*) what is ordered and disordered and (*b*) what is universal and particular. In the first place to consider the meaning of order and disorder, we would not approach this as we have regularity and irregularity, that is, by suggesting that the one consists in a lack of the other, rather in terms of the relative merits of an 'orderly' or a 'disorderly' end. And in these terms what we mean by an 'orderly' end is not what we mean by a perfect or univocal end, only what is adequate or sufficient in itself. Using the paradigm case of a living orchestra we need to address the difference between (*a*) what results from a certain craftsmanship (i.e. what is purely functional) (*b*) what is both active and idle (i.e. what is functioning).and (*c*) what is active in and of itself (what is disordered or functionless.)

If for instance you reflect on the craftsmanship that goes into the making of a flute *or* the skill of the musician in striking the right chord, then on both counts what you have is something functional rather than ineffective in its kind. On the other hand, in the way we compare what is functioning and what is functionless, what this really rests on is the question of adequacy or sufficiency as an end. A piano or harp for instance will mean something quite different in a solo performance than it will in a larger ensemble, even if there is no difference where it concerns the musician and the execution of any skill. When at the start of a concerto you observe the instruments that are being tested and attuned, it should be obvious in what sense they are also indistinguishable, or at least that what they evince is nothing more than a cacophony of sounds. In the living performance on the other hand, it is a particular *synthesis* that will ultimately enable them to achieve the result that they want. In this context therefore, what it means to be 'distinguishable' is only what it means to be strident, since no matter how well a single instrument may be played, this is not at all in keeping with that impression which will be generate overall. 'Functioning' therefore comes to mean what is adequate to such and such an end, 'functionless' on the other hand, to what is adequate as such and such a *means*.

So far as it concerns the relation between the universal and particular, we need to approach this through the consideration of what is meant by a proper whole and a proper part. *Conjunctivism* is a doctrine which asserts that for any two objects there will always be a third and which is composed of them. Thus, we need to admit both continuous and discontinuous objects, things that are not only in contact but also things that are distant in both space and time. With respect to a simple judgement or conjunct such as 'A and B', what this means is that if there are such things as rabbits and roosters, then there must also be a scattered object that embraces them both. In the same way, if the form of our judgement is 'not A' and 'not B', then this is not at odds with our earlier statement, since we can equally well affirm that two things do not exist as we can that they do. However, whether this is a consistent or coherent point of view is an altogether different matter. So far as we affirm that two things *must* make a third, it is also necessary that we deny that two things cannot make a third. But consider the following examples: (*a*) The class of all odd numbers may be different from the class of all even numbers, but together they constitute the class of all cardinal numbers. Hence the class of all cardinal numbers may be divided into what is even and what is odd, but the principle of being inclusive will always override the principle of simple exclusion. (*b*) The class of prime numbers includes both what is even and odd, but the class of prime numbers does not include all the numbers that are even and odd. Hence the principle of being exclusive will always override the principle of being inclusive. (*c*) The class of vertebrates may be different from the class of invertebrates, but together they constitute the class of all living things. Thus, although the class of living things may be divided into those that do and those that do not have backbones and skulls, the principle of inclusivity must override the principle of exclusivity. (*d*) The class of land dwellers includes both some vertebrates (e.g. birds) and some invertebrates (e.g. snails), but it does not comprise all vertebrates and invertebrates (i.e. it does not include such animals as lobsters and fish). Hence the principle of being exclusive must override the principle of being inclusive.

And yet it seems according to the doctrine we have just outlined such distinctions must be either chimerical or at least invalid. Where it concerns the meaning of a proper part, in strictly logical terms we need the idea of equivalence or what is coextensive as such. Take for example the class of equiangular triangles and then compare this with the class of equilateral triangles. These classes could be described as coextensive, since there are no equilateral triangles that are not equiangular and no equiangular triangles that are not equilateral. It is another matter however when the relation we are dealing with is one of simple inclusiveness, given the proviso that (*a*) there is a class, say class X, of which there is at least one member, say Y, and (*b*) there is a conjunct class, say Z, but which has no member that is not a member of X. The following should serve as a simple example. Given at least one member of the African nation but some Africans who are *not* Tunisians, all Tunisians are a 'proper' part of the African nation. On the other hand, and even granted that this may be an altogether sensible approach, we might begin by supposing that it is not the part that is dependent upon the whole but the whole that is dependent upon the part.

To this end, we might need to revise our thinking about the meaning of a part that is *overlapping* and the meaning of a part that is not. It should be obvious that what we mean by a part that is overlapping is a situation where two parts are being 'shared'—in these terms what we have is the creation of a new part from two parts that were already there. But what about the meaning of a spatial whole, in what sense might we regard this as comprising parts that are overlapping? Our first reaction to such a proposal might be one of outright incredulity, since what would seem to be implied is that a smaller volume may in some sense be the same as a larger volume, and which is surely quite absurd. Furthermore, this is by no means in keeping with our assumption that without at least some unit of measurement there cannot be anything that is measured at all. If two things are comparable and are found to be equal in length, then this is because we can ascertain how they might also be different, but we would surely not say that of any space that was empty. (A light year or a parsec is not the means of measuring different volumes but only very large distances in space.) If we assert therefore that a cavity within another cavity is also within the host of that cavity, then what we are arguing for is the autonomy of the latter and the dependence of the former. And our assumption is the same when we argue that a cavity within a host is also a cavity within any larger host. (That is, it doesn't matter what surrounds a hole, or whether it can be filled in later, the host is still the host).

Such reasoning however is perhaps not as solid as it might firstly appear—it certainly agrees with our intuitive sense, our everyday experience, but it may not exhaust the full scope of our knowledge. We might adopt an approach that is quite at variance with this; that is, there might be an overlapping space if we are prepared to countenance the puncturing of space, just as there might be an interrupted space if we are prepared to countenance the elasticity of space. (For the first of these, you might imagine an empty train rushing in and out of a tunnel; for the second, how a wave of light becomes distorted as with the Doppler Effect.) Thus, where it concerns the question of permeability, we would regard this as conjunctive with the removal of fewer and fewer *material* parts; and where it concerns the question of deformability, we would hold this as conjunctive with the addition of more and more *cavernous* parts. This in turn will shed a different light on the meaning of inclusion and exclusion per se, since the same thing may be both inclusive in one sense and exclusive in another. All that is required is to transpose the relation between what is 'inside' and what is 'outside', such that the former is inclusive in the sense of what is getting *smaller* and the latter is exclusive in the sense of what is getting *larger*.

But to return to our discussion about the meaning of a proper part, so far as it is the whole that is dependent upon the part and not the part that is dependent upon the whole, the implication of this may be demonstrated and in the following way. The continents of the world might be said to be seven in number, they being Africa, Asia, Europe, North America, South America, Antarctica and Australia. These therefore are all parts of the same whole and exhaustive of that whole. But we would not say that there is a distinct class that comprises *just* the inhabitants of Africa and Asia, just Australians and Europeans or just Eskimos and Zulus. Hence so far as there is a proper whole that is derived from the meaning of a proper part, then this can surely only be *some* Africans and Asians, *some* Australians and Europeans, *some* Eskimos and Zulus. Or let us take another example. The group of objects that comprises such things as paper, pencils and erasers we would generally call stationery. But we would not from this starting point argue for the existence of a subgroup that comprises just paper and pencils, just pencils and erasers, just rulers and ink. Hence so far as there is a proper whole that accords with any proper part, then surely this can only be *some* paper and pencils, *some* pencils and erasers and *some* rulers and ink.

Chapter 5
Principle of Individuation

To being our enquiry, we need to distinguish between the sense in which diversity in number *may* reflect diversity in kind and the sense in which diversity in number *must* reflect diversity in kind. In the former case, what we are dealing with is the basic difference between things that are liable to change and in the latter case, the basic difference between things that are constant throughout time. Consider if you will what we mean by an element such as nitrogen, or a prime number such as seven, or the angles inscribed in a circle, then it should be clear that these are all constant and in no way susceptible of change throughout time. On the other hand, what we mean by an ox or an owl, or any human product, say a table or a chair, are the sorts of things that inhabit a world that is constantly in flux. These two questions are entirely distinct, since what we mean by *identity* in the strict sense concerns only the former, that is, what is logically unique, not a comparison of two things so far as they may or may not be alike. The concept of identity has often been elucidated within the broader framework of time and space, as when it is said that the same thing cannot have two beginnings, that the same thing cannot be in two places at once, that two things cannot be in the same place at the same time, etc. This however is somewhat simplistic—it obscures the more important distinction between a change in location and a change in duration or at least, the comparison of one thing with respect to its motion and the comparison of two things when they may or may not be at rest. Consider the case of Siamese twins. Are they the same because they have some parts in common or are they different because there is a difference in their fingers and their toes? The answer can only be given if we know what is meant by the *norm*.

If we ask if it is the same thing in the same place at the same time, then this is a strictly *existential* question (that is, a question about space and the occupants thereof). If we ask if it is the same thing in the same place but at various times, then this is a strictly provisory question (that is, a question about the relation between time and space). If we ask if two things can be in the same place at the same or at different times, then this is a strictly *grammatical* question (that is, a question about the meaning of space). Now it is important to realize that these questions are not conjunctive but rather disjunctive in their kind, or at least so far as the first two may have any bearing on the third. We can define an object as something that occupies the same place at the same time or we can map the history of an object with a set of coordinates and in conjunction with a purely observational set of rules. If on the other hand we ask whether two things can be in the same place at the same time, or can have the same beginning in time and space, then this quite clearly is an appeal to our intuitive or analytic judgement. That is, we might consider that two things can never occupy the same place at the same time if we have defined a place with respect to some occupant or we might consider that two things can occupy the same place at the same time if they occupy one place qua one part of the whole or one place qua one whole in itself. Not only that, but we tend to regard the physical world as supportive of such a view, since we take it to be significant that 'X is to the left of Y', that 'Bath is to the left of Bristol' and that 'France is to the right of Spain'. The problem here is that it is not entirely clear how this could be said to constitute a relation (or at least what is *real* in any relation), since if X is to the left of Y, then Y *must* be to the right of X and we are none the wiser about any actual state of affairs—or at least what it might mean if there were any change in this state of affairs. Consider on the other hand such statements as 'John is the nephew of James', 'Two is the square root of four', 'Fame is the object of envy'—then in none of these we do find what is commutative or interchangeable in itself. (That is, there is a specific relation and not just the existence of quite different relata).

So far as it concerns a comparison between things that may or may not be alike, there are two entirely different methods we might employ: on the one hand, what could be called the discursive or analytic, and on the other hand the descriptive or evidentiary. What we mean by the former is a certain set of assumptions about the relation between quality and quantity, such that there is one kind of distinction for things that differ specifically and quite another for things that differ numerically. And the grading of these will be such that although material distinctions must always be encompassed in the meaning of what is formal, what is formal need not always be encompassed in the meaning of what is material. For what is undivided in the genus will always be divided in the species, but what is undivided in the species is in no way what is distinctive about the genus. Or we might pursue this through a discussion about the relation between existence and essence. If we suppose that one thing can be the cause of another's existence, then what exists in reality must also exist in potential, or at least, have the potential to exhibit this or that particular set of properties. The implication will also be that it is the whole that supersedes the sum of its parts, that division can only reveal what the whole contains and that the whole can never be generated by something partitive or discontinuous in itself. Thus, if we take the view that the whole is prior to the part in the sense that it may not be composed of divers parts, then what is essentially the same may be divided in such a way as is extensively quite different, but what is extensively the same cannot on its own account be divided in a manner that is essentially quite diverse.

Having said that, it should not be assumed that existence can only be encompassed through essence, or that the former has no relevance in and of itself. Quite clearly, if there is one existent then there are not two existents, and operations such as addition and subtraction could well be described as the backbone of mathematics, taken in and of themselves.

From a certain perspective, we might well say that essence is prior to existence since there is more specialty in the former, or at least, there is more specialty in any person than there is in any nationality or any race, but in a stronger sense might the pith of this be made to serve a very different end. So far, it could be argued, as there is more specificity at one extreme there is also less being, whereas at the other, there is not only more being but more completeness as well, that is, a more complete inventory of things. Consider the following passage from a work by Aristotle:

> Genera . . . are always prior to the species since they do
> not reciprocate as to implication of existence e.g. if there
> is a fish there is an animal, but if there is an animal there
> is not necessarily a fish.
>
> (Categories chapter 13 14b24)

The difficulty here is that there seem to be two things that are being run together, the *intension* and the *extension* of a term. What surely cannot, but appears to be argued for, is that there are two distinct groups, a group of things we call 'fishes' and a group of things we call 'animals'. The inference would seem to be that these groups cannot influence one another, but that there will nonetheless be more animals than fishes, since if they were paired off and removed, most of the former would remain. The reasoning however is somewhat suspect, since it is not existents we are comparing, rather only the more or less restricted meaning of a word. That is, what we are saying is that the concept of an animal does not contain the concept of a fish, but that the concept of a fish must contain the concept of an animal. So far as existence is concerned, this is necessarily inclusive rather than exclusive, since there can only be more animals if there are more of the things we call 'animals', and that does not discriminate between the form that it takes, be that a bird, or a fish or a mammal. Hence numerical identity must always be made subordinate to specific identity.

As opposed to the intuitive method, what we mean by the descriptive method is that it takes the individual as its starting point and does not assume the same quality will be exhibited in a variety of things, but regards each thing as comprising a complex of qualities, which *may* or *may not* be the same. So far as it concerns the question of 'essence' however, then a further distinction must be made between the competing claims that two things cannot be qualitatively the same and that two things may or may not be qualitatively the same. To consider the second of these, if we suppose that what is inclusive is what marks the difference between each and every *thing*, and what is exclusive is what marks the difference between each and every *kind*, then this is not very far from the traditional or scholastic approach. That is, what is indicative of the species qua species is what we call its *differentiae* and what is indicative of the individual qua individual is what we call its *accidents*. Or we might express this by saying that what is 'essential' is what is in the thing itself, and what is accidental is only in our point of view. According to Locke, properties such as extension, figure and motion could be said to be 'in' the things themselves, but colour, sound and smell are really 'in' the senses, that is, a kind of mediated knowledge that constitutes the sense data but not the 'thing in itself'. Further to this, we might define a synthetic whole as (*a*) something having an underlying or enduring element and (*b*) what is identifiable or classifiable or of such and such a kind.

On the other hand, we might take an entirely different line by suggesting that what 'essence' conveys is a complete agreement in both the macro and the micro—that if there is even the least discrepancy, this will suffice to account two things completely different in the way they should be viewed. And so, what we are arguing for is a difference between what something is by virtue of what it is in *all* respects and what it is by virtue of what is in *some* respects. Consider the way we might approach this through the relation between existence and essence. Since what we mean by 'essence' includes all the attributes of a thing, what it has and what it has in common, constitutes 'existence' in the only true sense of the word. That is, there is a difference when we say that something is inclusive by virtue of what it is in and of itself, and that something is inclusive by virtue of what it has which is peculiar only to its *kind*. Existence is something that binds things that are formally (or qualitatively) distinct and yet materially (or quantitatively) the same. Essence on the other hand is not binding at all; it no more pertains to what has quantity than it does to what has quality, to what is fleeting than to what is lasting, to what is fictional than to what is real. For example, although we would not say that Sherlock Holmes is real it does not follow there may not be different versions of what is essentially the same iconic and primordial character.

Where it concerns the question of individuality, there are three ways we might approach this: (*a*) at the existential, (*b*) at the empirical and (*c*) at the transcendental level. So far as it concerns the first, the issue that needs to be addressed is what makes something the same as itself given a particular conception of time, and what makes something the same as itself given a particular conception of space. Quite clearly, being vital and alive must entail a body that one can control, and having organs and structures that connect one with one's immediate environs. We know that the self is the same so far as it has the same hypostasis, that it has an intellect and a memory, and that there is a unified consciousness which connects it with a singular past, with a singular present and with a singular future. On the other hand, if we were to argue that identity concerns only the given space that a living body occupies, then we have reduced it to a mere cipher or any conjunction that may arise between the parts of time and space.

At the empirical level, there are several issues that need to be addressed, and these are a comparison of two things with respect to (*a*) their grossness and fineness, (*b*) their fullness and incompleteness (*c*) their symmetry and disproportion. What we mean by the quasi-qualitative approach is a comparison of two things that does not involve any distinction between the essential and the adventitious, but which regards all the qualities as relevant to just such a complex or whole. If we compare two things as regards their colour, their texture, and their smell, then there will always be some difference where it concerns the richness of detail. Either one will have more attributes or be more detailed, even if we consider that they are comprehensively or extensively just the same. On the other hand, if we wish to express the relation between quality and quantity as altogether inclusive and not exclusive, then we can do this by means of the Identity of Coefficients. If for instance, one considers something as comprising heterogeneous parts but of only two kinds, then how we distribute these parts may well be influential in what it is that results. Assuming their number and ratio to remain the same, it may be possible to achieve an entirely different result if we substitute one set of parts for the other. That is, what we mean by the whole is something that is represented *in* the parts, but not the part as something that is representative of the whole. As concerns the third point, what we need to consider is how we might arrange the parts in a manner that is most suitable and most pleasing to the eye. To this end an arrangement such as 3:5 and 5:8 will be more 'agreeable' than 2:6 and 6:8, since the ratio of the smaller to the larger part equals the ratio of the larger part to the whole.

Where however it concerns a comparison of all things, then what we need to consider is what it would mean if our world were not the least bit uniform in its kind. If our assumption is that a Supreme Being would not make two things exactly alike, then there must always be some ground for their difference, be that what is active or passive, what is manifest or latent, what is necessary or contradictory. Consider the following group of objects and the attributes they might possess. Object X comprises the properties 'a,b,c', object Y comprises the properties 'b,c,d' and object Z comprises the properties 'd,e,f'. Now if we treat this arrangement in terms of what is common and what is not, then in one category will we have the properties 'b,c,d' and in the other 'a,e,f'. If further we connect X with a and Z with 'e,f', then what we will arrive at are the primary constituents of each in addition to certain supplements, that being 'b,c' for X and 'd' for Z. This however is not the only way we might approach the matter, since it makes no allowance for what is and is not commutable *per se*. Certainly if we allow that for any two things, may there be a coincidence in number but not in kind, then there is no reason why 'a' cannot be substituted for 'd', nor 'b,c' for 'e,f'. On the other hand, if we consider that the common properties may yet be annexed to produce an invariant whole, then in no way do we have something that is reversible or interchangeable in itself (given the status of Y as a simple or invariant whole). By comparison the original entities (what is peculiar to X and Z) will appear as merely colourless shapes, indifferent in themselves but nonetheless diversified in their number. Depending on one's point of view therefore, we will have either a simple substance that is diversified in its parts or a cluster of properties that are undivided in themselves

How then might we characterize this in the manner we have expressed it, between the meaning of a *monad* on the one hand and a *modeme* on the other? In a certain context we might say to be one is to be composed of like parts and to be many is to be composed of unlike parts. Now in every homogeneous whole the parts participate in the form of the whole, as for instance, every part of fire is of the nature of fire. So far as it concerns heterogeneity, the parts do not participate in the whole, but each has a form which is peculiarly its own. Thus, it is unity or indivisibility on the one hand that contrasts with multiplicity or divisibility on the other. We may however choose to approach this quite otherwise, given that the self-replenishment of a part may be at the expense of the whole, and the self-replenishment of the whole may be at the expense of certain parts. If what we mean by a unified whole is that which is adequate to such and such an end, then just as there is a threshold for the fulfilment of any task, so must there be a threshold for the effectiveness of any part. It should be clear therefore that it is only in the removal of certain 'vital' parts that any mischief may be done, since whatever is idle or inactive can hardly be made more so, whatever the means one might apply. So long as there is sufficiency in the number of working parts, it is reasonable to assume there will also be sufficiency in the achievement of any assignable end. Where however it concerns the question of the energizing of such a whole and the replenishment of all its parts, this will occur only when there is a more even distribution, i.e.

when some of the more vital parts become less so and some of the less vital parts become more so. However, there may also be something quite at odds with this, a concentration of energy such that some parts assume a disproportionate influence in relation to all the rest. That is, some parts that were active and in a helpful way may become more active but in a somewhat discommodious way. And this is exactly what we mean by a modeme, an active but nonetheless roguish part, something that *sustains* itself through others, but only by disabling them and making them less effective at their core.

Chapter 6
Of Relations

There are two broad issues that arise with respect to a relation and they are as follows: (*a*) whether it is independent of or only subsidiary to our everyday world and (*b*) whether it is equal to or only an adjunct to those things it is meant to conjoin. Consider a simple statement such as 'David is the son of John'. Now there are two ways we might interpret this. Firstly, that 'sonship' is an accident that pertains to David and 'fatherhood' is an accident that pertains to John or that 'sonship' is a relationship having an equal status to what it refers to, so that John is only indifferently the father of David, just as David may be only indifferently the father of Simon. Hence there are two possible interpretations. We might say that since John is the father of David, David *must* be the son of John, but that if John is the father of David and David is the father of Simon, then John *cannot* be the father of Simon (diversity of content). Or we might say that if Michael and John are unrelated, but both Michael and John are fathers, it does not follow that if Michael has a single child, then John must have a single child (diversity of number). Or in the case of 'A precedes B', what we have are two terms and a relation that is fundamental to our understanding of time. But since the word *precedes* also has a form that enables us to place it at the head of a sentence, as in 'Preceding is the opposite of succeeding', it might seem natural to regard this subject as having just the same status as anything of a more manifestly concrete kind. It would also seem natural to regard the expression 'A is antecedent' or 'B is successive' as examples of a relation that holds between a term and itself, only here where it is something asymmetrical rather than symmetrical in its kind.

Or let us pursue our enquiry by comparing the statements 'A is younger than B' and 'B is younger than A'. Now we know that the meaning of these statements could in no way be construed as the same, but it remains a moot point how or on what grounds we might establish any difference per se. Certainly we can infer nothing from the presence of 'A', 'B' and 'is younger', since we have entirely the same set of elements in either case. Neither can this difference be ascertained if we consider a number of such statements, e.g. 'A is younger than B', 'B is younger than C', 'C is younger than D', etc. Consequently, the sense of such a sentence can only be adduced if we break it down in the following way, where there are (*a*) the terms A and B, (*b*) the relation 'is younger' and (*c*) the asymmetrical nature of each term if viewed in a certain way. That is, it should be clear that 'A is younger' or 'A is older' is a mere variation on what A is in and of itself, since there is both the question of its placement within any given complex and that complex in and of itself

On the other hand, what could also be argued is that if we treat any term merely in respect to its station then we have effectively reduced it to what is vacuous and aberrant in itself. That is, if one were to argue that the statement 'A is identical with B' is not the same as 'B is identical with A', then the instant it becomes a question of the content of both, then it is not at all clear how such a comparison might be made. Certainly, there is a perfectly obvious sense in which the brown briefcase that is sitting on *this* table is the same as the brown briefcase that was sitting on *that* chair, since we can observe its transit from t_1 to t_2. But if there were two identical briefcases sitting on the table, then surely this would be on account of certain common properties, not because the one just happened to be to the right or left of the other, as if it were necessary that this should be so. Thus, neither would it seem at one extreme that relational facts were simply the properties that different things exhibit, *nor* that there are only relations, and that it is from these that everything else must be built. In the present case, when we say that two briefcases are identical what we mean is that they are the same in this or that respect, and so it is some common property that antecedes that relation we call commonality. On the other hand, it may be an entirely different matter when it is some relation that is binding or essential for those things that are at hand. If two briefcases are sitting on the table then it is a contingent matter how they might be arranged, whether they are sitting beside one another, on top of one another or several metres apart etc… But then of course it is not a contingent matter how two things are arranged when they are bound by that relation we call causality, since if A causes B, then it cannot be the case that B causes A.

And if we were to deny that at least some relations are not necessary or in some respect situational, then we would be open to the charge that the things we call real are actually not as real as we might imagine them to be. If A exists and B exists, then it is only the case that AB *may* exist, given that there is some way they may be connected as a whole. But since the parts may exist in their own right just as the whole may exist in its own right, what should not be inferred is that there is one and only one relation that might make them both complete. Hence, we could say that the bottle of milk is sitting on the fridge or the bottle of milk is sitting in the fridge, but whatever the case, where there are two terms there must be two connections as well. If it were true however that the bottle that is sitting in the fridge *can only* be sitting in the fridge, then what we would require is a further relation to explain why this should also be so. We could thus imagine an infinite number of such 'relations' each one connected to all the rest. Looked at from the viewpoint of either a diversity of number or a diversity of content therefore, the argument against the reality of relations must be regarded as a somewhat compelling one.

However, it is not just a question whether we take relations to be something inherent or something adventitious, but also how the mind might be active in forming ideas that are general rather than those that are detailed. Since it is the judgement that not only joins but also separates the subject from the predicate, on no account we can accept that it is the latter alone that constitutes a relation. What we mean by 'the subject' is something that is qualified by that reality surrounding it, and what we mean by 'the predicate' is something that may or may not be affirmed of the subject taken in its more extensive sense. Thus, in the case of 'My sister is playing on the swing', 'my sister' is one aspect of reality and 'is playing' what connects her with the more generalized idea 'is-playing-on-the-swing'. Of course there are those who would argue that since you can say 'Tallness can be predicated of a milk bottle' just as you can 'The milk bottle is twenty centimetres tall', then what this proves is that the predicate is no more dependent on the subject than the subject is on the predicate. Not only that, but you can also compare the properties of tallness and shortness without any prejudice to either the one or the other. What the issue really hinges on here however, is what you mean by 'dependent'—are you using this in a linguistic sense, in an attributive sense or in an on ontological sense? Are you saying that tallness may be predicated of a milk bottle but not the number six, that tallness may be predicated of a milk bottle but not the desire to be rich, or are you saying there is an idea of tallness apart from any particular thing, that is, that tallness is a universal?

Such a consideration may also be relevant when we ask if the idea of diversity can only be grounded in the *reality* of what is the same, or whether diversity could be said to constitute something whole or unific in itself. Thus when we say 'A is different from B', is this sufficient to establish that relation called diversity or do we need to specify in what respect they are not also the same? No doubt the proposition has a sense so far as it expresses some idea, but this is not the same as the *relation* we call diversity, since for that what we need is a closer inspection of the *facts,* not a closer inspection of the *terms.* If 'A' denotes a bachelor and 'B' denotes a husband, then this does indeed assert a relation, the relation we call diversity, but that is not the case if 'A' denotes a husband and 'B' denotes a married man. The point is, in the way we employ a particular sign or a particular symbol it may depend just as much on the context as it does if we regard it in and of itself. For instance, if you use the symbol '+' in the context of '20 + 2 = 22', then this is altogether proper, but that is not nearly as apparent in the case of 'sign + post = signpost', since 'sign' may mean 'to sign' and 'post' may mean 'to post' as when you ask a person to 'sign and post' a letter. Hence, there is a difference between the way a set of signs and symbols may be applied in some appropriate setting, and the way they may be used when this is simply accurate or precise. It is not inconceivable that two persons could play a game of chess in a way that was perfectly consistent with the rules, but in no way connected with any end, or at least, with the end of actually bringing such activity to a close. (Even if the game ends in stalemate that does not mean they intended it be so.)

The point about all this is that there is a difference in the way we might handle such a question if it concerns just diversity in number or if it concerns both diversity in number and diversity in content. Number '1' is different from number '2', the numbers '1' and '2' make 3 but not 4, number '5' is half of number 10 but not 12, etc. However, in the case of content, what we need is something that *grounds* the concept of diversity; otherwise all we have is the connection between a symbol and any general meaning. Quite clearly in the case of A = A, although we have the symbol '=' what we do not have is a diversity of terms, and hence, what could properly be called a relation. However, in the case of A = B most certainly we do, but also one derived from those assessments and observations we might make. For instance, where it concerns the question of consanguinity or 'blood relation' then this could involve any number of things, since there are different kinds of relations, from that which is spousal, to that which is clannish, to that which is racial. We might say that two members of the same family have the same colour hair; that two individuals with a Catholic background were married in the same church; that two Indians from the same tribe speak a language they call Siouan. In the same way, there may be different shades of red and there may be different shades of blue, but without a colour chart and without the use of our sight, we could not say what was similar or dissimilar at all (i.e. similar with respect to colour but not necessarily shape, similar with respect to shape but not necessarily smell, etc.).

The next question that presents itself is this: In what respect is it the case that relations may be abstract but not universal and in what respect may they be objective but not ideal? It stands to reason that if we regard relations as being universal, then to this degree they must also be abstract, but does it follow that if we regard them as being abstract they must also be universal? Perhaps the way we might address this is through a comparison of the kinds of statements that evince either (*a*) sameness with respect to both content and number or (*b*) diversity with respect to both content and number. So far as it concerns (*a*) what we are dealing with is a simple identity statement such as 'A exists' or 'A is A'. So far as it concerns (*b*) what we are dealing with are two contrasting ideas, on the one hand, a certain mutuality between the terms and on the other a certain contrariety between the terms.

Let us examine this a little more closely. Relations such as 'is greater than', 'is the cause of' or 'is proportionate to' imply a certain contrariety between the terms at hand, and so preclude us from abstracting what is common to them both. If it is the case that A is larger than B then necessarily B must be smaller than A, but that is not to say there is any critical quantity that determines what is 'larger than' or 'smaller than'. Even if there were, it is impossible that the same accident could be in two entirely separate subjects or be passed from the one to the other. On the other hand, in the case of 'The ratio 1:2 is the same as 2:4' then there is no problem in asserting such a claim, nor that 'greater than' is the converse of 'smaller than' when there is no discrepancy in the meaning of these terms. However, although this shows that 'to be the same' is not necessarily to have a property which is common, that is not say one cannot abstract a certain property when this involves a further term. In the circumstances where segment A is in the ratio of 1:2 to B, segment B is in the ratio of 1:2 to C, then without any further information is it not the case that we can simply deduce that the relation between A and C must be 1:4? And is this knowledge any the less objective than that which could be said of the ideal?

In treating of the meaning of diversity, we have already noted how under one heading 'number' what it tends to lead to is a certain mutuality, and under another heading 'content' what it tends to lead to is a certain contrariety. Therefore so far as it concerns a basic formula, a relation should be said to comprise (*a*) two terms and no more than two terms and (*b*) two connections between these terms, understood either as opposite attributes or the same attribute present or absent (That is, if the connective is a relation such as *above* and *below*, then the issue resolves itself; otherwise we need 'is' and 'is not'). This obviates the kind of problem that arises when we think of two terms in relation to two pairs of attributes or a pair of attributes in relation to more than two terms. It is fundamental to our argument that in terms of the whole-part relationship, if A exists and B exists, then it is only the case that AB *may* exist and so not in a way that is completely invariable. It could be argued that if A is greater than B and B is greater than C, then A must be greater than C. The question however remains, is this statement about the relation between A and B or is it a statement about the relation between A, B and C? If our answer is in favour of the latter then the objection could be raised that this is to confound what we mean by a relation with what is simply a *deduction*. In other words, if there were another element D, and C was greater than D, then would you say this was a different *relation* or just another part of the *same* relation? And if the latter, then what of 'A is greater than D', would you approach this by saying it was the same or just a different kind of reasoning?

Hence, although our reasoning, or reasoning from a premise to such and such a conclusion may in some sense be said to be skewed, it does not follow that what we are a dealing with is a relation that must also be skewed. We can see the consequence of this when something such as 'is taller than' is taken to be asymmetrical, even though it is not clear in what sense one term must have priority over any other. It might be argued that if you consider some whole comprising A and B, and A and B have weight, then if their relation were reducible to some common property then it would be impossible to say whether A was heavier than B or B was heavier than A. The problem with this is that 'being heavier than' does not even raise the question of what is common in any relationship, and so it is begging the question to ask if it is also asymmetrical. If A is heavier than B, then it is *only from the perspective* of A that the relation is one of 'being heavier than', since from the perspective of B it is one of 'being lighter than'. Hence this is a reciprocal and not an asymmetrical relation.

Whilst admitting that relations do not adhere to things in the way that discernible properties do, or that they are just the different descriptions of what a thing *is*, neither would we concede that they have a being or a quiddity that is peculiarly their own. Let us approach this in terms of the distinction between an absolute and qualified *description*. Sometimes when we describe things, we do so in a manner that is altogether vague and imprecise, as when we call something large or small, heavy or light, clear or vague. In so doing, we do not suppose these qualities to be subject to any exact measurement, rather are they the judgements that we form based on our experiences as a whole. When a carrier says that such and such a vase is heavy what he means is that it is difficult to convey, or least that is, relative to his physical capacity not relative to a building or a bridge. When a connoisseur judges that such and such a wine is fruity what he means is that it is fruity in relation to how it tastes, not fruity in relation to his feelings or his thoughts. When a farmer says that such and such a watermelon is huge what he means is that it is huge in comparison to anything he has seen or encountered in the past. In other words, those cues that apply are in keeping with our experiences overall.

However, when we say that our descriptions may be qualified, what we mean could be understood in either of two ways: (*a*) where it concerns the existence of some internal measurement or (*b*) where it concerns the existence of some internal comparisons. So far as it concerns the former, this is a theoretical mean between two extremes, as when 'larger than' is taken to be the obverse of 'smaller than', 'taller than' of 'shorter than' and 'wider than' of 'narrower than'. This is essentially what we mean by a relation in connection with anything that exhibits a certain diversity of content. However, there is also the sense in which a relation is something that binds two objects such that we might call this the complex 'A and B'. For instance, let us say that A = a goalpost and B = a flagpole. In this case, height could be said to be a relation that binds these objects as the complex 'A and B'. On the other hand, to consider another possible conjunct, say the Eiffel Tower and the river Thames, in this case you would not say that the Eiffel Tower was taller or shorter than the river Thames and you certainly would not say it was the same in height. Hence what is relevant in the way we judge one circumstance may not be relevant in the way we judge any other.

At a more speculative level, what we mean by vestigial or incipient matter is that it is of the nature of any cell that it be either self-expanding or self-dividing and that it is only in the case of the latter that there is any real prospect for growth. This also underscores the idea of a *modemic* relation, or what is distorted and asymmetrical rather than what is flawless and self-contained. Consider the following set of objects and the attributes they might possess. Let us say object X comprises the properties 'a,b,d', object Y comprises the properties 'a,b,c' and object Z comprises the properties 'a,b,c,d'. Now in terms of what is common and what is not, if we compare the original objects X and Y, what we have is 'a,b' on the one hand and 'c,d' on the other. If we compare X and Z, then what results on the one hand is 'a,b,d' and on the other 'c'. If we compare Y and Z, then what we have is 'a,b,c' as common and 'd' as what is not. It is clear therefore there is a certain compatibility where each of these comparisons is concerned—certainly no violation of the rule that there be both the inclusiveness and exclusiveness of any part. On the other hand, if we make a broad comparison of all three objects, then a certain difficulty may arise, since Z is a composite of X and Y and so affords no ground for what is separate rather than for what may also be conjoined

Perhaps we can express this idea of mutuality in the following way. (1) X has the quality of being unique by virtue of lacking c (2) Y has the quality of being unique by virtue of lacking d (3) Z has the quality of being unique by virtue of having a lack or possession status different for c than it does for d. We may however consider another alternative such that it is not any original pairing that serves as a basis for comparison, but a fluid interchange of the objects just as they are in themselves. Let us say that object A possesses the property p but is lacking in q and r, object B possesses the property q but is lacking in p and r and that object C possesses the properties p and q but is lacking in r. Now from this perspective, it is only a comparison of the entire complex that will yield what is inclusive and what is exclusive per se. Again we might formalize this by adopting the following rules: (*a*) A has the quality of being unique by virtue of lacking q, (*b*) B has the quality of being unique by virtue of lacking p and (*c*) C has the quality of being unique by virtue of having a lack or possession status different from that of both p and q. In the first instance, what we have could be called a *monadic* relation and in the second, what could be called a *modemic* relation.[2]*

---

2   It should be clear that in the way we are treating of the 'monadic', we are not doing so by comparison with the 'dyadic', 'triadic', etc.)

Chapter 7

Of Abstract Ideas

To begin with, let us consider what is meant by *abstraction* and whether this involves any true separation or ultimately only the objects of sense and their copies as these are deposited in our minds. This might be viewed in either of two ways (*a*) the separation of certain qualities or (*b*) the separation of such and such a quantity from such and such a quality. Abstraction means the separation of matter and form—the separation of two things that ultimately enables us to discern a certain essence or a certain quiddity. The question then arises whether there be any end for such an activity, an unchanging or ideal form in which this activity must ultimately be brought to a close. We might approach this from the viewpoint of (*a*) a class or collection of things and (*b*) any singular or particular thing. Where it concerns the question of a species or class then what we are dealing with is both a specialty and a common bond, the former what distinguishes it from any given thing, the latter what connects it with any given thing. The question then arises whether there be a common nature in conjunction with the specifications for any particular thing, or just the specifications for any particular thing understood as the *potential* to be used in such and such a way. We might for instance define a table as something having a flat top, supported by pillars or legs, and used for eating, studying, conferring etc . . . But this would not be its 'common' nature, otherwise we could not distinguish it from any cupboard or any chair, that is, it would not be distinctive as a piece of furniture but only something that *may* be construed as having a variety of uses. When we think of 'furniture', we do not think of something that can be conveniently divided into matter and form, rather, something that supports a particular kind of *usage*. In other words, we may be able to use a cabinet to eat our food on, but it would be more appropriate if we used it to store a radio or a record-player.

Let us now consider how we might arrive at the idea of a single object, say perhaps a staircase or a desk. We could perhaps regard this as the different interpretations that are placed on it as seen through the eyes of a user, as seen through the eyes of an artist, as seen through the eyes of a maker. It is then a certain colour or a certain texture, a certain wood or a certain glue, a certain something to ascend from or a certain something to studying on. Or we might regard this in the manner of a single percept, what appears from this angle or from that, from in front or from behind. In all this however, we have nothing unific as such, only a particular datum, a particular aspect, a particular use. However, the fact that we may not discern anything ultimate or transcendent does not mean there is no such thing at all. Because we cannot proceed from the univocally 'real' to the univocally 'ideal' does not mean we cannot augment the sense of what a thing is by considering it in greater and greater detail, or be more sparing in any account we may provide. Suppose for instance you were asked to sketch the image of a bird or a fish, then this is not the same as what it would mean to sketch the image of a magpie or a gopher. In the first instance, you would need only a broad outline, in the second instance distinguishing marks such as colour and plumage as well.

But the question still remains whether there is any real comparison between something precise or distinctive and something of a more universal or generic kind. From our own perspective, it is clear that what this entails is only what we *intend* to convey the object, not a comparison of more and less detail, rather, whether 'sameness' is accomplished through the discernment of what is simple or 'sameness' is accomplished through the discernment of what is complex. Certain things cannot be apprehended in such and such a way because we do not possess the requisite means, certain others can, but not because they are the reconfigured version of something admitted from without. To consider the difference between the concept 'humanity' and any particular man or the concept 'animality' and any particular animal, it should not be assumed that the latter is simple whereas the former is not, that what is comprehended in humanity must be something quite complex, whereas a man is nothing more than an amalgam of divers and adventitious parts. Here the implication is that the mind is active so far as it is dealing with something complex and that the senses are active so far as what they are dealing with something simple. This however obscures the more immediate question: What is it that *prevents* us from apprehending something as a unity and what is it that *enables* us to apprehend something as a unity?

Perhaps the point can be made a little clearer if we consider the difference between a less and more 'perfected' whole, as discerned in the relation between a man, a mammal, an animal and a living thing. As we proceed in an upward direction, what we appear to be doing is filtering out more and more attributes such that there is less specificity in a mammal than there is in a man, and greater generality in an animal than there is in a mammal. But the question still remains whether what is involved here is a true separation, whether there are in fact parts that can be separated and whether there is in fact something that can be reconstituted as a whole. That is, what does it mean if we attempt to achieve a greater sense of unity at one extreme or a greater sense of precision at the other? Consider what would happen if you were to proceed from a whole man to the parts of a man—would this engender more or less precision overall? Certainly, there is a difference between being five feet or four feet tall, between having wavy or straight hair, but what 'adds' to our understanding of the difference between Mary and Jane is not necessarily what 'adds' to our understanding of the difference between a gibbon and a plant. Or in the case of Joseph Merrick, the so-called "Elephant Man" a greater degree of complexity should not dissuade us from the belief that this must still be counted as a man.

Or consider at the other extreme what would happen if we attempted to append the meaning of a living thing to things that were more spiritual or more ethereal in their kind. Could this or would this do anything to enhance our sense of what it means to be unified or would it rather lead to a wrangling over whether in fact there really were angels and bunyips, mermaids and elves? Thus what we are doing in passing from one rung to the next does not necessarily suggest what is more or less 'complete', but rather something opposed to the very idea of completion itself. The equivocation that has become apparent here could also be expressed in terms of a disjunction between existence and essence or what we have called a *specialized* nature and a *global* existence. What is common, as for instance what is common to any mammal, should not be seen as what is additional to the make-up of any mammal, but rather what is binding on any group qua a subgroup of any whole. To suppose there may be both a proper and a common nature (as did the Schoolmen) is rather misplaced, since we cannot filter out certain attributes without destroying the very ground for existence itself. And how could there be any category of being unless there were not instances or cases of precisely what this was?

Where however it concerns the question of greatness or a perfected whole what this involves is the apprehension of something quite distinct or transparent through and through. Consider an abstract figure such as a simple triangle. It should be clear that when we compare one type of triangle with another what we have are not different aspects of the same thing, that is 'triangularity', rather any number of figures quite unique and distinct in themselves. That is why the number of triangles is illimitable because we can conceive of them in so many shapes and sizes. And if further we were to take two mirror image triangles and rotate one through 180 degrees, then we can discern in what sense there may be strict identity rather and not just similarity in this respect or in that. We might also say of the isosceles that it strengthens the distinction between the equilateral and the scalene, of the scalene that it strengthens the distinction between the equilateral and the isosceles, of the equilateral that it strengthens the distinction between the scalene and the isosceles.

Thus, it is not any common feature but rather uniqueness that governs the individual both in its specific and more categorical sense.

Consider now, in conjunction with our earlier discussion, the difference between the concept 'rationality' or 'humanity' and the concept 'triangularity' or 'circularity'. Given a certain set of assumptions, what we might infer is that there is a universal idea achieved by the means of highlighting certain attributes and rejecting certain others. And yet although we might well say this with respect to the former, that is, what does or does not possess rationality, we would not necessarily say this with respect to the latter. What we mean by 'triangularity' no more pertains to 'being a triangle' than 'circularity' pertains to what we mean by 'being a square'. That is, triangularity is something that pertains to the apriori makeup of space, but not necessarily to what is 'in' space, and thus, so far as space is a synthesis then so also is triangularity, but no less so than squareness, circularity or anything else of a similar kind. Where it concerns the question of 'being triangular', this pertains to its type or its visual representation, be that isosceles, scalene or equilateral. What might be true in one case however is not necessarily true in any categorical sense, that is, it is something that any figure may exhibit, not however, what it must or must never exhibit. We do not consider a circle to be of such and such a type, because in this case there are no particular subgroups that may be different in form or design. Where however it concerns the question of just *being* triangular, what we are dealing with is a simple construct that bears comparison only to itself and just those parts of which it is made. And this we might also say of the act of apprehension, that what we conceive of as a triangle *must* be veridical so far as it is brought before our minds in precisely the way that it is.

Let us now address the question whether what we mean by an idea is the simple likeness or imitation of what is real, or whether it involves an act, the object of the act and what is binding on them both. In terms of our general argument the following points must be made. Firstly, what we mean by the sensuous is something within the scope of our reason but not the edges of our reason, not what must or cannot be, rather what may or may not be. At one extreme we have the idea of a transcendental being, what *must* exist of its very nature, and at the other an impossible object such as a three-sided sphere or a six-sided square. In between there are many other things, some we would regard as sensuous, some we would regard as abstract, and some we would regard as ideal. But we should also be clear about the difference between something that *must* and something that *may* exist by virtue of being placed before our minds, in the case of the latter, when this partakes of what is sensuous. The notion of an Infinite or Necessary being on the other hand, since it does not partake of what is sensuous, might be open to the charge that it is not the sort of thing that *every* mind would wish to entertain. Hence when we say 'must' we mean what must be rational, but of course, not necessarily what must also be real. In other words, because we can *conceive* of a Necessary Being does there mean there must be such a thing as well. (The Schoolmen were somewhat remiss in the case of the Ontological Argument).

The important point is that what is perceived must always be included within the gamut of what is perceivable, that a mental component the 'intentional object' must be added to the perceptual content and from which all our general knowledge is derived. To take an example in keeping with our earlier discussion, suppose a number of persons were observing the same object, say a brown carpet on a lounge room floor. Of course, what they 'see' are really different impressions that they then infer to belong to the same thing, viz. that rectangular piece of matting they are currently attending to. Consequently, to perceive here means to form a composite picture from those cues that have been automatically supplied. However, compare this with an approach to knowledge that is much more demanding in its kind. Although no one in the modern age has actually witnessed the power or ferocity of a dinosaur, there is no doubt we have a very detailed knowledge of how these creatures must have lived. We do not have merely a vague idea of what a dinosaur might have looked like; we can create an exact duplicate from its skeletal remains and draw up an epochal chart as well.

By linking the conceivable with the perceivable, what this also enables us to do is surmount the distinction between the active and the passive, or what constitutes the *source* of our knowledge and not simply what is immediate in and of itself. Looked at from one perspective, it is the spirit or mind that is the cause of our 'sensible' ideas, and since nothing can be known outside of what is knowable, what they refer or give rise to can only exist in the mind of some Infinite Being (Berkeley). Looked at from another perspective, it is the body that is the cause of our truly 'sensible' ideas, only here where they are traces or impressions of what is ultimately inexplicable in and of itself. But the assumption that the source of our knowledge emanates either from within or without, founders on the fact that wherever there is an image there must also be an object, and this does not discriminate between an adjunct to the mind and an adjunct to the senses. So far as there is a difference between an object and the image of that object, our conclusion can only be that what is delusional cannot be real and what is real cannot be delusional, to either the senses or the mind.

The question remains however, whether what we mean by delusional in the sense of what we take to be real, is the same as what is imaginary in the sense of what we take to be a *substitute* for what is real. We tend to regard an image or likeness as a substitute for what is real because (*a*) it is actually present at the time the object is not (an after-image) or (*b*) it is symbolic of what is real or is a copy of what is real (e.g. the wafer of bread that is taken by church communicants). But is this really the way we would wish to characterize the relation between any object and its image? A desert mirage is surely not something that corresponds to anything real, but then neither is it a substitute for anything that is real—it is merely what we *hope* might be real. Or consider the image of a chocolate mountain—to what extent is such a thing a substitute for what is real? Our answer here is that there may be nothing out of place, that we can both conceive of a chocolate mountain and that we can build a chocolate mountain—the existential status of the latter has no bearing on the former and the meaning of the former has no relevance for the latter. Of course, a mountain is not something that could naturally be composed of chocolate or any such ingredient, but that is not to say we could not construct a mound of chocolate and then transform it into something mountainous.

Consider also how this might have its corollary in the realm of ideal things. We can for instance have both the different forms of a circle and a triangle and the different orderings of a circle and a triangle. From a certain perspective we might regard the latter as 'less complete' than the former, since there may be different types of triangles but there can only be one type we call a circle. Or if we consider numbers as in the nature of what is ideal, then number 1 will have greater import than number 2 and any whole number greater import than any fraction. Or we might consider the difference between a pink and a scarlet shawl. For all practical purposes there is only a slight difference to be discerned, but we might suppose that scarlet rather than pink is a better approximation to what we call the colour red. Neither should we suppose there is any real 'contrariness' between a pink elephant and an elephant that is grey—our assumption about the colour of a thing no more interferes with our discernment of how it should act than does the regularity of any figure interfere with what is irregular overall. (A 'pink' elephant is something we tend to associate with a delusional state, but it is not an implicit truth that every elephant must be grey.)

Where it concerns the question of number, any definition must include the idea of what is similar, but that of course is what is similar in general not similar in this or that respect. In accordance with the tenets of a well-known logician3, we might treat number as a characteristic of classes or any class of objects. The number '7' thus comprises the class of all classes having such a number of members, as for instance the days of the week, the continents of the world, the hills of Rome, etc. What we would then be saying is that for any number does it constitute a class of similar classes, the things in one class having a one-to-one relation with the things in any other. In this way, we can overcome the difference between a specialized nature and a global existence, since every existent in these terms has been incorporated within some particular class. Where it concerns the question of a certain category of being on the other hand, such an approach may be not nearly so effective in its aim. For instance, suppose we make the observation that Paul is a good walker but that Peter is not or that Peter is a good swimmer but that Paul is not. And of course, one can certainly appreciate the truth of these remarks, but only so long as we do not change the category or province we are in. Although it is true that 'man' belongs to the category 'animal', it is not equally true that 'animal' belongs to the category 'man' and so we cannot sensibly maintain that 'All animals can walk' or 'All animals can talk'. Neither would we hold that what is true of the whole must be true of any part, since although all or at least most men have the use of both arms, we cannot say 'this arm is cowardly' or 'that arm is brave'.

Although number in some sense represents a kind or relation or at least a coincidence between ideas, what we mean by a *real relation* hinges largely on the apprehension of an object that is aggregated, and so ultimately on the meaning of what is sensuous but not ideal. All the things that inhabit our immediate environs can be broken into their essential constituents, even those smaller parts that may not be so visible to the naked eye. Thus, it should be clear in what sense two things cannot be the same, but at best be only similar, depending whether they be compared on account of their grossness, on account of their fullness, or on account of their proportionality.

However, we might also approach this from an altogether different viewpoint if we consider two jigsaws that are entirely the same in their size, in the shape of their parts, and in that image they exhibit. Let us say by a manual working we were to replace every part from the one with its equivalent from the other, then what change would this have wrought so far as any general observations were concerned? Quite clearly there would be no change in their general appearance, since everything remains as it was to begin with. On the other hand, so far as the pieces themselves are concerned there will indeed be something different. If for instance the pieces in the first set are labelled 'X,Y,Z', and their places 'a,b,c', the pieces in the other 'U,V,W' and their places 'd,e,f', then at the end of this activity

'X,Y,Z' will be connected with 'd,e,f' and 'U,V,W' with 'a,b,c'. Thus X has the precise characteristic of having moved from a to d, Y from b to e and Z from c to f. What this also enables us to do is establish certain basic differences or, at least, a certain difference in their *relationships*. We might consider this from the viewpoint of: (*a*) a comparison of properties (i.e. the shape of the parts), (*b*) a comparison of places (i.e. their contiguity and separation) and (*c*) a comparison of times and places (i.e. the pre-and post-arrangement of the parts). And so what we are saying is that although it may not be possible to bring out a difference in the case of the first, nor the second, or at least so far as it concerns their places vis-à-vis one another, it may well be where it concerns the third, since it surely matters whether U is moved before W or W is moved before U. (The parts cannot be magically transposed, and if there is a *cause* of change, then there must be strict antecedence in the way this is done).

The important point about this is that in the way we treat of properties and numbers we would tend to regard the former as having a distinct form and the latter as having a condensed form. That is, properties can be combined in a manner that enables us to exhibit that relation we call 'being similar' or 'being diverse', since we do not regard the object as being limited to just the form it might assume at any given time. We can imagine two objects that are the same in colour but not in shape, the same in shape but not in colour, or the same in both their colour and their shape. On the other hand, we can conceive of number no otherwise than in terms of that relation we call diversity. A pair of slippers is not the same as a pair of gloves, but they are as one in what they represent, that is, the number 2. In the list of chemical elements helium has the same number as Sylvia II Remus, but that is not the same as the way two twos may combine to produce the number 4. Hence in these instances, 'similarity' is not a concept that can be juxtaposed with any other, rather, it is a formal requirement for connecting things that in the first instance may be really quite diverse.

3 Bertrand Russell: Principles of Mathematics 1903 Ch.11 Definition of Cardinal Numbers.

Chapter 8

Of Judgement

Although, as we have already seen, there is a difference between the way we apprehend a certain object (as between the simple and the complex), what we mean by its appearance in this or that respect is not exactly what we mean by a mode of apprehension. Certainly, we can grasp something as a unity because it presents itself as a unity or as a concretion because it presents itself as a concretion, but that has more to do with the object than it does with any *act* per se. So far as it concerns the act there will always be a degree of diversification, since we may also *imagine* that something is so, we may also *believe* that something is so, we may also *judge* that something is so. In the case of the latter, this is how in its propositional form, we connect a subject with a predicate, that is, we judge that something is such and such or in such and such a state. Consider for instance the following assertions, (*a*) it is raining today and (*b*) it is sunny today. Now also consider that (*a*) if it is raining and I judge that it is raining today, then my judgement is true; (*b*) if it is raining and I judge that it is sunny today, then my judgement is false; (*c*) if it is sunny and I judge that it is not rainy or cloudy today, then my judgement is true and (*d*) if it is sunny and I judge that it is raining or cloudy today, then my judgement is false. What is involved here, as in the case of any hypothetical state of affairs, is the acceptance or rejection of that state of affairs, although in a case such as 'All unicorns have single horns', then this judgement is about a representation and not something strictly denotative.

The important thing to keep in mind is that falsity proceeds not from the manner in which any judgement is made, but rather the actual state of affairs as this is known or discerned. That is why a unicorn is a figuration and not a denotation, because its status can in no way be influenced by any judgements that have or will ever be made. The question of what is factual must thus be distinguished from the question of what is dispositional, since a judgement with a negative import may be factually true, just as a judgement with a positive import may be factually false. Consider this from the viewpoint of the same person both affirming and denying that something is so, and different persons affirming or denying that something is so. In the one case what we have is a certain vacillation, a movement back and forth, in the other case, either complete unanimity or a totally different point of view. What we mean by this latter however is not what we mean by true contradiction, since there is only a contradiction in the reckoning of what is true, not any variation in the opinions about what is true. It may be a matter of opinion whether cigarette companies are the cause of heart disease, whether gays should have the same rights as 'straights', or whether whaling should be banned in the southern ocean, but it is not a matter of opinion whether Neil Armstrong set foot on the moon in the year 1960, 1969 or 1972.

Let us now consider what could be called a double judgement or something that incorporates the idea of both an affirmation and denial. (*a*) 'There is an A and A is B' or (*b*) 'There is an A and A is not B' are not just simple affirmations and denials, rather a certain existential status in conjunction with an affirmation or denial. Within the categorical table, consider instances such as 'some S is P' and 'some S is not P'. If we take this to be in the nature of a double judgement, then we might cite as an example 'There are trees and some trees are deciduous' or 'There are trees and some trees are not deciduous'. On the other hand, if we do not believe that there are trees (as we might also say perhaps of gargoyles), then it is of no account what qualities they might possess, whether or not they have leaves, whether or not they have quills, or whether or not they have roots. Hence the judgement 'All trees are deciduous' and 'No trees are deciduous' would essentially be just the same, given that there can only be disagreement if there are trees, but not if there are not. From an existential viewpoint therefore, we might regard the I and O type statements as complementary, just as we might the A and E type statements, that is, 'Some S is P' and 'Some S is not P' as well as 'All S is P' and 'No S is P'.

But now let us consider something a little more complex, say perhaps the statement 'There is a sporting event down at the local arena'. Given that this may or may not be the case, we also need its complementary 'There is nothing happening down at the local arena'. In this instance how do we distinguish between the kind of judgement that affirms a particular state of affairs and the kind of judgement that denies a particular state of affairs? That is, in the latter it seems that there is not only less stated but also less that needs to be proved and in the former not only more stated but also more that needs to be proved. If it is the case that (*a*) there is a sporting event down at the local arena, then what is requisite is that there be both a local arena and something presently occurring down there. On the other hand, if it is not the case that (*b*) there is a sporting event down at the local arena, then all that is requisite is that there be no local arena. A certain equivocation has arisen here because we do not only have the double judgement 'There is a P, and S is or is not a P' but also its disclaimer 'There is no P'. Unlike the earlier example where there was an implicit connection between an object and its properties, there is no connection here between the object and what may or may not be happening at any particular time. Thus, there are two ways to prove it wrong but only one way to prove it right. In order to avoid confusion, what we could perhaps say is that what the proposition is about is not the same as what is being *judged about*. The object understood by 'the local arena' is certainly not what the judgement is about, since that involves a more abstract connection between the parts, that is, the complex that joins the object not just with any assembly but with some particular use.

If however, we attempt to extend this to what is ultimately also *affirmative* in itself, then we will be caught between the rocks of Scylla and Charybdis, either as it concerns the objectum of any judgement or what any judgement *must* also be about. (By 'objectum', we mean its objective representation.) To consider the first of these, it is difficult to discern any real difference between the statements 'There is a sapphire on the dressing table' and 'This sapphire is blue', if the implication is that the former is somehow assumed or implied in the latter. We have only the trite observation that whatever exists must also be representational in its *being*, but that does not commit us to the further claim that what is chimerical must also be real. We need therefore to be clear about the difference between existence in the sense of denotation, and essence in the sense of connotation, otherwise 'there is an X' will mean nothing more than 'there is a quality embodied in X'. We do for instance have as clear a conception of 'being winged' as we do of 'being blue', of 'being blue' as we do of 'being rainbow-coloured', but does that mean that a griffin or the coat of Joseph must exist just as surely as does the ocean or the sky? Or to express this in the words of a famous pedagogue: 'A hundred real thalers do not contain the least coin more than a hundred possible thalers' (Kant: CPR Transcendental Dialectic).

So far as it concerns the second point, we need to be clear about the meaning and content of any judgement and what may or may not suffice with respect to those judgements that we actually make. Consider the following propositions: (1) 'There is no such thing as the local arena' and (2) 'It is the case that the local arena does not exist'. If the first is true, then it must be the case that the second is true, but what could also be argued is that the relative clause 'that such and such is so' is not the same as the sense of our original assertion. Perhaps this can be more easily grasped when we compare the negative statement, 'It is not the case that the local arena does not exist' with our initial assertion 'The local arena does not exist'. But the question is whether there really are two different 'senses' or whether it is simply the *form* of the one in relation to the *form* of the other. There seems to be a suggestion that it is the 'reality' or the 'objectivity' of a judgement that reflects what is real or what is true, and thus, the fact something is so must be contained in the simple belief that something is so. Quite clearly however, so far as any verification is concerned the statement 'A does not exist' is no different from the statement 'It is the case that A does not exist', since if A does not exist then both are true, and if A does exist then neither is true. It is not the 'objectivity' of any particular judgement that imports meaning into such and such a state of affairs, rather the verification of what is true that supports those judgements that are actually made. (We will argue later that 'sense' has relevance only with respect to denotation)

Let us now consider the question of a compound judgement or the kind of judgement exhibited in the following schema: (*a*) A and B, (*b*) not (A and B), (*c*) not A and not B, (*d*) not (not A and not B), i.e. A or B and (*e*) not A and B. The first pair could be described as conjunctive affirmations and denials, the second pair disjunctive affirmations and denials, the last as both an affirmation and denial. Looked at from another perspective, (*c*) could be called the existential opposite of (*a*) just as (*d*) could be called the existential opposite or (*b*). With respect to the relation between (*a*) and (*d*) or (*a*) and (*e*), what could well be argued is that these are compatible, or certainly if you accept compatibility between any whole and any part. Since a part of A is compatible with the whole of A, and the whole AB must be compatible with any part of it, a part that is 'not A' is certainly not incompatible with any part that is B. Likewise, if there is a complex 'this A and this B', then what otherwise could A and B be if not part of just such a thing?

However, we may also treat of this in terms of a whole-part relation that is much broader in its meaning. If A and B are *exclusive* parts and what they comprise is an exclusive whole, then clearly, they will be opposed to the non-existence of A and B, since collectively 'not A' and 'not B' do not constitute anything. On the other hand, if A and B are *inclusive* parts, then the supposition that there is a whole that comprises A and B does not necessarily exclude the existence of a part that is either 'not A' or 'not B'. Now let us investigate the relation between (*b*) and (*d*). If A and B are simply exclusive of one another, that is, if A is not B, then quite clearly a part of A or a part of B must be distinguished from the sum comprising A and B. On the other hand, if A and B are inclusive parts, then 'not A' and 'not B' could well be a composite that includes A and B, and hence, not one whole as distinct from any other, but one whole as distinct from any *part*. Thus, it is not necessarily the case that A and B qua the composite is qualitatively different from the parts that constitute such a composite. How then might we regard the relation between (*a*) and (*d*) or (*a*) and (*e*)? If the parts are exclusive, then it is a simple case that A must exclude 'not A'. And if they are contiguous, then it is a simple case that A or B is merely a part of the whole AB. On the other hand, if the parts are inclusive then the situation is altogether ambiguous, since A and B as a whole neither inclusive nor exclusive, cannot be compared with any part that is both inclusive and exclusive, as must be the case if what we mean by 'not A and B' is what is non-inclusive and yet inclusive.

Now let us address the question we have earlier dealt with, whether, for any two objects, there *must* be a third and that is composed of them. As an example, take the class of odd and even numbers in conjunction with the class of positive integers. In what sense would you say that the first two make or combine to produce the third? Although this may be true from the viewpoint of how we divide something 'in abstracto' it is not true in the sense that chocolate, for instance, can be divided into cocoa and butter or the colour green can be divided into yellow and blue. All that we are really entitled to say is that the class of odd numbers *excludes* the class of even numbers or that the class of positive integers *includes* the class of even numbers, but it cannot be both. (That is, in itself it can only be inclusive or exclusive, in the latter case exclusive, or at least exclusive of negative integers). And even where it concerns concrete things these remarks are no less to the point. Although it may be fairly argued that the class of Chinese and Taiwanese do not exhaust the class of Orientals, what cannot be fairly argued is that the class of Orientals and the class of Occidentals constitute the class of all living things. On the other hand, when what we are dealing with has the character of a true whole-part relation, then our surmising will be different yet again. Consider for instance the relation between the class we call vertebrates and the class we call reptiles. In the case of the latter, there is clear evidence of what is both inclusive and exclusive—what is inclusive in terms of what is broader or larger, and what is exclusive in terms of what is simply coordinate. There is indeed a third thing (i.e. the class of vertebrates) that is composed of two or more things (birds, reptiles, fishes, etc.).

And this in turn illuminates the meaning of a 'proper' whole, since if there is something on which the parts are dependent, might there not also be something on which the whole is dependent? The meaning of a proper part can be illustrated quite simply as when we say 'The citizens of New York are part of the citizenry of the United States'. To deny the relation called a proper part, we would either have to (*a*) deny the emptiness of New Yorkers outside the class of all Americans or (*b*) assert the emptiness of Americans outside the class of all New Yorkers. On the other hand, it is perhaps not nearly so clear what we mean by a proper 'whole', or at least, what it means to be dependent on the existence of such and such an exclusive *part*. But perhaps we could look at it from this viewpoint. We know not only that New Yorkers and Bostonians are part of the United States, but also that they are not part of one another. In what sense therefore might there be a proper whole which comprises just New Yorkers and Bostonians? Might we not say that it comprises just some New Yorkers and some Bostonians? In this way, we will have the comprehension of a whole that is not the same but rather less than the sum of its constituents, at the same time of course, as we introduce a certain randomness into how this might be achieved. (Jut as we do with compulsory military service by simply drawing marbles from a barrel)

There is also the question of the modality of any judgement—that is, the traditional distinction between the assertoric, the apodictic and the problematic. The assertoric is a simple assertion of whether the predicate does or does not agree with the subject, the apodictic, whether there is a *necessary* agreement or contrariety between the two, the problematic whether there is a *possible* agreement or disagreement between the two.

This however should not be confused with the distinction between the necessary, the possible, and the impossible, where we have, say, the idea of what is necessary in itself, the idea of what is possible in itself or the idea of what is contradictory in itself. In this case, what we are concerned with is not the simple conception of such and such a thing, but rather the existence of such and such a thing, that is the necessity, the possibility, or the impossibility of it having any being.

The classification of something as apodictic or problematic on the other hand does not concern the question of being but rather the question of quiddity, and on what grounds we might infer anything distinctive as such. An assertoric judgement is not really of the 'modal' variety, it is simply concerned with what is or is not the case, with what is or is not any actual state of affairs. The apodictic and the problematic have to do with the *intension* of a term, whether the subject and predicate are in perfect agreement, in partial agreement or in complete disagreement. If we consider something such as a square circle then it is clear there can be no agreement, and the statement 'There are no square circles' would be apodictic in its kind. (If it were assertoric, then we could ascertain this through a simple inspection of the facts.) On the other hand, if we consider something such as an Infinite or Transcendental being, then the question could well be asked: Is it the nature of such a Being that it permits the commission of evil or the suffering of those who are innocent? The answer to this is somewhat problematic, since a non-believer would certainly argue in the negative, whereas a believer might be more circumspect, or at least, he might refer to the original fall of mankind.

One of the issues raised by all this is whether there should not be some broader distinction to reflect the difference, say, between the meaningful and the meaningless, or what is verifiable and what is not. Consider for instance the following statements: 'My sister has a heart of gold' and 'My computer has a heart of gold'. The first of these is not true if you take it in any strictly literal sense, since if it were, there could be no circulation of the blood, but of course that is not to say it must be devoid of any meaning. The second of these is not true either, but in this case because it is meaningless and not just metaphorical. And so, would it not seem reasonable to regard both of these as in the nature of the assertoric? Well certainly the latter, but in the case of the former it may be problematic if my sister does in fact have a heart of stone. (Or at least, if she was miserly and not generous)

Or consider statements of the following kind: 'There is an early hominid and it existed in northern Europe exactly three million years ago' or 'There are extra-terrestrial beings and they inhabit a planet that is circling the star Alpha 2000'. What is at stake here are claims that in themselves may or may not be true, but not in the sense that there is only a partial rather than full agreement between the subject and predicate. The question is, is this something we would regard as pertaining to the assertoric or the problematic? Looked at in terms of our present day knowledge we may well be inclined towards the latter.

Chapter 9

Analytic and Synthetic

As we will later see, by discursive knowledge what we mean is a method that draws inferences based on a principle that is fixed or unyielding, such that the outcome will always be implicit in those postulates or assumptions from which we began. However, we might approach this more directly in terms of the distinction between concepts and objects, or a faculty that unifies the data it receives and those materials from which such activity is derived. It also raises the question whether we take completion to mean what is not complete but can be *made* complete, or whether we take completion to mean what has been completed, and hence, what is not subject to change or renovation throughout time. And in respect to these different surmises is it the latter that pertains to the analytic and the former that pertains to the synthetic. By an analytic proposition we mean one in which the predicate is either openly or implicitly contained in the concept of the subject. By a synthetic proposition we mean one in which the predicate lies outside the concept of the subject, but is connected with it nonetheless. (We say proposition not judgement, since in the case of the latter, the truth of this can only be discerned through the senses and not the form that any statement may take.)

In order to elucidate the meaning of the analytic, compare the following: (*a*) A heptagon is a seven-sided figure, (*b*) A heptagon is a six-sided figure and (*c*) A heptagon is not a seven-sided figure. The first of these is manifestly true or true by definition, the second and third are manifestly false or false by virtue of the law of contradiction. Note however in overall terms that the second and third have an equivalent status, if not in form then at least in content. We would not say that (*c*) was less complete than (*b*), since although the latter is more descriptive it is no less false, just as it is no truer that a heptagon has seven sides than that its angles are equal to nine hundred degrees.

So far as it concerns the meaning of the synthetic, then in these terms, to apprehend something is to provide a fuller and more complete description, not a fuller and more detailed breakdown of those elements of which it is composed. And if, as we might argue, there is no such thing as ideal or unchanging form, then so also, we would deny that there is any such thing as an inadequate or indefinite object, rather only different degrees of determination, a comparison of things so far as they are more or less complete. It is certainly true, for instance, that there is more detail in a palomino than there is in the meaning of a horse, but that does not attest to the fact that the latter is 'incomplete' whereas the former is not, only that there is more precision in the former than there is in the latter. You might for instance say that a man is more determinate than a mammal, and that a mammal is more determinate than an animal, but does it follow that what is living is more determinate than what is dead, or that a man is more determinate than any ear? It all depends on whether you say the whole is more determinate than the part, or that what is animate is more determinate than what is not.

So far as it concerns the perceptual object, we might regard this as what is more or less 'clothed', or at least at the other extreme, what is lacking in colour, what is lacking in colour and shape, what is lacking in colour, size and shape, etc. If we suppose that something is a metre in length, then it is certainly not half a metre or two metres in length, and that is because in this respect is it completely determinate in itself. Or at least, even if we take the case of a balloon that is expanding, we would not say it was the object that was getting larger but rather the space that was getting larger. Similarly, something brown (like a piece of chocolate) or something green (like a piece of grass) is completely determinate with respect to its colour, but of course, that bears no relation to how much it weighs or whether or not it has a set of legs. Does it follow therefore, that something indeterminate with respect to its weight, or indeterminate with respect to its length, is also indeterminate in itself? Of course not, since even though the colour green does not incorporate length or weight, it does not exclude the concept of what has length or weight, since there may well be a class of objects that are green and a metre long, just as there is another that is brown and a metre long. It may however be true that what is more determinate in its being encompasses the meaning of what is more determinate in its colour, as we have already seen in the case of a horse and a palomino, but this is just the *degree* of its completeness—it has nothing to do with things that are altogether different in their kind. (We would not describe a palomino as a complete object, just as we might a horse, as something incomplete.)

And the same applies *mutatis mutandis* in the case of something that is not real, a fabled beast perhaps such as a griffin or a sphinx. Since no one has ever observed a collection of such things, it is difficult to say how any attribute might be combined or separated from any other, even though what we are dealing with is by no means an absurdity or some irrational thing. What is clear however is that if there really were griffins and sphinxes, then they would have to conform to the meaning of a griffin or a phoenix, since in principle it is not easy to say what parts might be appended to what others, whether the wings of an eagle *could* be appended to the body of a lion or the body of a lion to the head of a man, etc. (Quite clearly, there are certain restrictions that must be placed on such a concretion, and so what is inconceivable is what we believe it is inconceivable nature might produce.) In terms of an imaginary object such as a chocolate mountain (Meinong), then in this case we would not say it was 'incomplete' *because* it violates the law of excluded middle, rather, that the law of excluded middle has no application in the case of something that is simply not real. Of course, a chocolate mountain is neither taller nor shorter than Mount Blanc, but that is because of the unqualified status of the latter not the intermediary status of the former, as if to be something chocolate was a prerequisite for what it means to be Mount Blanc.

A question might also be raised about the prospect of an impossible object, although in this case it is not a question about the physical constraints but rather the linguistic constraints that must be strictly adhered to. In the case of a 'round square', if we allow that some spatial objects exhibit the quality of 'being round' and other objects exhibit the quality of 'being square', then to the degree that space is a unity it may just be the case that certain objects cannot be produced in the way that the rules are applied. It may therefore not be a question of ontology, but how far you can stretch the bounds of sense, since even if you allow that a 'round square' has some discernible status (i.e. it was some kind of shape), would you say the same about a 'red hypotenuse' or 'a prime number that was noisy'? Similarly in the case of 'the A that is not an A is an A' and 'the A that is not an A is not an A', then even if there is no difference in the way they are constructed (or at least in their essential elements) there must at some point be an apprizing of precisely what it is they convey. And so, because something can be said in a manner that is syntactically sound does not mean it can also be *sensibly* or *cogently* said.

Let us now consider whether there may not be an indeterminate object in the sense of what is incompletely or inexactly judged about. As we have already seen, there may be some equivocation where this concerns the question what something is about and what it is that is being judged about. Take for example the following: 'The present consul of Rome is left-handed' and its negation 'The present consul of Rome is not left-handed'. Now there may be a legitimate distinction between the object that is in the judgement and what the judgement is about, that is between its truth value and its descriptive value, but does it follow then that the former is just as determinate as the latter is quite the opposite? It seems that some confusion has arisen here and we need to clarify this by comparing a conditional with what could be termed a complex judgement. We could of course have expressed ourselves by saying, 'If there is a present consul of Rome, then he may or may not be left-handed'—in which case there is no ambiguity whatsoever, but that is not to say there is either in our original statement if we take this to be a possible combination of those parts that are in fact involved. That is, what is absurd is not the same as what is just putatively right or wrong. If it is the case that there is a present consul of Rome, then it may or may not be the case that he is also left-handed. If there is no present consul of Rome, then of course neither could such a one be deemed to be either right- or left-handed. This however, has only to do with the way we regard certain suppositions, not how certain facts may actually be brought to light—it may be no different from something such as: 'Cornelius Scipio was a Roman Consul' or 'Cornelius Scipio was left-handed'.

As we have already seen, and in keeping with the treatment by Hume, there are three ways we may forge a connection between ideas, and that is by a comparison of (*a*) their properties in the case of resemblance, (*b*) their places in the case of proximity and (*c*) their times and places in the case of causality. To begin with resemblance, on what grounds might we say that something does or does not bear a likeness to something other than itself? Let us approach this from the viewpoint of how something might change, although quite specifically in its character and not the intensity of its being. Suppose that the complex ABC becomes CDE, then EFG and finally GHI. How then might we infer that there is something transitive throughout, given that what results has nothing in common with that state to begin with? Quite clearly, what is in evidence can only be a certain resemblance between the *parts*, BC being similar to CD, DE being similar to EF and FG being similar to GH. There is no thoroughgoing change but only a gradual transformation in all the parts, one thing being phased in and something else being phased out. So far however as it concerns the question of any single property, what is needful in this regard is some specimen or a unit of measurement. The T-square for instance could be said to be an objective determinate of parallel lines, the altimeter an objective determinant of height, and the avoirdupois system an objective determinate of weight. We might also say that the ear is an objective determinant of sound so far as it can distinguish between sounds and tastes, that the tongue is an objective determinant of taste so far as it can distinguish between tastes and smells, that the eye is an objective determinant of sight so far as it can distinguish between sights and sounds.

A measurement is something we may use not only to compare but also to contrast, or at least a tongue for what is bitter but neither sweet nor green, an ear for what is raucous but neither soothing nor hard. What we mean by resemblance therefore is the approximation to such an ideal, what we aspire to but not necessarily what we can attain (that is, agreement but not identity). The metre bar in Paris is the ideal embodiment of a length that is accepted by all. Greenwich Mean Time is a recognized standard for the regulation of time. There may also be the ideal embodiment of a colour in the form of a wavelength, but we need to be careful here about the difference between the percept and how it is regarded in a strictly scientific way. So far however as there are different assessments on no account would we say there is anything that underpins similitude per se—what is similar is only similar in this or that respect, and that follows from an inspection of the facts, not the categories of thought. We would no more use a barometer to measure length than we would a chronometer to measure height, but what that proves is that certain things may be connected in a way that *makes* them alike, not that it is clear how this ought be achieved.

It is important to realize that although what we mean by a quality or characteristic may something quite distinct, what we mean by the 'same' thing is not merely the same quality, but also, a possible combination of things quite diverse. No doubt, the different shades of colour are different from any colours on a chart, and the contour of a sculpture is different from any piece of marble, but that is not to say we cannot combine a certain colour and shape to produce what is distinctive as such. It has sometimes been claimed that what we mean by the different relations or resemblances exhibited in any whole are what is 'real', but that any single character or attribute is a mere *ens rationis*. Further on and in a completely different context we will see how mistaken this can be (Ch.21), but the problem here arises because of a simple misdirection, i.e. because something of a certain colour is indeterminate with respect to shape and something of a certain shape is indeterminate with respect to colour, then what we are dealing with is an object necessarily indeterminate in itself. In order to dispel this illusion, let us suppose we are given the following figures: (*a*) a blue prism, (*b*) an orange cube and (*c*) a red sphere. Let us say for argument sake that the prism and the cube have a certain similarity in their shape (they are both angular) and that the cube and the sphere have a certain similarity in their colour (they are contiguous on a prism). Now on what grounds might you assert that similarity in shape was a logical adjunct to dissimilarity in colour or that dissimilarity in colour was a logical adjunct to similarity in shape? Or alternately, that dissimilarity in shape was a logical adjunct to similarity in colour or that similarity in colour was a logical adjunct to dissimilarity in shape?

Moving now from what is sensuous to what is *ideal*, it is not a question of what is similar but rather, what is certain, just as, at the other extreme, it is not a question of what is diverse but rather what is contrasting. Since it is altogether certain that a rectangle is not a square, so is it altogether certain that a triangle is not a circle and that an octagon does not have ten sides. We also need to distinguish between a formula or a definition and what is intuitively or immediately given, since what is transformable or adaptable is not necessarily the same as any present intuition. We have already seen that colour is one of the characteristics of sensuous being, but that is not to say that the complex ingredients of any object will prevent us from apprehending what is simply the colour red. To make this point a little clearer, consider what it means to compare a cherry with a letter box. Depending upon our point of view, we might regard this as resting on either (*a*) a comparison in their size, (*b*) a comparison in their weight or (*c*) a comparison in their colour. Whereas the first two express what is broadly dissimilar, the last expresses what is broadly alike. Or perhaps not just 'alike' but even identical, given that what is one in essence (a given shade) may yet be many in aspect. The colour red is a generic quality that we intuit just as it is, but we cannot express this as a general formula since there is nothing more in the concept than there is in the object. On the other hand, in the statement 'Red is not green' or 'Orange is not blue', then what we have is something both necessitated in our thought and reinforced through the senses.

To ask however whether such statements should be styled synthetic or synthetic *a priori* is very much a matter for debate. There is certainly no doubt that when we say 'Aqua is more like green than it is like red', what we have is something synthetic of its very nature, but that is not so readily the case for 'Being coloured is not the same as being blue', since in the latter what we have is something *conceptual* whereas in the former that relation we call resemblance. But to return to our original assertion, since there is nothing more in the concept than there is in the object, it is difficult to say whether the concept of one colour does or does not include the concept of any other. For instance, although it is by no means obvious that the colour green corresponds to a wavelength between 495 and 535m, nor that the colour blue corresponds to a wavelength between 470 and 475m, what is certain is that the wavelength 473 m cannot be the wavelength 510 m and so in this respect the colour blue cannot be the colour green. On the other hand, since a change in the percept can only be achieved by insensible degrees, there appears to be no reason apart from our physical knowledge *why* one colour encompasses such and such a range or *why* there may not be the perception of something as greenish-blue.

So far as it concerns the question how we obtain full knowledge, there are those who would argue that this is only possible through a discernment of what is synthetic *a priori* and not just synthetic *a posteriori*. Whether we take analysis in its qualitative aspect, as a regress from any consequence to any ground, or in its quantitative aspect, as a regress from any whole to any part, this cannot in any way afford true knowledge or what is progressive and not perfunctory in its kind. Thus, in order to achieve that end we hope for, it is necessary to incorporate within the whole something that fuses both the knower with the known, and the content with the prospect of what is knowable in the main. Let us consider causality as a case in point. Since at the atomic level there appears to be nothing in the behaviour of matter that binds it in any indispensable way, events could just as well be random as they are in any sense designed or engineered. Given the prodigiousness implied in cause and effect, it seems at another level then no matter how far we go with our analysis this will not lead to anything we call the 'cause' or a principle that invariably leads to just the one and only result. Where it concerns mathematics and the truths of logic, then the issue is whether what we are given in certain outcomes is the same or something *more*, than what we were given at the outset. If for instance, there are ten marbles sitting in a row, then it is a purely arbitrary matter whether we divide these into an odd or an even number just as long as their total remains the same. And in which case it is really only a certain synthesis that determines how things will work out. That is, whether we add 7 to 3 to make 10, or 6 to 4 to make 10 it is not incidental but rather necessary that we achieve the result that we do, only however, by *completing* our actions once we have commenced on our task.

This also raises a question whether we know or are aware of something because we *perceive* it to be true, or whether something is true by virtue of the way it comes to be known. Since language is an objective determinate of the world we occupy, it follows that what makes it useful is what is true in itself, not what is imposed by some devious or clandestine mind. Hence the question could well be asked: If there is a set of propositions we call synthetic *a priori*, then on strictly logical grounds, why is there not also a set of propositions we call analytic *a posteriori*? Presumably, the answer to this stems from the fact that the analytic precludes any possible reasoning from experience, whereas the synthetic does not preclude any possible intervention of the mind.

Perhaps we might approach this by beginning with either an analysable object and then proceeding to its parts, or a system of postulates and axioms and proceeding to its grounds. Colour for instance is something we take to be a generic property, and this then must come in advance of any theoretical division of its parts. (That is, the parts *qua* separable do not impinge on its being *qua* qualitative.) On the other hand, if something is regarded as a mensurable whole, then we may be able to proceed from this to its theoretical supports, as with any system of geometry. One of the services that Riemannian geometry has performed has been to establish an ordering or prioritization that had hitherto been thought impossible. Instead of beginning with certain postulates—the point, the line, the plane—what we are doing is working back from our everyday world to achieve a different ordering of the parts in their relation to any whole. We have in the figure of a circle the ratio of the circumference to the diameter and this will always be pi (3.141592). But if we begin with a sphere and not a plane, then since the diameter is a little longer will this ratio be a little smaller. And this has important implications for our original set of postulates as is the case for instance, in the axiom of parallels. On whatever grounds we might deduce that two lines are parallel, this can only be in terms of what is comparatively *straighter* and not 'straight' or 'arrayed' in itself. We might further strengthen our argument by the introduction of a geodesic and the denial of any parallelism whatsoever.

But to return to the question why there cannot be something analytic and *a posteriori,* consider the definition of number we have previously cited

(Ch.7). What would you say of this - is it knowledge of the kind that is synthetic *a priori*, analytic *a posteriori* or neither of these? Our answer quite clearly is that it belongs to the *a priori* rather than the *a posteriori* but also to what is quantitative and not just qualitative. Certainly, there is something here that concerns both the real and the ideal, but what conclusions might we draw on the strength of what we have just been hypothesizing? If you consider a group of objects such as the appendages on a hand, or the planets in the solar system, then what we mean by the object is surely something simple and unanalysable, not those particular qualities that pertain to it as well. When we think of a planet in the context we are discussing, we do not think of it as having a certain size, a certain shape, or a certain colour. (Although of course we may of certain qualities that make it a planet *pace* Pluto). Therefore, in the sense in which we might say that the heads on Mt Rushmore are the same as the suits in pack of playing cards, we are not doing so with respect to any specific characteristics but how this may be viewed in the main. In the case of number, the important thing we need to keep in mind is that it may have either a formal or material aspect, so that if it is indistinguishable with respect to its form it is not necessarily indistinguishable with the respect to its matter. The equation "6 + 7 = 13" is not the same as "13 = 13" in respect to its form, but it is in respect to what it denotes. And that is why the former may be regarded as synthetic, or at least to some degree, but the latter not at all.

Suppose on the other hand that you were to argue that 'A has the characteristic of being yellow' means that A belongs to a class of object that are similar to a sunflower. Or 'A has the characteristic of being sweet' means that A belongs to a class of objects that are similar to a cachou. Now of course what results from this may be two entirely different sets of objects but then again it may not. The modus operandi here however is entirely different from what we have just discussed, since there *must* be two mutually exclusive classes if there is a number for each. On the other hand, if we inspect a range of items that are familiar to us there may be at least one object that is both yellow and sweet (say a piece of honeycomb). The constituents of a thing therefore, or what it can be broken down into, may for certain purposes be viewed quite differently than what it connotes as such and such a whole or such and such a numerical class.

Chapter 10

Language and Logic

Where language is concerned, what we need to appreciate is that it comprises two quite distinct and yet equally important aspects—first, there is its *physical* aspect or what it is in itself, and secondly, there is its *practical* aspect or what it is designed or intended to do. Since language connects us with both our fellow human beings and that world in which we live, its primary purpose is to illuminate or 'bring out' what initially lies hidden and concealed. Consider the difference shadings that are implicit in either a command, a request, or a reproof. Depending on his sensitivity the respondent may experience either a degree of compliance, a degree of incumbency or a degree of remorse. Thus, there is quite clearly a sense in which the 'shared' character of our language underscores a certain fellow feeling, or a set of values and beliefs that bind us to some common good. On the other hand, as signs and symbols are the words we use alive and active so far as we are aware not only of their potency but also of their limits, so far as we recognize that they have both a reasonable aim and a necessary base. The thoughts and feelings that are incommunicable are not the thoughts and feelings that we do not choose to express, rather only the gibberish that ensues when there is a breach of the rules, so that it is the structure of our thought that must accommodate itself to the structure of our grammar, not the structure of our grammar that must accommodate itself to the *possibility* of how we think or feel. Of course, it is true that the sense or meaning of our words cannot always be encompassed in any particular object to which they refer, that there is a legitimate distinction between asserting and describing, but that is not to say the former should override the latter in each and every case. If that were so, we would not be able to construct a language from a language or treat it in any purely formal way.

So far as it concerns our practical reasoning, or the kind of judgements we make about the world which surrounds us, there will be few limitations on what our language may or may not do. The words *this* and *that, now* and *then,* do of course serve to circumscribe the parts of time and space, but that is of no great relevance where it concerns the kind of observations that could or might be made. When we say for instance, 'This chair is not jocular' or 'This lampshade cannot fly', then of course, there is a restriction on two fronts, in the first place, how any property may be *casually* related to any object, and in the second place how any property may be *causally* related to any object. In the act of perception there are two things to be discerned, first, something by means of which the object can be fixed or represented, and secondly, the different impressions or appearances that enhance our sense of what it is. Quite clearly, there is a difference if our attention is directed to a dog that is lying on the lawn, a rake that is lying on the lawn or a brick that is lying on the lawn. We do not simply take any object as a complex of properties and divide it in any way we might wish; rather, do we regard the substratum as that which is *evinced* through such and such a set of means. What we mean by the appearance of an object is thus a more and not a less detailed explication of its being—otherwise there would be different 'realities' for each appearance just as there are different appearances for each reality. The difference nonetheless between the fixed and the indeterminate remains as before, only in the case of the latter where we begin with an attribute and proceed to its embodiment. You might after inspecting the items in a room conclude that they were (*a*) blue in colour, (*b*) angular in shape and (*c*) firm in texture. Hence the determinate part is either the species we call colour, the species we call shape or the species we call texture, and the indeterminate part is just these specific syntheses, bearing in mind that not all furniture is blue, square and hard.

With respect to the relation between *meaning* and *denotation*, what we can say is that there may be both agreement in the object and yet a difference in the meaning or agreement in the meaning and yet a difference in the object. In the first case, what we have could be called a definite description or some phrase that may be substituted for the subject, and in the second, an attribute or characteristic that may be predicated of any subject. On the whole however, the issue at stake here is by no means an easy one to discern, rather, what it requires is a careful examination of all the components that are known to be involved. Compare and contrast the following: (*a*) The meaning of the first sentence in Conrad's *Heart of Darkness* is the same as the meaning of 'The Nellie, a cruising yawl . . . swung to her anchor . . . and was at rest' and (*b*) the meaning of 'the first sentence in Conrad's *Heart of Darkness*' is not the same as the meaning of 'The Nellie, a cruising yawl . . . swung to her anchor . . . and was at rest'. In (*a*) meaning and denotation are in perfect accord, since we begin with a particular denotation and then elucidate all its parts. In (*b*) on the other hand, these are not in perfect accord, since if we begin with a particular meaning then we must also exclude *all* those things that it does not contain. Or to express this a little differently, although the meaning of 'the first sentence in Conrad's *Heart of Darkness*' may be the same as the meaning of 'the first sentence in Lawrence's *Sons and Lovers*' that of course, is not entirely the same sentence and so is by no means the same thing as that to which it *refers*. What this might suggest therefore is that although every denotation must have a meaning, not every meaning must have a denotation. And so, we should not assume that every sentence that has a meaning also has an object, but rather, that just as there are strict rules for the use of one so must there be strict rules for the use of the other.

(The statement "There are angels in heaven" may well have a meaning but that is not to say it must also have a reference).

There is another possibility in the way we might view the relation between meaning and denotation, and that is if we do not suppose a denoting phrase but merely treat any sentence as a purely arbitrary set of signs. For instance, in the case of $x = x$ and $x = y$, identity of content cannot be the same as identity of form, otherwise there would be no way of accounting for the difference between x and y. Of course, we might just be playing a game in which we attribute identity to x and y, but not say, to y and z, but if these are true signs, then they must also have a meaning different from what it is they describe. We are familiar with this in the case of our everyday language, since not only can different words mean the same thing in different languages, but the same word can have different meanings in the same language. The word *grimalkin* can mean either a cat or an ill-tempered woman and the word *bow* can mean either a looped knot or an instrument for shooting arrows. On the other hand, the same object may be signified in many different ways, as the word *boy* in English is the same as *knabe* or *ragazze* in German and Italian. The implication thus is that it is not just the predicate that adds meaning to any subject, but the subject that may be meaningful in and of itself.

We might also consider this in terms of the difference between a literal and metaphorical description, or the different descriptions that may be relevant given such and such a change of circumstance. 'The Bank of England' for instance, could well be deemed a literal description, but we would surely not say the same of 'the Old Lady of Thread needle Street' even though they are one and the same thing. Or we might say that at one time of day Venus is called the morning star and at another the evening star. The point can also be made by comparing what we have said about the way that meaning and denotation are related and the way that sense and denotation are related. The meaning of 'The first sentence in Conrad's *Heart of Darkness*' may be the same as the meaning of 'The first sentence in Lawrence's *Sons and Lovers*', but we would not say that the sense of the first sentence in a paragraph was the same as the sense of the first sentence on a page, even if they are entirely one and the same set of words (Frege's distinction between sense and meaning).

A 'sense' therefore is something we connect with the same denotation, be that the planet Venus, a bank, or a page, a 'meaning' on the other hand is something we connect with a denotation but not in any fixed or invariable way.

Let us now consider more closely what we mean by the binding or communicative aspect of language and how we tend to treat it more as a means than we do as an end in itself. That language has a communicative role could be viewed in either of two ways. On the one hand, we might say that having or sharing a language means having or sharing a universe, that everyone understands the same words and that the same set of words describe the same set of things. Thus, the great majority employ the same language to express a particular cultural, religious or political point of view. Or we might say that everyone has a set of beliefs and cognitions that are reflected in their everyday language, and that to some degree this will influence how they think and feel. In terms of the analytic-synthetic distinction, this may also be relevant in how we approach the question of knowledge, since what underlies it is a threefold distinction between certainty, uncertainty and the impossible. Thus, to assert that the analytic proposition is one in which the predicate is contained in the subject is really only to say that the predicate is *assumed* to be in the subject, whereas in the case of the synthetic, it is *assumed* to be not. And this raises the question in what sense it conveys indubitable knowledge about truth and falsity, since although the former is precise and definitive, the latter quite clearly is not. That is, since we can never know of a synthetic judgement precisely where it stands, but only that it *may* be true or false, in what sense could it be said to convey anything really genuine at all? On the other hand, a logician might attack this by suggesting that it puts the cart before the horse, that we cannot know what a proposition is, unless we know that it be true or false.

Perhaps this can be demonstrated a little more clearly if we ask what it means to be false, rather than what it means to be absurd. In the case of a synthetic proposition what you have may be either true or false, but what would you say of a proposition if it simply contradicts itself? Whilst it is true that something such as 'All triangles are bounded figures' is indubitably true, what would we say of the opposite, that it is meaningless or simply that is untrue? Since a logician is someone who wants to know if any proposition is falsifiable, he is probably more inclined to be generous towards the latter and not limit it to what is purely nonsensical. We have already stated that a unicorn is something representative and not something denotative, but that is not to say we would also categorize it as what is meaningless rather than meaningful. And the same might be said for the case in point—whilst the sentence 'Not all triangles are bounded figures' may not be true, we would surely not describe it as a *logical* absurdity. There is a difference between saying 'Triangles are not bounded figures' and 'Triangles are not bounded territories.'

There are many things that do not belong to the realm of real things, but that does not mean they cannot be apprehended as if they did. Even in the case of a 'round square', although we might describe this as synthetically impossible this is not to say it contravenes our sense of what is clear and distinct, any more than it does if we conceive of a sapphire that is red. It just so happens that the property of being angular excludes the property of being curved, but we would not know that unless we *judged* that it was so. Hence we need to be careful not to confuse nonsense in a grammatical sense with nonsense in a conceptual sense—and if language sets the boundaries for the way we think, then what is absurd can only be what is grammatically absurd, not what contravenes the general belief that a predicate *must* or *may* only be contained in any subject.

The attack on the traditional account of analyticity also rests on the claim that it obscures the very distinction it is supposed to be laying bare. That is, by reducing certain statements to the status of what is meaningless, it surreptitiously raises emptiness to the status of what is meaningful. To the degree that the predicate is only partly contained in the subject, then this may appear to convey at least *some* knowledge, but it is a different matter if the predicate merely reiterates what is in the subject. 'A triangle is a triangle' would not appear to be as significant as 'A triangle is a three-sided figure', but that is not to say they are not equally analytic or, at least, that they do not equally conform to the requirements of grammar. And thus, it seems all we really have is a prescription for excluding what is incoherent. In the same way, it is difficult to say what is conveyed in the words 'A bachelor is an unmarried man' if only to exclude the apparent absurdity of a married man who is also unmarried. Worse still it may cause us to attribute analyticity to propositions that are certainly not analytic, as for instance 'The father of Edward VI, king of England, was king of England' or 'A fruit that is orange is also what we call an orange' (In the case of the latter, there is clearly no *necessity* that an orange be called an orange).

And so, let us suppose from the outset that truth and falsity concern the character of that world which we inhabit, and that to be the subject of a sentence is to be a *concretum* and not merely an *abstractum*. This is essentially the way that Bolzano handles the question in the *Theory of Science*. If we take a simple sentence such as 'A loaf of bread costs sixpence', then there is no doubt this has a referent, but it does not have the kind of detail that would enable us to ascertain whether it also be true or false. Hence, we need to make explicit what in some sense is already implicit, that is, we need to have a further specification regarding the time and place. We might therefore say, 'A loaf of bread costs sixpence in London' or 'A loaf of bread costs sixpence in London on 2 July 1942' and in such a way as to furnish evidence for judging it to be either true or false. We might also wish to consider a range of options for how such a sentence could be altered or varied. Instead of London, we might substitute Amsterdam; instead of sixpence, we might substitute threepence; instead of a loaf of bread, we might substitute a leg of ham. Of course, in the case of determinants such as time and place, these are the parts of a sentence that must always be variable— otherwise, we could not say under what circumstances something was or was not the case. The validity of a proposition thus concerns the ratio of true-to-false outcomes when a certain number of substitutions are made and within a given range. If all the sentences that are generated through certain substitutions are true, then its validity is 1 and if all these sentences are false then its validity is 0. If for instance we said, 'A loaf of bread costs sixpence in every British city on 2 July 1942', then this would produce a number of different outcomes, but if it were true in half the cases, then that would be its validity.

On the other hand, where it concerns the question of invariability, this will proceed on two fronts. If there is no idea that can be varied without altering its truth or falsity, then this is what makes the proposition *analytic*. If there is at least one idea that can be varied without altering its truth or falsity, then this is what makes the proposition *synthetic*. Thus in the case of 'God is omnipotent', we would characterize this as analytic, not synthetic, since omnipotence is something we invariably associate with God just as God is something we invariably associate with being omnipotent (Of course this is not necessarily what we would say of a notation such as 'Every object is B or not B'). In the case of "Not all marshmallows are white" on the other hand, since this is not self-contradictory, it must also be regarded as what is *synthetic*. In brief, what makes something analytic is not the fact that it is indubitably true, but rather, that there is no change in its original *sense,* so that it retains what it was from the beginning. The notion of invariability in this case is not being contrasted with what is variable; rather might we describe the latter as what was transformable, and the former as what was *fixed*.

Now let us consider the implications this might have for something else—what we mean by the extension or intension of a term. Traditionally what we call the extension of a term is the totality of all things to which that term applies. What on the other hand we mean by its intension is the sum or total properties that are therein implied. But whilst there is no controversy with respect to the first of these, it is an altogether different matter where it concerns the second. That is, there is an issue where it concerns the meaning of a simple or crystalline idea or, at least, the isomorphic relation between any object and its idea. No doubt there is a difference between the concept of a vertebrate and the concept of a bird, but then the question arises: Does this imply a difference in intension or only the interpretation of different terms? That is, in what sense is 'being a bird' contained in the idea of 'being what is vertebral' and is this the same as the way that 'being a hand' for instance is contained in the idea of 'being what is functional'? It could be argued by those in favour of a more extensional approach, that there are no true ideas but only true propositions, and that if a proposition consists of parts, then so also must there be for those ideas that it contains. Thus, meaning can only be achieved by a compounding of all the parts, as well as any change as the result of such compounding. There is no difference in content if we compare 'A callous father of a tender child' and 'A tender father of a callous child'; it only raises an issue if we ask whether their *meanings* be the same. And so, if meanings can only be generated through propositions that have parts, then we cannot say there is an increase in intension at the same time there is a decrease in extension, or that there is an increase in extension at the same time there is a decrease in intension.

And yet perhaps we are not altogether comfortable with this approach, perhaps we are not so convinced that an *abstractum* is really illusory in itself. In the first place, we need to be clear about the sense in which something is inclusive, as we might say of any true existent, and the sense in which something is either inclusive or exclusive, as we might say of any essence. Where it concerns an inventory or collection of things then we tend to approach this quite casually, by supposing that the part of any part must also be the part of any whole. Thus, if we divide '10' into the parts '2,3,5', then in ascending order the part of any part will be the part of any whole. But we need to be aware that some things that are inclusive in one way may not also be inclusive in quite another.

As we have already seen (Ch.5) it is very easy to treat different classes as if they were different things, as for instance, the class of fishes and the classes of animals. Hence, we need to be clear that what we mean by an increase or decrease in extension is not the same as what we mean by an increase or decrease in intension. There is a difference when we say that the meaning of one term is included in the meaning of another, and that the extension of one term is included in the extension of another. In the case of the latter, it is self-evident that what we mean is something purely quantitative in its kind. In the case of the former, we need to be clear about the difference between a comparison with respect to *character* and a comparison with respect to *content*, taking 'content' to mean the amount of detail exhibited in and of itself. Thus, a term whose meaning is included in another may be said to have more detail but less character, since 'thisness' is the point of unity and 'accident' is the point of difference. The feline family may be said to comprise such things as lions and tigers, whereas the mammals comprise such things as lions, tigers and marsupials. But we would not say that the term *feline* has more content than *mammal* in any true or univocal sense, rather that it only has more detail as opposed to more *form*. Thus, it is not more and less detail that is being compared, rather more diversity at one extreme and more completeness at the other. Another point that needs to be made is that what makes a class is very rarely what makes it comprehensively the same, whereas what makes a class may also comprise descriptions that are very *different* in their kind. With respect to a particular station, e.g. the prime minister of Great Britain, we may be able to qualify its intension without in any way influencing its extension, by incorporating different qualities just as they arise e.g. the quality of being female or the quality of being of African descent.

In the case of 'This triangle has angles that are equal to two right angles', what makes it analytic follows from an examination of its meaning, not an examination of its parts. We know that triangularity is a point of unity for certain attributes, and that this includes having internal angles equal to two right angles. On the other hand, if we adopt the view that it is analytic because a single term can be changed without any change in its general sense, then what needs to be proved is that the invariability of such a whole is compatible with the invariability of all its parts. In the present case, it needs to be demonstrated how all the parts must contribute to the whole and not merely what kind of substitutions will effect the same result. There is no doubt that the word *triangle* pertains to the generic quality we call 'being triangular' and thus that it matters little whether we express this in the form of 'this triangle', or 'that triangle' or 'all triangles'. However, such does not preclude the prospect that the word 'this' may be used in a variety of other contexts. In the case of 'This hieroglyph is extraordinarily detailed', it is clear that what we are arguing for is certainly not a class of hieroglyphs that are equally detailed. In fact quite the reverse—what we are saying is that there is something about *this* symbol that makes it quite unique. In the same way, we would not say that *this* Peugeot is the same as *that* Peugeot if one has air bags and the other does not.

Chapter 11
The Limits of Knowledge I

If we wish to express ourselves in a manner that is clear and coherent, then we need to do so within the framework of certain laws, and these are what we call the basic laws of thought.

The Law of Identity states that whatever is, is and must remain so, throughout any argument or any rational speech. It is neither the part of any object nor the part of any idea, but only the whole of any object or the whole of any idea, and so it neither includes itself nor excludes itself nor is conjoined to itself. And yet if we examine this a little more closely, then it should be clear it does not consist in the simple tautology 'A is A' or 'B is B', rather, it proceeds from a comparison with what it means to be different or diverse. In order for something to be what it is, it must it also be different from what it is not, and that, to the same degree and in each and every respect. We cannot know what sameness is unless we know what it means to be similar or what it means to be diverse.

With respect to the Law of Excluded Middle, this is the means for protecting our 'real' world from what is illusory or nugatory as such. The Law of Excluded Middle may be taken from the viewpoint of what is true or the viewpoint of what is false: (*a*) Either proposition X is true or proposition X is not true, or (*b*) Either proposition X is false or proposition X is not false. It goes without saying that the proposition in question must be something that pertains to some *possible* state of affairs and so what can categorically be affirmed or denied. And since what we are dealing with is the actual or palpable make-up of things, what we do not have is something either absurd or self-evident, rather what is admissible as a corpus or body of facts. It is important to realize too that this law concerns just the general import of what we experience, not how this might change given any change in its time or its place. The truth value of our judgements is indifferent to either the time or the place they are uttered—rather, this is implicit in their meaning and not just added as an afterthought.

The Law of Contradiction states that 'Nothing can be both A and non-A', understood as applying to the same subject and a predicate applicable at the same time and in the same regard. However, properties in relation to objects are not the same as objects in relation to classes, and so we need to be careful when comparing 'All X' with 'Some X' that we do not do so in the way we might 'All X' with 'No X'. What we have in respect to a proposition that pertains to any class is a subject of such and such a form and a predicate of such and such a variety or type. Thus the form that is the genus may be expressed through those particulars that are its members, but there is no necessity in how this is done, rather, a certain positive unity at one extreme (the individual) and a certain negative unity at the other (the genus). To say that A is either 'b' or 'c' expresses a kind of negative unity, as when the insect is either this type or that or the species is either this genus or that. To say that quality 'a' belongs to B or C on the other hand, expresses a kind of positive unity, as when the jacket is either tweed or serge, the carpet is either tasselled or plain, the horse is either chestnut or black.

Let us now consider the difference between (*a*) ambivalence, (*b*) contrariety and (*c*) contradiction. *Ambivalence* is something that pertains to the particular import of our words and phrases, what exhibits a certain tendency or bias, which is either time specific or place specific. Our vocabulary is replete with words that exhibit a certain subtlety or colouration, and it is inconceivable that two speakers could have exactly the same 'sense' for all the phrases and catchwords that they use. It is clear that the words *rich* and *poor, weak* and *strong, brave* and *cowardly* will mean different things to different people depending on their cultural links, their social ties, the age or period in which they live. In the same way, a certain spatial or temporal framework will influence what they mean by 'here and now', 'then and there', 'before and after'. In the case of *contrariety*, what we are dealing with are two propositions that are opposite with respect to their quantity, but not necessarily with respect to their quality. Thus 'All snakes are venomous' is the opposite of 'No snakes are venomous', but that does not mean they are contradictory, since they may both be false but they cannot both be true. In the case of *contradiction*, let us compare what is physically impossible with what may at least be open to conjecture, or what is devoid of meaning with what may have some significance or sense. In the classic case of a Cretan or an inveterate liar, the statement 'All Cretans are liars' cannot have any meaning if uttered by such a one, since there cannot be any issue concerning his motive or the reason for acting as he does. In order for something to be true, it must be possible to enunciate such a truth, whereas there is a certain lack of logic in supposing that the truth can be expressed in a manner or a spirit that is completely out of whack. To be meaningful in this case therefore, does not mean to be grammatically correct but rather to be pellucid and clear.

In the way we have treated this matter, we have chosen to do so in terms of the relation between the speaker and the spoken word, but that is only to emphasize the content of our language and not its structure. However, within the classic categorical table let us see what happens when we compare the E (No X is Y)- and the A (All X is Y)-type statement together with the E- and the I (Some X is Y)-type statement. How we go about this may not be altogether in keeping with the standard or conventional approach, but what we need to keep in mind is that it is I and O, not I and E, that could be regarded as complementary in their kind. The statements 'All S is P' and 'No S is P' are certainly incompatible as regards their quantity, since if there is at least one member of a class then there cannot be none, but how, or in what way, there may be ambivalence in respect to their quality, really hinges on the evidence for what is and is not the case. It may be the case that all snakes are venomous or no snakes are venomous, and it may be the case that some snakes are venomous and some snakes are nonvenomous, but it is the general evidence that will attest to either the truth of one or the falsity of them both (i.e. the falsity of both if our subject is lacking in material being). What we need to keep in mind however, is that it is the complementarity of I and O that permits us to deny the truth of both as well as the truth of either. What we mean by the contradictory therefore, is that which denies the mutuality of I and O, and it cannot do this if it in any way supports the matching of A and O in conjunction with I and E. Would you say for instance that the statement 'All S is P' differs from 'Some S is not P' in the same way that 'No S is P' differs from 'Some S is P'? Consider the following alternatives: (*a*) There are snakes and all snakes are venomous or (*b*) There are snakes and some snakes are nonvenomous. Now compare these with the following: (*c*) There are no snakes and snakes may or may not be venomous and (*d*) There are snakes and some snakes are venomous. In the case of the former, what we have is a clear contradiction, and in the case of the latter only a possible disagreement about the facts.

Looking at the relationship between these laws, the thing that strikes one is the similarity or rather subtle connection between the law of identity and the law of contradiction. When we say '$2 \times 2 = 4$', is this not the same as '$2 \times 2 \neq 5$' or at least, are we not simply affirming one thing at the same time as denying something else? If what we mean by necessity, is the constant conjunction of ideas that are formed in our minds, then why does this not include a constant disjunction, as when we explicitly refuse to connect '2×2' with the number '5'? Or to put it another way, if what is, is not what is not, and what is not, is not what is, then non-being is simply the analogue of being, and in no way could there ever be a mistake in their identity. In principle therefore, why might we not regard these laws as having just the same fundamental ground? The answer lies in the fact that where it concerns identity what we are dealing with must always take a propositional form, and thus, must always be constituted of the parts we call 'subject' and 'predicate'. In the case of contradiction, what we are comparing are always the objects of thought, not intuition, thus not different parts or aspects of the same thing or the same thing but at different times. This is also why it can be applied to a wide range of categories; it can be stated about an attribute or an individual or a class. On the other hand, in the case of the law of excluded middle it is mistake if we suppose that this forbids us to think that two contradictory attributes may be *absent* from the same subject at the same time. Rather, this only begs the question where the boundary may be drawn between the existent and the non-existent. As we have elsewhere seen, a case could be mounted for saying that there are certain 'incomplete objects' that lie between the existent and the non-existent.

There is also a sense in which the first two laws may be subsumed under the third, but on no account would we attempt to subsume the law of contradiction under the law of identity. However in order to do this, what we need is the more primitive distinction between an analyzable and an unanalyzable object. In keeping with Russellian logic, we need to appreciate the sense in which something may be said to belong to a group by virtue of its denotation, not necessarily its meaning or its general import. For the most part, when we think of an object or an entity as belonging to such and such a class, then this is on account of certain qualities we take to be defining—a set of attributes that pertain to just this group. On the other hand, if you also consider such groupings as the fingers on a hand, the pips on a playing card, or the days of the week, then what is 'defining' is not necessarily what makes them all the same. That is, although it may be true that all the cards in a playing deck have the same size and texture, there may also be a sense in which the suits are the same as the number of the stars in the constellation Crux. In other words, the class concept 'playing suit' may not be the same as the class concept 'star', but that is not to say that one term in one group may not correspond to one term in the other. An article of clothing, say perhaps a glove, can be correlated with a stocking or a shoe, and that is because we know they always come in pairs—the same may be said for any class, be it closed or unrestricted in its scope. When we add up the pair of gloves or the pair of shoes, no matter how many there are they will always be represented by the number 2—even though of course, we would not say that the shape of a glove was the same as the shape of a shoe, or that the purpose of a glove was the same as the purpose of a shoe. What any single thing comprises in terms of a number of properties (and these may vary in the extreme) is not what affords it membership of that class of classes which is similar to any other class of classes. In this case, what we are arguing for is extension but in a most peculiar sense—we are treating the object in connection with a concept but not in a way that this might normally apply. (That is, we are not saying that a shoe is similar to a glove because they are both made of leather.)

What this also shows is that an object that is analyzable in one respect may nonetheless be unanalyzable in another. When we ask ourselves how many members there are in any given class, then we are dealing with the class as a numerical whole, that is, we are assuming that one item has the equivalent status of any other. And it does not matter whether these existents have feathers or gills, whether they are purple or black, whether they are wrinkled or smooth. And we may also be able to stretch the meaning of what is unanalyzable to include certain properties as well. The proposition 'Circles are not squares' is certainly something we would take to be analytic, but that does not concern the question how such an object may *potentially* undergo such and such a change. A piece of plasticine may at one time be soft and at another time be hard; it may also be moulded into the shape of a ball or the shape of a brick. On no account however would we ever describe as what was not one and the same piece of plasticine. If you were to strike middle C on the keyboard and did so more heavily than the C that was an octave higher, you would not then say it was a different *note* that had been struck. In the case of colour, we have a clear indication of something that cannot be affected by change, or at least not in itself, only through a medium that may alter it in this respect or that. A rainbow is something that may appear quite suddenly, but only when the heavens open and the clouds unleash their fury.

What we mean by a blue object therefore, cannot be separated from the concept 'blueness', just as a red object cannot be separated from the concept 'redness', and *ipso facto* all such propositions must be deemed synthetic. ('The colour red is not the colour blue' is plainly synthetic, since you cannot experience colour otherwise than as something distinct, and if you are experiencing red, then you are not experiencing blue, and if you are experiencing blue, then you are not experiencing red.) In the case of taste or smell however, then this is a little different, since it may be analyzable in one sense and yet unanalyzable in another. The peach that was ripe may well be the peach that is rotting, and so there is no doubt there may be a change in its taste without any change in its origin. But that does not preclude the prospect we may also have entirely different experiences at exactly the same time, as might happen if you mix honey and vinegar. Thus, the experience may be 'analyzable', but not in the way that different things are divided, rather, in the way that different objects are combined.

To address the question how or in what sense the law of identity could be said to be subsumed under the law of contradiction, we need to consider the class of all things, that is the universal class, and the class of no things, that is the empty class. If the universe of discourse contains all things that are sensuous and real, then the null class will include gorgons and griffins, and logical absurdities such as straight parabolas and three-sided squares. We also need to distinguish between what can and cannot be real and what may or may not be real, that is between a meaningful and a vacuous string of words. Whilst in one sense it may seem preposterous to combine the idea of an eagle's wing and a lion's body, in another sense it may not. However, if we are dealing with the question of extension rather than intension, then there is a critical difference between the class of tables and the class of griffins, since the former are numerable whereas the latter are not. To return to our subject, if what we mean by the class of real things lies between the class of imaginary things and the class of no things, then it must be subsumed under the law of contradiction, since this expresses the quantitative difference between what is ultimate or complete and what is vacuous or unreal. That is, no matter what class it is that we specify, it will always be included within the class of all things without being *identical* with the class of all things.

So far as there is a question how the law of excluded middle may be comprehended under the law of contradiction, we need to attend to our study of classes, and the difference between what is inclusive and exclusive in its kind. Consider the following means for subsuming any object under some broad scheme or classification. 'A has the characteristic of being blue' means that A belongs to a class of object that are similar to a sapphire. On the other hand, 'A has the characteristic of being brittle' means that A belongs to a class of objects that are similar to a wine glass. Now of course what results from this could be two entirely different classes, but then again it might not, since it is by no means inconceivable that there is at least one object that incorporates both these qualities (not a bluebottle since that is hardly brittle, but perhaps the egg of a bird). Therefore, we need to approach this a little differently if we are to demonstrate how the law of excluded middle may be made conformable to the law of contradiction. Perhaps what we might say would be as follows. The statement 'A has the characteristic of being non-blue' means that A does not belong to a class of objects that are similar to a sapphire. The statement 'A has the characteristic of being non-brittle' means that A does not belong to a class of objects that are similar to a wine glass. Thus, there is a sense in which what is exclusively one property may be subsumed under the general distinction between one possible complex and another, without specifying, of course, what is or is not the case.

Now let us consider the implications this might have for our overall conceptual scheme. In contradiction, one thing is self-mediated by the non-being of its other. In other words, in terms of what is positive or negative, the positive considered in itself is reflected into self-equality, and the negative considered in itself in reflected into self-inequality. The maxim which states a contrast or opposition controverts the maxim of identity: in the one case what we have is self-relation, in the other case self-disruption. However, in respect to what we might term the monadic and modemic, the law of contradiction could be said to constitute a kind of dividing point, only here, where the former is something that assumes it and the latter something that transcends it.

.In the case of the monadic, what we are dealing with is the law of identity, or where interconnectedness must be viewed as an implicit attribute. In other words, in terms of what is positive or negative, the positive considered in itself is reflected into self-equality, and the negative considered in itself is reflected into self-inequality. That is, if something is proportionate then it is in the nature of what is positive, and if something is disproportionate then it is in the nature of what is negative. In terms of a whole-part relationship which is homogeneous, then a part is something which may or may not be incorporated within any whole. Or at least in this case, the whole is simply the sum of all its parts. On the other hand, in the case of the modemic, what is in question is whether the part is more important than the whole or the whole is more important than the part, that is, in the first place, what it is we mean by an *intrinsic* whole. In terms of a whole-part relationship that is heterogeneous, then there are two ways we might approach the question of what is overarching, and they are (1) when we isolate or focus on the dominant feature or (2) when we isolate or focus on any particular one. In the case of the dominant feature, this will express itself in terms of what is either functioning or functionless. This may also have implications for the way we regard the Law of Excluded Middle. In the case of the monadic, what this implies is that from an enumeration of any set of predicates then either some predicate or its not-being, can be predicated of any particular thing. In the case of the modemic on the other hand, this also raises the question of what is intermediate, since the colour 'grey' may be regarded from the viewpoint of either black or white, just as the colour 'orange' may be regarded from the viewpoint of either yellow or red.

Although as we have already argued, there are grounds for both the analytic *a posteriori* and the synthetic *a priori*, what we really mean is that there are grounds for what is both perfectly and imperfectly analytic, together with what is strictly or broadly synthetic. Thus, the general schema we might adopt would be as follows. What we mean by (*a*) the analytic, is what is restrictive of the senses, what we mean by (*b*) the narrowly synthetic, is what is restrictive of the understanding, and what we mean by (*c*) the broadly synthetic, is what is inclusive of them both.

In terms of the relation between the analytic and the *a priori*, what we need to appreciate is that although the latter must always be conjunctive with the former, the former may not always be conjunctive with the latter. For instance, to the degree that we hold '6 × 2 = 12' to be an intuitive or *a priori* truth, this is only so because there is an explicit relationship between the parts, not because one part could be said to be *contained* in the other. That is, '12' is not contained in either '6' or '2', but we would nonetheless say there was equivalence between '12' and '6 × 2'. On the other hand, if you consider the statement 'All Cretans are liars' and 'Not all Cretans are liars' if uttered by the Cretan Epimenides, then in the one case there is an implicit contradiction whilst in the other there is not. However, to say that the latter is false is not also to say that this is explicitly so, only, that it will be invariably so no matter who has uttered these words.

The point about all this is that in the way we might regard language, it is either (*a*) a means or mode of communication or (*b*) a set of signs underpinned by a set of rules. In order to play the game of chess you need to know the rules that govern it, just as, in order to play the game of language you need to know its grammar and its syntax. In the case at hand, what we are given are the rules that forbid certain moves, but these are not the only kind, since there are others such as 'A man is a man who is not a man' even if this not be true. There is a difference however between something that can be directly intuited by our minds, and thus, what is strictly analytic, and a method for 'juggling the pieces' just so we can continue the game. If we take the analytic to mean any proposition in which the subject is contained or simply repeated in the predicate, then this could lead to any number of possibilities, as for instance 'An orange fruit is also what we call an orange'. Or consider the statement 'All brothers are male'. Now although this is certainly analytic, on no account would we call it *a priori*, since what is lacking is just that relation which would make it complete. On the other hand, if we were to assemble all the persons who are called 'brothers', then what might reasonably be inferred is that they must also be male, but that is only so if we take the view there are sufficient grounds for arriving at such a conclusion. In principle, it may be no different from trying to ascertain whether all giraffes have long necks, and the statement 'All giraffes have long necks' is certainly not *a priori* in its character. Leaving aside the case however, where the repetition of certain parts of a sentence is not indicative of what is strictly analytic, a definition as such is not what we would call perfectly but rather imperfectly analytic.

To define a cube thus as 'a regular polyhedron with eight vertices and six sides' may be analytic, but it is not *a priori* (or at least not in the sense that it makes explicit what in some sense lies hidden). The statements 'A cube is a polyhedron with twelve edges' and 'A cube is a polyhedron with six sides' may be synthetic but they are certainly not analytic, and that is because in the case of the former the subject could actually be an octahedron, and in the case of the latter a pentagonal pyramid. On the other hand, in the statement 'The whole is greater than the part' what we have is an *explicit* relationship, since the whole could also be less than the part, and from which it follows that this truth is something immediately apprehended by the mind. (A proof might be something as follows. For any two objects A and B, if A is equal to a part of B, then A is less than B, and if C is equal to A, then C is less than B, from which it follows that the part must be less than the whole.) So far as it concerns the relationship between the synthetic and *a posteriori*, then given that there is no limitation of the one in respect to the other, an empirical truth is simply one that comes to be known through some testable or verifiable states of affairs. 'My brother has red hair' is therefore altogether different from 'My brother is male', since the first of these could only be true if the meaning of 'being a brother' is limited to 'being red haired', whereas the latter can never be false, otherwise there would be no such thing as custom or convention at all.

Let us now address the question whether the propositions of arithmetic are (*a*) analytic, (*b*) synthetic or (*c*) synthetic *a priori*. So far as it concerns the kind of truth that rests on a simple operation such as addition or subtraction, what we can say is that this is *a priori* rather than *a posteriori*, since the result is surely predetermined, no matter what the means we might employ. Thus, it will always be the case that '7 + 5 = 12' and '5 - 2 = 3' even if it is not always obvious how this result has been obtained. Consider also the relation that holds between a circle's circumference and its diameter. If you divide the former by the latter, then the expression '3.141592' is certainly more precise than anything the senses could inform us of, and so, is what is intellective in its kind. It has sometimes been argued that what we mean by an axiom or postulate is not really a product of the mind, but a product of the senses, and that this applies not only in the case of geometry, but in any true system of thought. In any simple operation, say the addition of '2' and '3', what we have achieved is not complete unity,but only some agreement with the number 5, since we need to know how many groupings there are and in what way they are disposed to behave as they do.

On the other hand, what could also be argued is that if all we have is some collective consensus, and we would need to repeat this to confirm our result, what this would do is undermine the very nature of such activity, and replace it with what is only probably true. Of course, we might endeavour to save the argument by claiming that we do not need any number of trials but just the one, the 'correct' observation and to which all others agree. Again however, this is really only a kind of *petitio principii*, since it confounds the means of verification and our confidence in this, with what is the case on strictly *a priori* grounds. If, with the aid of an abacus, you were asked to add the number '6' to the number '7', then with reasonable care there is no doubt you could accomplish such a task, but what if you were asked to add 12,462 pistachios to a group of 15,290 almonds—how confident would you be and no matter how many times that you tried?

Another claim that is made is that there is nothing in the analysis of the terms of a simple equation that indicates what *result* we might obtain, since in the equation '11 + 6 = 17', there is nothing on the left-hand side that points to the number '17', just as there is nothing on the right-hand side that points to the numbers '11' and '6'. Thus, the operation of addition is something extraneous to the terms of an equation, and it is only when we undertake a particular *synthesis* that we arrive at anything different or really new. But even if we accede to this, there is still the more substantive question how the different parts of an equation are to be linked, that is, according to the relation we call equality, or the relation we call inequality? Fundamentally, we can only say either (*a*) 11 + 6 = 17 or (*b*) 11 + 6 ≠ 17, and from which it should be clear it is only the former that cannot be denied without contradictory. Hence, simply to point out how two things may be synthesized is not also to demonstrate how two things may not be synthesized, and quite clearly it is not any physical operation which underscores the meaning of what is contradictory rather than merely false. The assumption that underlies the belief in a synthesizing of terms is that if there is a change in the form of an object then there must also be a change in its *esse*. Hence the only truly analytic statements would be those of the kind 6 × 2 = 2 × 6 or 3 + 4 = 4 + 3, whereas 2 + 10 + 5 = 4 + 13, 4 + 13 = 17 and 2 + 10 + 5 = 17 must all be regarded as truths that are differently founded. However, consider the following possibilities. If we have a notational system that is based on the fingers of both hands, then it will undoubtedly be true that 1 + 4 = 5. If however, we have a notational system that is based on the fingers of one hand, then it will undoubtedly be true that 1 + 4 = 10. Are we then to say that the existence of one hand is incompatible with the existence of two? Quite clearly, there is a difference if we think of one number being abstracted from any two, or one number being composed of any two, but that is not to say *how* we arrive at a particular result, must precede the purpose for which such action has been taken in the first place.

On the other hand, where it concerns the basic axioms of arithmetic—the laws of commutation, association and distribution—a much stronger case could be made for saying that these are synthetic rather than analytic. When we ask 'does $a + b$ equal $b + a$, $a-b$ equal $b-a$, $a \times b$ equal $b \times a$ or a/b equal b/a', what we are asking is, 'Is there any meaning in the *order* of these terms?' This therefore is a question for which some verification may be necessary, independently of what can be gleaned through the simple operation of our minds. To begin with, suppose you were given several items that were placed in a row, as the following *****. Now the question is, to what extent does this imply any order or arrangement in and of itself? Quite clearly, it matters little if we begin with one item at one end and add 4, or two items at the other end and add 3, since it will always be the case that $1 + 4 = 4 + 1$ and $2 + 3 = 3 + 2$, no matter how we proceed. Likewise, the grouping $(1 + 2) + 2$ will be indistinguishable from $1 + (2 + 2)$, just as $(1 + 1 + 1) +1 +1$ will be indistinguishable from $(1 + 1) + (1 +1 +1)$. Further to this, if you create a figure that comprises a row of five items and a column of four items, then it is surely a matter of indifference which you begin with in order to ascertain what is the product of them both. And so 5×4 must equal 4×5. If we then proceed to something having three dimensions, this should enable us to deduce that $5(4 + a) = 20 + 5a$. Where it concerns subtraction and division on the other hand, this conclusion will not be so readily to the fore, since there is a problem when we are attempting to subtract a greater from a lesser number, and also, when we are attempting to divide a lesser by a greater number. In the first case, although we can adjust our sign from the '+' to the '-', this does not mean that what we have arrived at is a truly discernible result. In the second case, what results will always be something *less* than what is whole, whereas when we are dividing a greater by a lesser number, what results will always be something *more* than what is whole.

Although to this point, we have had no problem with the idea of what is allowable or permissible, an issue may arise when it is not language that is the instrument of thought, but thought that is the instrument of language. In the kind of reasoning that is called a paradox, certain unacceptable conclusions may follow from a set of premises that in themselves appear to be reasonable and sound. Thus, the way we respond may be in terms of any of the following: (*a*) We might accept the conclusion as valid, (*b*) We might reject the kind of reasoning that leads to the conclusion or (*c*) We might reject the premises altogether. Consider the sentence (S_1) 'What I am now saying is not true'. Now if S_1 is true then what it says about itself must also be true and so it must be false. But if S_1 is false, then what it says about itself must also be false and so it must be true. Or to express this a little differently, the sentence 'What I am now saying is not true' is true, if what I am now saying is not true, but false, if what I am now saying is true. The inference that might then be drawn is that S_1 is neither true nor false and that it somehow lies in a hole between the two. However, what if we were to replace S_1 with S_2, that is 'What I am now saying is either not true or it is meaningless'? Again we are caught in a circle, since if the sentence is true, then it cannot be true, and if it is false, then it cannot be false, and if it is meaningless, then it is what it says it is, that is, what is true.

It seems that in order for there to be a proper definition of truth then for the kind of statement 'X has the property Y' to be meaningful, it must also be testable, that is, there must also be some independent state according to which it can be compared and assessed. And so in the case of S_3, 'This daffodil is yellow', S_3 is true if the daffodil in question is indeed, the colour yellow. But to compare the form of the sentences S_1 and S_3, what we should really be saying in the first instance is not 'What I am now saying is not true' is true if what I am now saying is not true, but rather 'What I am now saying is not true' is true if what I have *specified* as not true is in fact true. That way, we can avoid the kind of circularity that arises when we have not stipulated what the sentence is concerned with or what it is about. These examples have convinced some logicians (Tarski, Kripke) that our concept of truth is incoherent and that the medium for its expression is not adequate for the task that is required. The problem appears to stem from the fact that something within the language is being used to describe what the language is in and of itself, when in this respect it contains nothing descriptive at all. A solution can only be found if we construct a metalanguage to go along with the object language—that is, a device that prohibits self-reference as it emerges in each and every case. The general idea is as follows. In what could be called the base language, there is no such thing as a predicate that is true for just those sentences that are true. At the next level, there are some sentences that predicate truth or falsity, and some that do not. Sentences of the former type however only pertain to those sentences drawn from the language at a level beneath them. Sentences of the latter type only pertain to that language at a level above them. What this schema does is to ensure that no language is able to disqualify itself from a set of predicates at its own level and potentially from a set of predicates at a level above it (Tarski's solution to the problem).

Something that is implicit in this kind of strategy is that when we account a sentence as neither true nor false, then we must also account it as meaningless—in keeping with the law of excluded middle. However, it remains to be seen if there is some completely unambiguous means for separating what is false from what is more properly devoid of any meaning. To be meaningless it could be said, involves a contradiction, but as we saw in the case of S_2, the circle that encloses what is false also encloses what is meaningless. Or it might be argued that what this concerns is the idea of a category mistake, that is, the attempt to apply a particular predicate to a range of subjects for which it is neither relevant nor fit. A property such as colour or sound is only relevant in the case of a sensuous object, not for abstract or ideal entities. A quality such as courage or cowardice is only relevant in the case of a rational being, not in the case of a mosquito or a flea. Quite specifically, the overriding claim is that there is one set of rules for sentences that are self-referential and another for sentences that are not. It remains to be seen however whether sentences that are neither true nor false must also devoid of any meaning as well.

Apropos this question, consider the following possible groupings: (*a*)(i) Number 2 is even, (ii) number 2 is not even and (iii) number 2 is odd; (*b*)(i) the envelope is open, (ii) the envelope is not open and (iii) the envelope is closed; (c)(i) the algorithm is pungent, (ii) the algorithm is not pungent and (iii) the algorithm is odourless. We might characterize the relationship between (a)(ii) and (iii) as what is logical, between (b) (ii) and (iii) as what is interchangeable, and between (c)(ii) and (iii) as what is grammatical. The important point however is that while there is a logical nexus between (i) and (ii) in (a) (albeit one of opposition rather than identity) and a certain equivalence in (b) (albeit of what is *actually* the case), there is no such relation in (c). What we are saying in the case of (c) is that although these sentences may be grammatically sound, it is a moot point whether colour or smell could ever be sensibly ascribed to what was simply algorithmic in its nature. A further consideration is that any appeal to meaning may not also be an appeal to truth but rather to the *context* in which something is said or the *use* to which something is put. Suppose by a slight change, our original sentence (S_1) becomes (S_4): 'What I am now saying, viz. that the sky is blue, is not true'. Then this would be false, given that the actual state I am describing is in fact true. What we have in the second instance is something false and in the first instance something contradictory, but nothing withal that could be called an absurdity. That is, the contradictory nature of S_1 only springs from the *lack* of any context; it only proves that self-reference may not suffice in and of itself.

Thus, although Tarski suggests that we need a metalanguage as well as an object language, we might adopt the view that it is not so much a question about the meaning of words as it is about the question of their *use*. Suppose you were standing in a room, say room 201, and you were to write on the board 'There is no sentence on the board in room 201 at this time, which is a true statement'. At the same time, there is someone standing in an adjoining room and what they write on the blackboard is as follows: 'There is no sentence on the board in room 201 at this time, which is a true statement'. In the first case, the sentence could be viewed parenthetically, that is, not true because it posits no conditions that could make it true, and in the second instance true. because there are such conditions, and these most assuredly have been met. But what if the sentence in 201 really read something like 'This sentence has eight words and fifty letters?' Such a change would make no difference to the status of the sentence in 202, but it would for what was in 201—what was 'not true' in the original sense could not be compared to what was 'false' in this altered sense. And so if our original sentence is neither feckless nor false, then what otherwise could we conclude but that it has a value that is dependent upon such and such a context or such and such a use? Or you might express this by saying that the sentence in room 201 is indeterminate with respect to a comparison of both times and places, whereas the sentence in room 202 is indeterminate with respect to a comparison of times but determinate with respect to a comparison of places.

Chapter 12

The Limits of Knowledge II

Turning now to an approach that is strictly synthetic, we need to distinguish between the concept of a thing in connection with the absence of any part and the concept of a thing in connection with the presence of any part. If the world we inhabit is essentially heterogeneous rather than homogeneous, then in order to grasp its true meaning we need go no further than what has being in itself, that is, how it is represented in this respect or in that. The table that I am presently seated at comprises just those qualities that may be discerned and from a particular point of view—it is a collection of angles from the viewpoint of a geometer, a collection of colours from the viewpoint of an artist, a collection of styles from the viewpoint of an artisan. And so, to classify a table as being of such and such an era, or of such and such a type, to apply a set of criteria to either its meaning or its use, is not to add a 'proper' to a 'common' nature, rather, to adopt a set of guidelines that at best can only be loosely applied. What thus we mean by the connotation and not the denotation of a term, can only be the result of those particular associations that we form, a way of grouping things according to our estimate that they essentially all the same. What may count as a piece of furniture in seventeenth-century England is not necessarily what would qualify in nineteenth-century France, just as a vehicle or a mode of transport in the age of the horse means something altogether different from it does in the age of the diesel engine. Any two objects therefore, no matter how closely conjoined, can only ever be more or less alike, and that depending on our point of view or what our instincts dictate.

We also need to be clear about the difference between a change by sensible and a change by insensible degrees. A good example of what is meant by an intensive or continuous whole is something like the spectrum of light; we may analyze it or break it down, but we cannot alter it in any substantive way. In this case, it is not evident to the naked eye at what point orange becomes yellow or yellow becomes green, but it is evident at the extremes how violet is not the same as either orange or red. On the other hand, where it concerns a change and by discernible degrees, there is ample opportunity to be deceived where sameness or unity is concerned. For instance, if we consider a series of changes beginning with ABCD, then proceed to ACDE, ADEF and AEFG, then it is clear there is an enduring part that we call 'A'. However, in the series of changes that takes us from ABCD to CDEF to EFGH, there is certainly nothing in the end that was there from the beginning. We might easily confuse these processes if there is some specific aspect we are attending to, say perhaps, whether there is any common element that connects two adjoining parts. If A is larger than B, and B is larger than C and C is larger than D etc . . . then what we are attending to is what makes each change a smaller composite than the last. But that only begs the question what makes something one and all the same—is it the same because it has the same *relation* or is the same because it has the same essential *part*?

Let us now treat the Law of Excluded Middle in relation to (*a*) the Law of Contradiction and (*b*) the Law of Identity. The Law of Excluded Middle states that one property of one kind cannot be the same as another property of the same kind, and that something is either P or not P, but that does not mean they cannot be combined in such and such a way or, at least, that something cannot be *partly* this and *partly* that. Thus, a cow cannot be both brown and white all over, but it may nonetheless have different patches that are brown or white. The propositions 'All cows are white (completely)' and 'No cows are white (completely)' cannot both be true and they could both be false, but that is not because there may be some exception to the general fact that *some* cows may not be white. Both statements would be false in the circumstance where not only (*a*) some cows were white and some cows were not white, but also (*b*) some cows were white and some cows were a mixture, including the colour white. If it were the case that all cows were a mixture, which included the colour white, then at least one of our original assertions must be true, but if it were the case that no cows were a mixture which included the colour white, then it would be an open question whether any cows were a mixture at all, and hence, whether either of our original assertions was correct. Hence there may be exclusion where it concerns the different kinds of properties, or what these properties are in themselves, but that does not pertain to the question how they *might* be combined, or what limitations exist with respect to the way different things *could* be combined. (A cow may be partly white and partly brown, but a billiard ball cannot be partly straight and partly curved, otherwise it could not have the *use* that it does.)

To put this in a general setting, now let us address the question of the postulates and axioms of geometry. Would we say that these were (*a*) analytic, (*b*) synthetic or (*c*) synthetic *a priori*? Quite clearly, it cannot be the first, since there cannot be space unless there is something we can envisage as being *in* space, and thus something that bears relevance to what space is in itself. We would not be able to draw triangular or circular figures on a blackboard if there was not a 'space' that contained them, and so a space that in some sense was explicable as well. By that we are not suggesting that the axioms of geometry are simply conventions lacking any real ground, rather, that geometry is a branch of mathematics and not the other way round. And so if, as we would argue, they are synthetic and not analytic, would we say also *a priori* ? Quite clearly, there is a sense in which any body of knowledge might be regarded as *a priori* if we take that to mean what is broadly deductive, that if we begin with certain axioms, then certain consequences will always ensue. On the other hand, what could equally well be argued is that if there is no 'privileged' geometry then there can be nothing *a priori* as well, or at least that if there are some theorems beyond doubt, then there must be others that are open to question.

Perhaps this point can be illustrated in the following way. Although in Euclid's original system there are certain undefined terms such as 'lies on', 'lies between' and 'is congruent', a certain set of different postulates could be adduced and by the following means. Let us say we begin with a straight line—then necessarily for any three points, one of them must lie between the other two. Thus for the points 'A,B,C', exactly one of the following must hold true: (*a*) A lies between B and C, (*b*) B lies between A and C or (*c*) C lies between A and B. For any points on a line comprising 'A,B,C,D' and assuming their order to remain unchanged, the following must hold true: (*a*) B will lie between A and C, (*b*) B will lie between A and D, (*c*) C will lie between A and D and (*d*) C will lie between B and D. From this it should be clear that A and D are never between even once, whereas B and C are between points and exactly twice. Now let us suppose we join the ends of this line to form a circle that has the points 'A,B,C' (D has been merged with A). In this case as before, there is no problem if we describe any point as lying between the other two (just once), since so far as this relation goes it is entirely beyond debate. (We might however choose to stipulate that if the points are equidistant, then what we are dealing with is only the larger arc.) Up to this point we have had no problem with the idea of 'betweenness' or the idea of enclosure, since this will be either (*a*) the end points in the case of a line or (*b*) the common point in the case of a circle. But suppose from our simple circle we were to construct something three dimensional, say perhaps a torus or a sphere—would these relations be the same as they were first of all? If we regard a closed curve as equivalent to the cross-sectional part of a torus then the result will be exactly the same, but what if we are dealing with a closed curve that is formed around the centre of such a figure? Three such curves may well create a relation of order, but this is not necessarily privileged in terms of what it means to be 'between'. That is, B will lie between A and C in the order 'A,B,C', C will lie between A and B in the order 'B,C,A' and A will lie between B and C in the order 'C,A,B'. However since the portion B divides A and C, whereas either A is divided by B and C or C is divided by A and B, then in order to be consistent, what we really need to say is that (*a*) A and B are *enclosed* by C, (*b*) B and C are *enclosed* by A and (*c*) A and C are *enclosed* by B. Thus, when there are an odd number of portions the general rule will be that it is the larger number that is enclosed by the smaller number. When there is an even number of portions, then the general rule will be that the whole can be divided arbitrarily and that any point has an equal status in relation to all the rest. And perhaps this is a good illustration of what we mean when we say that the postulates of geometry may be broadly synthetic but not *a priori* if this concerns a purely linear conception of space.

In terms of the relation between the Law of Identity and the Law of Excluded Middle, on no account we would argue in any strict sense that the one may be made conformable to the other. The Law of Identity states that if an object undergoes change throughout time, then it nonetheless retains something that is peculiarly its own. There must therefore be a relevant distinction between essence and accident, just as there is between uniformity and variability. What is essential will always supersede what is subsidiary, just as what is unified will always supersede what is fragmentary. Of course it is merely an empty tautology if we say 'A is A' or 'whatever is A is not "not A"', but sameness may nonetheless be a fruitful idea if we connect it with what is not essentially the same, as perhaps we can with respect to equality and inequality, congruence and incongruence, simultaneity and succession. Since concrete things are impervious to any relations that may hold between them, and since a red object for instance, is not aware that it is not green, what is requisite is that there be some external means, some dispassionate observer, to ascertain in what respect two objects may or may not be the same. And if indeed there is some discernible difference, then this is what we call their *unlikeness*; if however, there is no discernible difference, then this is what we call their *identity*. It is important to realize however that in the case of diversity what we have are not just two terms but two relations as well. Diversity of content is not just the adjunct to identity of content, in the sense that the former has two terms and one relation whereas the latter has one term and one relation. As could well be argued, if a milk bottle has a relation to the fridge, then it may either be *in* it or *on* it, but we can only conjecture which of these is the case. Neither is there any ground for a reciprocal relation—the fridge is no more invariably 'in' the bottle than the bottle is invariably 'in' the fridge.

So far as the Law of Identity is concerned, there may be no discernible difference in either the form or the content, as when we say 'all A is A', but in the case of the Law of Excluded Middle, there must be at least some difference, if only in regard to the content. Such notwithstanding, there is at least one instance in which we might adopt a more strictly descriptive approach to the question of identity, and that is in terms of what could be called the *Identity of Coefficients* (Ch.5). Consider what in perceptual psychology might be termed a reversible figure; say perhaps the image of a white vase on a black background or two silhouetted faces on a white background. If you examine this for a few moments then it might appear to change, showing one aspect and then the other. Now let us suppose we use a series of gratings with bars and spaces of various widths to highlight the difference between a figure and its ground. A grid containing broad bars might be said to have low spatial frequencies and one containing narrow bars might be said to have high spatial frequencies. If we were to fill the outer regions of our image with high spatial frequencies and the inner regions with low frequencies, then the effect would be to bring out the faces and make them more distinct. Similarly, we could highlight the vase if we filled the inner region with higher spatial frequencies. Suppose, say, there were thirty bars in one grid and only six in the other, then no matter how we separate or connect them, such a relationship would remain essentially the same ($30x = 6y$ or $6x = 30y$).

In terms of the meaning of what is broadly synthetic, we might approach this through either the percept or the concept, not however because of the way they might be prioritized, rather, because of their overall relevance. In the first place, let us consider some of the objections that have been raised to the Law of Exclude Middle. In mathematics, certain questions have been raised about the soundness of an indirect proof, that is, when it is assumed that if P is not the case, then 'not P' must be the case, or if 'not P' is not the case, then P must be the case. The conventional proof that the square root of two is irrational is a good example, since the idea here is to demonstrate that if it is not irrational then it must be rational, and yet that if it is rational, then what this leads to is an absurdity (*reductio ad absurdum*). The doubt that is raised concerns the question whether we are justified in applying it in the case of an infinite number or any proof that requires an infinite number of steps. The number 'pi' for instance when decimalized reads something like 3.142857 . . How though might you address the claim that somewhere in this number is there the sequence '787878' or that nowhere in this number is there the sequence '787878'? If neither has ever been verified, then in what sense could either be said to be true? Another question might be whether there was some last prime such that n - 2 was also prime, and if not, how we might demonstrate that such a relation implies succession without end. In a similar vein, although with any finite group of numbers we can investigate their contents and ascertain what is or is not the case, this is much less clear where it concerns something that is infinite in extent—rather do we need to invoke a particular rule for whatever inferences we might make. In the case of (*a*) every A is B or (*b*) it is not the case that every A is B, it is only by way of abstraction we can hit on any useful result. (That is, we may be able to address this if we have some discernible whole and what or may not be the part of such a whole, but not if what we are dealing with is something infinite in extent).

. These objections, however, although relevant in the area of higher mathematics are not necessarily to the point where it concerns our everyday world and those claims that are derived from it, since to make a meaningful statement is not necessarily to be bound by the caveat that it be verifiable as such. For instance, you might make the claim 'There is another star and another planetary system that contains intelligent life not dissimilar to our own' or you might say 'There is no other intelligent life in the universe'. Thus, while this may be in keeping with the Excluded Middle it is not necessarily in keeping with those conceivable means that exist for ascertaining which is true. That is not to say that verifiability may not be an issue, only we do not need the means of verification to know that at least one of these *must* be true. Or consider statements of the kind 'My sister is a gifted singer, but she will not be performing tonight because she has a frog in the throat' or 'My uncle was very unhappy the other day because he is the sort of person who wears his heart on his sleeve'. Here there is not even any question of verification, only the broad sense of what is conveyed and certain indicators as to what or may not be the case.

Another objection is that the Law of Excluded Middle fails to entertain the prospect that there may be something between the extremes of actuality on the one hand and insubstantiality on the other—that is, something that could be called an 'incomplete' object (Meinong). In the case of a triangle for instance, what could be argued is that '*the* triangle' is different from any triangle because it lacks the specifications that make for any particular one. This way, we can avoid the vicious circle that results from saying it *must* embody all the properties of such and such a figure. Individual triangles may be equilateral, they may be right-angled, they may be many-angled—the triangle *in abstracto* however is 'incomplete' because it does not embody any of these features, nor does it claim the status of what must be fully 'clothed'. Rather does it lie somewhere between what is fully determined and what is altogether non-existent. The only problem here is that it is difficult to say how we might compare what is sensuous with something that is not. That is, since there is no such thing as a class of triangles that can actually be counted how can we be sure that what is meant by the one and only triangle is what is unified in and of itself? Fundamentally, what we mean by the triangle can only lie between the *a priori* nature of space on the one hand and any physical description that might be given on the other. A triangle with all sides equal is what we call an equilateral triangle, a triangle with two sides equal is what we call an isosceles triangle, and a triangle with no sides equal is what we call a scalene triangle. But it does not follow that if we removed or combined all these qualities what we have could be called the 'essence' of a triangle.

There is also the suggestion that what we mean by 'complete' is in some sense derived from the meaning of what is not—that we should proceed from the abstract to the concrete rather than the concrete to the abstract. For example, if you observe someone moving towards you then before you can gauge whether it be a stranger or a friend, what is firstly requisite is that you be able to identify it as another human being. In the same way, if you observe an animal moving around a paddock, then before you can ascertain whether it be a Suffolk or a Clydesdale, it is at least requisite that you be able to identify it as a *horse*. The question however in what sense what is less specific can also be regarded as what is less complete, really depends on our set of assumptions, and that point from which any comparison can be made. Certainly if you take the class of all men as some unique and determinate *number*, or the existence of a man as comprising some unique and determinate *complex*, then this will in a sense be more 'complete' than is the mere concept of a man, just as the concept of a man is more 'complete' than is the concept of a mammal (in the sense that a species, for instance, is more *specific* than a genus). But then again, what is to stop us from adopting the same approach just beginning from the opposite end? That is, why might we not say that the class of all men was 'less complete' than the class of all things that have two ears and two lungs? In these terms, a person with one lung or one ear would be deemed less 'complete' than a bobcat or a deer, assuming of course that the latter satisfy that criteria we have already applied.

Further to this, there is the claim is that the Law of Excluded Middle has no inherent value, since it can only be construed as a statement about (*a*) everything, such that anything could be expressed in every different way or (*b*) nothing, such that there are clear and explicit rules for how any characters might be separated, but no rules to indicate how in fact they might be combined. In answer to this objection, what we need to keep in mind is that the aim of such a law is to safeguard the authenticity of our world, not to place it on any absolute or unconditional footing. For instance, in pointing to a flower in the garden it is hardly likely you would say, 'This flower has petals, but it is not clear whether they are bowed or straight'. Rather, we are more likely to establish an order from the general to the more specific and from the less to the more complete. It may be next to useless to make a statement that is so broad as to convey nothing relevant whatsoever, but it is not entirely trivial if we say, 'This flower has a pungent smell and it is not the colour blue'. It is only more useful if we can say, 'This flower is green, it has straight petals and a scented smell'. Or perhaps we can bring this out a little more clearly in the following way. Suppose we have a collection of objects consisting of (*a*) a blue pyramid, (*b*) an orange cube and (*c*) a red sphere. Let it be granted that the pyramid and the cube have a certain similarity in their shape (i.e. they are both angular) and the sphere and the cube have a certain similarity in their colour (i.e. they are contiguous on the spectrum of light). Now the question that might be asked is this: To what extent would you say that resemblance in shape was the necessary adjunct to a difference in colour or that resemblance in colour was a necessary adjunct to a difference in shape? Suppose we make a slight alteration so that the objects are now (*a*) a yellow pyramid, (*b*) an orange cube and (*c*) a red sphere. What would you say about this—would you not say that the parts of the whole were just *more* alike than before, that is, more alike in colour but not less alike in shape? Hence, there is no such thing as a *relation* of diversity that must be matched by any *relation* of resemblance, rather only a clearer and more explicit account of that which is real, and a hazier and less explicit account of that which is not.

As we have already seen, the difference between the analytic and synthetic hinges on the nature or character of any particular *proposition*. So far as it concerns the difference between the deductive and inductive however, what this hinges on is the character or nature of any particular *argument*. By a deductive argument, what we mean is one in which the conclusion follows necessarily from the premises so that denial of the latter also entails the denial of the former. The truth of the conclusion is thus something that could be said to be established on *a priori* grounds (that is, we need no knowledge outside of that contained in the premises). By an inductive argument, we mean that the conclusion does not follow necessarily from the premises, but that there are fit and reasonable grounds for any conclusion that has been reached. The truth of the conclusion is thus something that has been established on *a posteriori* grounds. The difference between the two has sometimes been expressed by saying that in the former, we proceed from the general to the particular and in the latter from the particular to the general. This however is somewhat misleading, since although deduction may well concern an inference from the general to the particular, it may be applied not only to individuals but to classes as well. It is certainly true that from the premise 'All lemons are bitter' could we deduce that 'Some lemons are bitter', but this is no less the case than if from the premise 'This object is a fruit' and 'This object is yellow' might we deduce that 'This object is a yellow fruit'. Or from the premise 'All Bostonians are American' and 'All Americans are Occidental', might we deduce that 'No Bostonians are Oriental'.

Of course, although this may constitute a formal distinction where it concerns deduction and induction per se, it is quite another matter where it concerns the methodology of science, since here there is room for what is both inductive and deductive in its kind. Fundamentally induction concerns the kind of argument that is based on (*a*) an enumeration of individual cases and (*b*) a comparison of analogical cases. In the first place, if we have a number of individuals 'a,b,c' that are observed to be P (say perhaps a duck) and these in turn without exception to have Q (say perhaps webbed feet), then it might be reasonable to conclude that all Ps are Qs, that is, all ducks have webbed feet. In a similar vein, if we have a number of ducks that are R (say perhaps mallards) and these in turn without exception have S (say a bottle green head and a white collar), then it might be reasonable to conclude that all R's are S's, that is, all mallards have a green head and a white collar. Or we might express this in a statistical form by suggesting that if a certain percentage of a certain sample evinces a certain quality or characteristic, then this will also hold for the population as a whole. Someone who canvasses the political views of a small section of society is working on the assumption that this will hold good for the community as a whole. (Although as history shows, incumbency may also have its benefits). So far as it concerns the meaning of induction by analogy, then here what we are *not* trying to do is infer what may be the case in every other instance, but rather, only in the next that we encounter. And this may be so restrictive as to involve just two examples. The strength of such a method will hinge on certain key factors, but principally it will be *less* effective where (*a*) there are fewer cases to be compared and (*b*) there is some property that past cases do not have in common with the present, or there is some property in the present case that is altogether lacking in the past.

How and in what way science also supports the method of deduction hinges on the difference between an inference in conjunction with the facts, and a reason or explanation that is supported *by* the facts. Deduction may be useful on occasions when there is no direct or immediate evidence for what is and is not the case—as for instance, when we are dealing with some unobservable property and there is a dispute about what it is that best fits the evidence at hand. The following might serve as a simple example. From early times, it was well known that in order to drain liquid from a barrel it was necessary to have an opening at both the bottom and the top, otherwise the liquid would hold fast and not be released from the vessel. This was also the case with something such as a clepsydra—plugging the upper orifices prevented any exit through the lower. The seeming explanation was that there had to be a tendency for matter to cohere in order to prevent a vacuum, in this case the remaining space once the liquid had left its container. But since this notion of an 'empty space' was itself an *ens rationis*, little wonder the Ancients could never overcome their prejudices and fears. That the material universe must be 'full to the brim', that it must be 'replete with being' that it was not susceptible of improvement— these were all untested assumptions without any basis whatsoever. To underscore this point, consider the following thought experiment. Let us say you have a straw that is filled with water and the water is at rest, being held at one end by the pressure of a thumb and at the other by the pressure of a finger. Now suppose that you remove and replace the finger at one instant and at another remove and replace the thumb. Or perhaps, remove and replace the thumb and then remove and replace the finger. Since the order in which this is done of no particular account, and hence, are not two causally connected events, the question that needs to be asked is as follows: If neither event can achieve a discernible change, then how, through the simultaneous occurrence of both, could the result be any different? Thus, it should be clear that there is something more than the coherence of matter that is at work here.

A more credible hypothesis was that there must be a sufficient amount of pressure before any liquid could be made to rise, and also, that there must be a limitation in terms of any height that could be reached. Thus, we are surrounded by a body of air able to exert a particular pressure such that the pressure exerted in one direction must be matched by the pressure exerted in the opposite. The behaviour of the drinking straw can be explained in terms of an upward and downward pressure at both ends, in conjunction with that unilateral force exerted by the earth. When the top of the straw is opened, there will not only be downward pressure but also an obstacle, which prevents any release; when the bottom is open, there will be both an upward and a downward pressure, but a prevalence of the former (air pressure over gravity); when both ends are open, there will be air pressure in opposite directions on the one hand, and the prevalence of something downward (gravity) on the other. So far as it concerns the value of these different surmises the latter must be undoubtedly preferred—there is ample evidence for the creation of at least a partial vacuum in terms of the disparity between one thing (the weight of any physical object) and another (the weight of any body of air).

Deduction may also be important where it concerns the testable consequences of any theory, and in extending its scope beyond that for which it was originally intended. For instance, given that one of the most notable features of light is that it travels and is reflected in straight lines, what one might suspect is that it is in some way corpuscular in its make-up. That is, it obeys the laws that govern the motion of all bodies, not only does it exert a force but may also be impeded in its turn. One of the testable consequences of this is that light, when passed through one prism and then another, can be recombined or reconstituted so as to resemble or mimic its original form. Another consequence is that light should travel faster in a refracted medium than in something such as air, since there will always be a certain impetus when one force is exerted in conjunction with any other. This is something that has well and truly been tested and observed, although of course, it does not address the question whether light travels faster in any medium than it does in the absence of any medium—something that may serve to either prove or disprove our initial result.

Another example of a very testable theory is the law of attraction or gravitation. This is also a good illustration of how it is that the theory may sometimes follow the facts rather than the facts that follow the theory, or at least, how what is insightful may not be just that, but rather, a synthesis of all the knowledge hitherto gained about the planets and the stars. Thus, not only did the systems of Copernicus and Kepler inspire a more radical or inventive thought, but they themselves were the testable consequences that supported it as well. And there were also its auxiliary effects, the motion of the tides, the precession of the equinoxes etc... On the other hand, the more general the theory the more liable it is to any discrepancy in those effects it was intended to explain. A case in point would be the irregularities that were observed in the movement of the planet Uranus. In view of this discovery, the available options were either (*a*) to completely revise or abandon the initial hypothesis or (*b*) to introduce a new hypothesis but in a purely ad hoc way. By adopting the latter approach, this not only saved the original model, it also led to the discovery of a new planet, the planet Neptune. Such a strategy however is not always so fruitful or to the point—in the case of the Michelson-Morley experiment, there was hardly any point in postulating something to explain the existence of something that had not even been proved to exist.

In an earlier chapter (Ch.9) we addressed the question whether causality concerned something in the nature of the synthetic or the synthetic *apriori*. It has often been argued that the relation between cause and effect implies something that is both unique and quintessential—that for any series of events there must always be some reason or some ground from which this proceeds (Leibniz). On the other hand, there is also the kind of argument that starts with a distinction between what is evident and what is necessary and then concludes that it is only empirical truths that can be denied without contradiction (Hume). That is, it may equally well be true if we state, 'Event A will succeed event B' or 'Event B will succeed event A', since there is no way the denial of either could be said to be a necessary falsehood in and of itself. However, both of these are extreme viewpoints, in the one case, as the outcome of an unhealthy rationalism, and in the other, an unhealthy scepticism. To address the first of these, there is nothing prior to experience that compels us to order or arrange things according to what must eternally or incontrovertibly be true. The fact that science has progressed in the way that it has clearly indicates that it is our observational powers that have improved, not our deductive skills, since to the degree that the universe is ordered there can only be so much order to be discerned. As to the second, although it may be true that no degree of belief can furnish what we take to be certain, it does not follow that this also supplies the ground for what we take to be untrustworthy. If the laws of nature have been dependable up to the present, there is no reason why they will not continue to do so well into the future.

In the context of classical physics, what we mean by 'cause' is closely connected with what we mean by 'force'—that is, an *internal* force that compels a body to remain at rest or in uniform motion, and an *external* force that compels a body to undergo change, be that speeding up or slowing down (Newton). The gist of this is that if it were possible to know the position and velocity of every particle in the universe then we could predict with complete certainty how every particle must behave. As we now know however, the state of the universe of very far from being a piece of clockwork, since at another level there is a very different picture to be discerned. According to quantum theory, the relation between light and matter is such that it is impossible to determine whether, in any given instance, either is strictly a particle or a wave. Observations of photons do not support the conclusion that they have both a determinate velocity and a determinate position—rather, that if they are determinate in one respect then must they be indeterminate in the other. This leads to the rather quirky surmise that a particle may be able to 'interfere with itself', that it may be able to 'be in two places at once' that it is a mere 'probability function' when we are not apprised of its actual place.

Chapter 13

Truth and Reality

One of the legacies of the great system builders of the seventeenth century is that they tended to adopt an approach that was cogent rather than simply inductive, and hence by working from something with rational form and proceeding to something with Necessary Being. The power of corporeal things was not something derived from any finite source but from the omnipotence of God, and no matter how varied in appearance nature be construed no otherwise than as emanating from just such a one. The doctrine known as monism has a number of recurrent features and these could be described as follows: (*a*) There is only one whole of which there may be many versions, there is only one truth of which there may be many expressions (*b*) Judgements and beliefs are true, not so far as they agree with any outside reality but only so far as there is agreement amongst themselves, that is, so far as they are consistent but in no way verifiable. (*c*) Judgements must have objects but these alone are not sufficient, rather, every relation modifies the terms of that relation and no term can be judged of apart from that corpus of all relations. One of the consequences of this is that if there is one part of reality that is completely known, then every part of the whole must be known, as in the system of Leibniz. Conversely, if it is the whole that is completely known, then this must involve knowledge of its relation to each and every part, and this in turn to what each part is in and of itself, as in the system of Spinoza. These are the doctrines called monadism and pantheism.

We can illustrate this in the following way if we consider its implication for the question of diversity: Let us suppose that A = a milk bottle, B = a fridge, ArB = sitting in a fridge and BrA = holding a milk bottle. If we assume that A and B differ when A has the adjective 'different from B', then 'different from B' must contain the adjective 'different from "different from A"'. And if 'different from A' really means 'different from ArB', i.e. holding a milk bottle, then 'different from "different from A"' must surely mean something like holding a tin of sardines. Conversely, if we suppose that A and B differ when B has the adjective 'different from A', then 'different from A' must contain the adjective 'different from "different from B"'. And if 'different from B' really means 'different from BrA', i.e. is sitting in a fridge, then 'different from "different from B"' must mean something like sitting in a cupboard. In itself of course, this does not disprove the doctrine called monism— rather does it confirm it, since an infinite regress in this context only means that there are no such things as relations or at least only a finite number of properties connected in a finite number of ways.

A more telling objection concerns the way we would ordinarily conceive the relation between identity and diversity. As we have already seen, an analytic proposition is one in which the predicate is contained in the idea of the subject and a synthetic proposition one in which the predicate is not contained in the idea of the subject. But it seems that if there is no such thing as a different *aspect* of truth, then there can only be room for the former, since what we mean by the predicate can only be construed as what is *part* of the subject. Or let us approach this in terms of the difference between (*a*) analysis and synthesis as they pertain to a difference in process and (*b*) what we have called assertoric and apodictic judgements. In the case of an object D that is broken down into the parts 'a,b,c', it is not unreasonable to suppose there are different relation that have also been produced thereby (we might regard 'a' in relation to 'b' or 'c', 'b' in relation to 'a' or 'c', and 'c' in relation to 'a' or 'b'). But if we proceed in the opposite direction, then it is important to distinguish between synthesis when what we mean is something reductive and synthesis when what we mean is something conjunctive. If there are two related wholes AB and BC, then by a simple operation, we might reduce this to the whole ABC. But it should be clear that this involves a certain ideation, it involves a fusing of the parts which is not at all like the process of mixing red and blue to produce the colour purple. And so also on the question of what is internal and what is external—in the case of analysis this might be called an internal operation, but we would not in the same way call synthesis an external operation, only when the product is something altogether new. We cannot make oil into water or water into oil, but we can make water into steam or cocoa into chocolate.

Another problem with any activity that draws inferences based on some incipient whole is that it tends to confound the object of ideation with the product of ideation in the way, for instance, that it tends to regard classes and sets as just as 'real' as the members that make them up. Thus, when we say that AB and BC becomes ABC, what we mean by this is that some part has been incorporated within the whole. On the other hand, the claim that the more elements you connect then the more varied will be the whole, is a little like the scholastic argument that there *must* be one species for each individual if it is incorruptible, but many individuals for each species if it is not. (We will deal with this more fully in our treatment of universals, but suffice to say that clarity in respect to quantity is very different from confusion in respect to number.)

As regards the difference between the apodictic and the assertoric, then as we have stated previously, this concerns the intension of a term in the case of the former, and the extension of a term in the case of the latter. What however we mean by the intension of a term, should not be confounded with any reality on which it is based, or any implicit agreement as concerns the necessary and the hypothetical. Whether there is or is not a Divine Being may be a debatable issue, but the question addressed by an apodictic judgement is what qualities He must possess if indeed He does exist. Therefore, in terms of the relation between logical and causal necessity, in no way should the one be grounded in the other or be joined to the other through the medium of what is called the hypothetical.

Another consideration is how we might arrive at anything other than what it means to be coherent or self-consistent. It seems that if there is no relevant means for ascertaining what is false, then all we have is a sliding scale taking us from the less adequate and the less complete to the more adequate and the more complete. If the whole truth is not an aggregate of truths but only something that can be apprehended *through* truth, then all argumentation would be in vain, all reasoning would be in vain, and all observation would be in vain. In the final analysis, our conjectures would be as empty as our daydreams, our achievements just as pointless as all our failures and our discoveries just as fruitless as all our misadventures. Not only that, but if the truth is just as clear and pellucid as our monist would suppose, then must this not also be the case with any instrument that uncovers our darkest thoughts? But again, we have entered upon a bed of thorns, since the structure of our language does not reflect the purity of our thought, and the content of our thought does not reflect the content of what is real. In respect to what we have previously said, consider the case of a Cretan when he utters the words, 'All Cretans are liars'. Now the kind of quandary that derives from this is not one that is strictly semantic—it is more about the relation between the speaker and the spoken word than what it is permissible to say or what such a person might in fact *think*. The statement as it stands is logically absurd if uttered by a Cretan but not if uttered by a non-Cretan. In the same way, if a Cretan utters the words, 'Not all Cretans are liars', then this is not meaningless but false, just as it would be if uttered by a non-Cretan. Quite clearly, if there is just one truth, then there cannot be one set of rules for what we can say in expressing what we think, and another set of rules for what we cannot say but which is not in contradiction to what we think.

Logical holism as it is frequently called is opposed by the doctrine called logical atomism. The intuitive idea here is that what counts are not judgements and beliefs, but the objects of judgements and beliefs, and the facts or things that result from a constructive approach where the elements of experience are concerned. To begin with, let us consider the various qualities that are discernible through our senses, say colour and shape for the eye, sound for the ear, taste for the tongue, etc. We might then say that these are certain kinds of assortments, as for instance bitter and sweet tastes, harsh and soft tones, pleasant and pungent smells. We can then combine these by suggesting that certain tastes and smells, certain colours and shapes, are present together at a certain time or in a certain place. Even language supports the claim that the things we regard as qualities may also be regarded as substantives. Not only can we say that 'this is a lump of sugar' and 'this sugar is sweet', we can also say that 'sweetness is a property exhibited in something such as sugar', 'sugar is sweet' and 'this is sweet'. Therefore, in the case of 'this is sweet', what we have is an atomic proposition that reflects the basic fact that 'something is such and such'.

However, we need to be careful not to confound a basic fact with a basic meaning, since a basic meaning may be more or less complex, depending on whether it is more or less autonomous. Sometimes we can only apprehend a subject through the manner in which it is described, not through a simple inspection of what it in fact is, as for instance when we say 'Henry VIII had six wives', 'Henry VIII founded the Church of England', 'Henry VIII died in 1547'. The reason for this is that where there is a question about denotation rather than connotation, we may need to be especially careful about the words we employ. It may be perfectly clear what we mean by the expression 'the one and only Richard Nixon', but there is a difference if we say 'Richard Nixon was a former president of the United States' and "Richard Nixon is the current president of the United States'. Leaving this aside, wherever there is complexity of meaning this will invariably involve a greater complexity in any terminology as well. Thus, for an atomic fact, there are just two ways it might be construed. and that is as either true or false. (In other words, 'something is such and such' or 'something is not such and such'.) This is important for the principle of bivalence. But quite specifically where it concerns the addition of such words as *if, or* and,

and, what is simple will become what is complex and what is atomic will become what is molecular. This then raises the prospect that where there are different facts there may also be different outcomes, depending on the operator or connector we are using at the time. When however, we describe 'and' or 'or' as being in the nature of connectors, it should be clear we mean connections between the facts, not simply between the nouns or parts of speech. Whilst it is true that atomic propositions can contain only one verb, there is no limit to the number of nouns they may contain. And of course, that raises the further question whether by a verb do we mean something necessarily relational or an abbreviation for something much more inveterate in its kind. Consider the following propositions: (*a*) 'John loves swimming and skiing' and (*b*) 'John loves fishing, but he hates swimming'. Quite clearly, the latter is molecular but that may be no less so in the case of the former, since this is really an abbreviation for 'John loves swimming and he loves skiing'. It would be a different matter however if we had a specific relation word such as *exchange*, since in that case something like 'John exchanged his sandals for his slippers' would clearly be atomic and not molecular.

In saying that atomism and holism are opposed, it should be clear we do not mean 'opposed' in the sense of different theories that explain the same observations or the same set of phenomena—it is not like the dispute about light as to whether it is composed of particles or waves. Rather the one is a theory about reality and the other a theory about the nature of truth, such that, the issue is really whether reality should be viewed through the prism of truth or truth should be viewed through the prism of reality. So far as it concerns the former, this is expressed in terms of the belief that if there is one subject, then this must be what comprises the totality of all things, and if there is one predicate, then this must be what comprises the properties of all things. So far as it concerns the latter, if predication is itself an end, then not only are there many things but also those relations that connect these many things.

However, if there is a problem with holism there may also be a problem with atomism. When we say that 'John loves fishing' (aRb), 'John loves skiing' (aRc) or 'John hates swimming' (aRd), these can be combined in different ways to produce what is molecular in its make-up. But whilst this is true of any proposition, it is not necessarily true of any particular fact. It all depends on what you mean by a monadic relation. If you take the basic constituents of reality to be sense data and nothing more, then the quality that a thing exhibits could be said to bear a relation to itself. On the other hand, if you consider things to be more than their particular constituents then in comparing them you would tend to do so on account of both their identity and diversity. As we have already argued, the way we compare the Eiffel Tower and the river Thames is not the same as the way we would compare a flagpole and a goalpost. In neither atomism nor holism is there any attempt to compare things that are truly heterogeneous in their kind—it is just a question whether we should begin with a coherent body of facts that are also relational or a coherent body of truths that are also not absolute. For our own part, we would tend to resist any urge towards unity, since the best that can be hoped for is an inclusive relation between quality and quantity, or the whole being represented through the parts rather than any part being representative of what is whole. And this applies not only to the meaning of reality but also to the meaning of any *belief.*

There are two ways that the relation between knowledge and belief may be viewed: on the one hand, where they are mutually exclusive and, on the other hand, where the former is grounded in the latter. Under certain circumstances, it would seem odd if a person were to say he simply *thinks* something is the case if he knows it is the case, as for instance 'my name is so-and-so', 'there are five toes on each of my feet' or 'I am seventeen today'. But this tends to be the case only when knowing is compared with disbelief (or at least uncertainty), not when there are different degrees from what is less to what is more certain. Thus, it would seem very odd if Woodrow Wilson in 1914 had uttered the words, 'I believe I am the president of the United States', but in a sense it would be no less odd if a lunatic had uttered the words, 'I *am* the president of the United States'. Opposition between knowledge and belief in this instance is therefore based on the difference between clear and delusional thinking. However the reason we are more partial to the view that knowledge must be based on belief is that there is a difference in the way we say something when this pertains to what our words are about, and the way we say something when this pertains to our degree of conviction in using the words that we do. For instance, if two people with no knowledge of the present weather conditions were asked for their advice and one said, 'Bring your umbrella. It is windy and rainy', and the other said, 'Bring your sombrero. It is sunny and warm', then it is difficult to say what the actual criteria for choosing might be. That does not mean you may not *guess* right, but neither does it mean you would be any wiser if you did. On the other hand, suppose you were to show someone a stamp and his response was 'This stamp was minted in India'. You then show the same stamp to someone else and his response is 'This stamp was minted in Indonesia'. Now with no knowledge of your own but aware that person A was a trained philatelist and B a trained geologist, who would you be more likely to believe? In this case, what we have is a degree of knowledge or what could be called a *justified belief.*

There are three principal conditions for knowledge and these could be stated as follows: (*a*) The agreement of a proposition with some actual state of affairs, as for example 'This orchid is purple', when the object currently before me is indeed the colour purple, (*b*) the acceptance that a speaker has for the truth of what is being conveyed and (*c*) a justification or reasonable ground for believing that such and such is the case. What this implies is that there are certain basic beliefs or certain indubitable grounds and on which all others beliefs must depend. It is also important to be clear that in the relation between acceptance and belief there is both a point of agreement and a point of divergence. If a person knows that something is the case, then he also accepts that something is the case, and if a person accepts that something is the case, then he also believes that something is the case. It is a moot point however whether someone who knows that something is the case also believes that something is the case, or at least 'believes' in the weaker sense. It could be argued that 'to know' implies being in a special or privileged state and that language clearly attests to what is provisory or passing (as in the case of supposition or conjecture) and what is sure or certain (as in the case of axioms or rules). We need to be careful therefore about what is truly justifiable, not merely what accompanies any fancy or any whim.

Of course, there are numerous objections that could be raised to such a formulation, but let us consider just two of the counter examples cited by Edmund Gettier[3]. Let us say that James and John are applicants for the same job and that James has a justified belief that his opponent will be successful. He also has a reasonable belief that John has exactly ten dollars in his pocket. James therefore concludes that the person with exactly ten dollars in his pocket will also be the person who gets the job. However, John does not get the job, and unbeknownst to him, James has exactly ten dollars in his pocket. In what way therefore is our initial belief connected with what is true or with any precondition for what it means to know the truth? In response to this it should be clear that what we mean by 'justified belief' concerns only the criteria or the likelihood of being successful—it no more requires that a person have ten dollars in his pocket than it does he has two hundred. Implication in a logical sense means only the kind of outcome that could be inferred in a *reasonable way*, not just according to what does or does not turn out to *be* the case. If it happens that James had been chosen not because of anything he has in his pocket but say perhaps, his eyes are blue rather than brown, then likewise, there is no way this could have been inferred in any reasonable or predictable way.

In the second example, let us say that James has a good reason to believe that John is the owner of a motorcycle—such evidence concerns John's own testimony, his laudable remarks about the sport of motor racing and his extensive knowledge of their different makes and models. Let us suppose that James also has a friend called Simon and that Simon is a jet-setter whose whereabouts is rarely known. From this, James then

---

3   E.Gettier 'Is justified true belief knowledge?' *Analysis* XXV (1963)

considers the following options: (*a*) Either John owns a motorcycle or Simon is in Rome, (*b*) either John owns a motorcycle or Simon is in Venice or (*c*) either John owns a motorcycle or Simon is in Paris. Now given certain permutations, it is possible that any one of these might be true or that none of these might be true. But let us suppose that John was really lying and that he does not really own a motorcycle. And let us suppose that Simon just happens to be in Venice at the time of such surmising. It thus appears that what we have is an evident disjunct that is not true (i.e. John owns a motorcycle and that Simon is not in Paris, Rome or Venice) and a true disjunct that is not evident (i.e. Simon is in Venice, but that John does not own a motorcycle). Again however, what this does not prove is that a true state of affairs is derived from a false and not a justified belief. The false belief that John owns a motorcycle is not the reason for the truth of such a disjunct, but rather that Simon is in Venice, and that is not something about which anyone might have any reasonable belief, at best just a hunch. Hence a justified belief can only be compared to a fancy or unfounded belief, not something that is true but only accidentally so, otherwise we would be arguing in a circle, and no belief could be justified unless it was derived from what was absolutely so.

In order to address the problem of circularity, it has sometimes been suggested that we add a rider stating that if 'p' was true, then S would believe that 'p' was true, and that if 'p' was false, then S would not believe that 'p' was true. But again, this would be to place certitude at a level far above the actual capacities of men. Let us say you were standing at a roulette wheel and there were two options for the present spin—that it would or would not land on zero. Given just these conditions then you would surely be justified in believing in the latter. However, if someone placed his money on zero and the ball just happened to land there what would you say—that his predictive powers were stronger than your uncertainty, or that if you had known differently, you would have chosen differently? Surely neither is the case, since the law of probability is the only thing which makes any real or true sense. What this proves thus is not that knowledge and belief are incompatible, rather, that there are different ways they might be conjoined. It is not simply the case that you can only 'hit on' or jag the truth, rather, there is the viewpoint of what we know as conditional upon what we believe, or what we believe as conditional upon that which we know. For a belief to be 'coincidently' true or false, it must be the case that either (*a*) it would still be believed in the event it was false or (*b*) it would not be believed in the event it was true. In the case of (*a*), if there is no evidence that a particular herb can provide a cure for gout, then neither is there any reason for believing it might work. On the other hand, if a person is known to be an incessant liar (as in the fable of the boy who cried wolf), then this produces will be a state of general disbelief, even on those occasions when the subject may be predisposed to tell the truth.

In the way we have treated of justification, we have tended to do so against the backdrop of the kind of knowledge that is mediated, rather than what may be termed immediate or direct. As we have earlier stated, in the absence of any direct evidence as to where a stamp originates, we are more inclined to accept the word of an expert than someone who has a purely passing interest. This itself however may be somewhat problematic, since if there were no terminal or fixed beliefs we would be caught in a vicious circle, taking us from our initial belief to the antecedent justification for any number of similar beliefs. Thus, in the way we conceive of knowledge might we do so in the form of a pyramid, each of the parts at one level bearing an asymmetric relation to those at the next, and the whole ascending from many parts to that which was singular at its top.

In suggesting that justification must also in some sense address the issue of what is self-justifying, it should be clear we do not intend this as a counter cry to the kind of scepticism about internal states, but only to the evidence about external events. Cartesian doubt begins with the question of what we can really know about ourselves, and then attempts to resolve this by appealing to certain 'clear and distinct' ideas. This however is not the panacea that it appears to be, since all it really does raise a more sinister prospect i.e. doubt about the existence of minds beside our own. The tenor of such an argument might be something like the following. If a person were to utter the words, 'my hands are feeling numb', then a sceptic could argue that what this proves is nothing more than that these words will be accompanied by such and such a particular *belief.* But this belief, the belief of someone else, is not the same as experiencing numbness in one's own case. And since we do not need words and signs to accompany our purely inner states, there is a clear schism between what our body language might suggest and what is in fact the case.

To argue in such a way however is really only to confuse the symptom with the disease—that a person is able to lie or dissemble does not mean that this is incompatible with his capacity to communicate his feelings or his thoughts. In fact quite the reverse. It is a little like saying that a doctor only has the capacity to diagnose a disease if he has the disease himself, or that a patient can only be cured if he has simply faked it and was never really ill. On the other hand, this is very different from the way a sceptic might handle the question of *causal* relations, by suggesting that they have no real relevance apart from what we have simply imagined but not truly inferred. Whether it concerns a certain priority in respect to time or contiguity in respect to place, we need to explain how this supervenes over the basic constituents or those orderings we call time and place. For that therefore, what we require is a form of knowledge that is self-justifying in the way we have already suggested, precisely as is afforded in the axioms of science.

As we have already seen, logical holism is the kind of doctrine that is supported by an infinite regress, since it makes the relative value of each belief conditional upon the value of the system as a whole. Where foundationalism is concerned the strategy is altogether different, since what we are attempting to do is to avoid the circle that encloses all inferences and all conclusions that may or may not be justified. It is not inconceivable however that there may be a system of thought neither supported by an infinite regress nor imperiled by an infinite regress, as is evident in the case of geometry. In terms of what is called traditional geometry, this is the kind of system formulated by Euclid and consisting in certain basic tenets, from which are then deduced a number of proofs and theorems. However, in no sense we would say that this was supported by an infinite regress or necessary to counter such a prospect. If the former, then it would be inconceivable there could be any other system than the Euclidean, and this is certainly not the case. If the latter, then the whole of geometry would have suffered with the rejection of the fifth postulate, whereas in fact, all it has really done is spawn other geometries equally privileged in themselves. And in a sense this is what might be said of a system of basic relations, the more primary being what we call the modemic, and the more subsidiary being what we call the monadic. Let A be an object that possesses the property 'l' but is lacking in 'm' and 'r'. Let B be an object that possesses the property 'm' but is lacking in 'l' and 'r'. Let C be an object that possesses the property 'l' and 'm' but is lacking in 'r'. Now what makes this a primary relation is that 'r' is also a composite, say the composite 'no'. By comparison what we mean by a secondary relation is one that will be lacking at least one of these parts, be that 'n' or 'o'. And so let U be an object that possesses the properties 'l' and 'o' but is lacking in m. Let V be an object that possesses the properties 'l' and 'm' but is lacking in 'o'. Let W be an object that possesses the properties 'l,m,o'. Alternately, let X be an object that possesses the properties 'l' and 'n' but is lacking in 'm'. Let Y be an object that possesses the properties 'l' and 'm' but is lacking in 'n'. Let Z be an object that possesses the properties 'l,m,n'.

Chapter 14

Universals and Particulars I

So far as it concerns the question of universals, there are two broad ways we might approach this: either in terms of what is descriptive or in terms of what is discursive. So far as it concerns the former this a method of drawing inferences based on past and present observations, such that these observations will always remain open to scrutiny in the future. Individuals are arranged into different classes or different categories and the words for these classes are what we mean by their universal being. So far as it concerns the latter, this is a method for drawing inferences based on a fixed principle, such that the outcome will always be determined by those assumptions from which we begin. Hence in these terms, it may be possible to separate existence from some more primordial or transcendental being.

But there is also another issue that arises from the discursive method itself, and that is about the relation between specific and numerical identity. On the one hand, we might adopt an approach which presumes that the latter is contingent upon the former and, on the other, an approach which assumes that the former is contingent upon the latter. Looked at in one way, it could be argued that existence is contingent upon essence and hence that numerical identity must supersede what is *specific*. In a stable world what this means is that every individual is its own type and every specimen is its own species. On the other hand, in a changing world what this means is that diversity in form will be mirrored by diversity in number, and in such a way that the latter is merely an addendum to the former. In this respect however, if we take the number of species to be entirely indifferent to that which they signify, it drives a wedge between the idea of a thing and the idea of a class. This in turn obscures the broader distinction between the ideas of *inclusion* and *exclusion* per se—the existence of the species is not supported by the existence of all its members, rather is the latter indifferent to the former.

So far as it concerns the relation between whole and part, the implication must surely be that the one is contained in the other, and that what *is*, is wholly in all the parts and not just in several or any given one. Working from this assumption, the problem then becomes how we might consider that what is part of the individual may not *suffice* for any individual, but that what is outside the individual may yet be what is singular and indivisible in itself. If for instance, we consider 'humanity' as the whole of what is human, then this might be said to comprise the humanity of Hannibal, the humanity of Pericles, the humanity of Xerxes, etc., such that each instance must add to the *whole* of what is human. But then if the arm of Xerxes or the thigh of Xerxes is part of the whole of Xerxes, then why might not Xerxes himself be regarded as what is universal and not particular in its kind?

Or we might approach this a little differently and yet with entirely the same result, if we consider the relation that holds between the species and the genus or the species and the individual. Certainly, it may be true that the genus is equal to the species and the species to the individual so far as it concerns some essential *form*, but from another perspective this is clearly not the case. Necessarily there will be fewer members of any subspecies than there are of any species, just as there will be *mutatis mutandis* concerning the relation between the species and the genus. On the other hand, if we regard a species as what is common to any number of its members, why we might we not also regard the individual as what is common to any number of its parts? The problem of universals thus becomes the problem of the one and the many, or in precisely what sense we can say that something is a collection of things qua such and such a collection, or something is a collection of things qua what is discernible or recognizable in itself.

An approach that runs counter to this is that essence is contingent upon existence, but in the sense that specific identity must supersede numerical *diversity*. What we mean by the individual therefore is that *specific* complex of qualities by which each thing comes to be known, but not in addition any 'common' nature that ties it to others. In this case there is no room for universals, since if there is nothing that could be said to be 'common', neither is there anything distinctive other than what is distinctive in this respect or in that. The question is however, whether by starting with the least significant are we then entitled to advance to the claim that this must be the greatest as well. That is, it takes for granted that if there is a difference in *some* respect, then this must count for what is different in *all* respects. If in a formal sense it is true that any two bodies *must* occupy a different place at the same time, is one to infer that this is what makes them entirely distinguishable throughout each and every moment of time? That is, if object X is to the right of Y at time t_1 and object Y is to the right of X at time t_2, then they have not really 'swapped places' but retained that place each had from the outset. Or as another example, let us say you witnessed a recital of the same musical piece but at different times, and noticed a slight variation from one occasion to the next, would you then conclude that these performances were altogether different and not essentially just the same? If you are going to argue that it is because two things are numerically distinct they must also be specifically distinct, then sameness could only mean similitude and there would be nothing identical at all. Not only would the red ball over here be different from the red ball over there, it would not even be true that it was the same *shade* of red that was discernible at all.

The question of whether two things are similar or the same can often be decided through inspection, as for instance when we inspect two patches of colour or two musical sounds. What we mean by 'exactly the same' will thus be what is indistinguishable to either the eye or the ear and this gives us a sense of confidence about the judgements we make, as it does when we vacate a room and on returning discover that it is exactly as we left it. But it still remains a moot point whether our senses are something on which we can always rely. As another example let us say you were to measure the length of two bodies, and using the metre bar in Paris, you concluded that one was exactly two centimetres longer than the other. Consider on the other hand a personal quality such as courage or veracity, then in what sense could these things be compared, in what sense could one person be said to have more courage than another and in any way that was quantifiable as such? Of course, we can and often do make these assessments, but that is not because there is any clear rule, rather, because we take them to be discernible if not in an altogether accurate way.

Thus, in the way we treat of a quality such as courage we do so as a matter of simple convenience, because it suits us to say that this person is courageous but that that person is cowardly, or that this person is veracious but that that person is not. And if this is true for less evident qualities then why should we not extend it to those things that are more perceptible, since the perceptible may also pertain to what is universal in its kind. If you were asked what was common to a lemon and a sloe, then the answer you might give is that they are bitter in their taste. On the other hand, if you were presented with two lemons and judged them to be equally bitter, then on what grounds would you say they were any less the same in either their shape or in their colour? The point is, it suits us to regard qualities as existing independently of one another because it gives us greater confidence in any assessments that we make.

Perhaps the best way to resolve these differences is if we maintain a firm distinction between existence and essence, rather than running them together, or treating them as just the same. By essence what we mean, is something which is peculiar to some things but not what is common to all things. In one respect, the approach we adopt is removing certain qualities to bring out the meaning of the generic, in another, garnering certain qualities to bring out the meaning of the idiosyncratic. We might regard the relation between the genus and the species as one of simple inclusion: in the first place where it is a question of quantity (or what is quantified) and in the second place where it is a question of purity (or what is purified). Quite clearly, there will be fewer members of any species than there will be of the genus, just as, there will be less clarity in the latter and more differentiation in the former. We would not say therefore that the species is compounded of the genus and the differentiae; otherwise, we would be using the genus to create a greater indistinctness and not the species to create a greater degree of precision. The relation between the species and the individual on the other hand could be described as one of simple exclusiveness: in the first place because what is 'essential' to the individual is not what is 'essential' to the species, and secondly because what is distinctive about the species is what can be *divided* in the species, whereas what is distinctive about the individual is what is whole and not divided.

Or we could express this a little differently by saying that the species and the individual are coequal in number but different in nature, whereas the species and the genus are coequal in nature but different in number. Let us pursue this in a little more detail. The individual and the species are coequal in number in the sense that the whole and the parts are coequal, that is, so far as what we are dealing with is an aggregate and not what is indissoluble in itself. On the other hand, they may also be regarded as what is different in their nature, since although the 'accidents' are inherent in every member of a species, the 'differentiae' are not inherent in every species, only what distinguishes one species from any other. Where it concerns the relation between the species and the genus, it should be clear they cannot be coequal in number, since the members that comprise the genus must be greater than the members that comprise any subgroup. However, what we mean by the essence of the species must always be inclusive of the genus, since from this perspective it is the former that has its grounding in the latter, not the latter that has its grounding in the former. Certainly, there will be more complexity in the species than in the genus, but that does not also mean greater coherence, since it is only by the removal of what is diverse we can see what is clear and pellucid in itself.

If therefore as we would maintain, the meaning of particulars can be connected with a specialized rather than generalized *nature* and universals with a global rather than specific *existence*, the question still remains in what sense the latter could be said to have any true verity at all. That is, do we mean by 'existence' what inheres *in the mind* as a concept or what we project as an image, or do we mean by 'existence' what inheres in a world that we know to be real? Let us approach this in terms of a distinction between (*a*) the possible and the impossible, (*b*) the real and the apparent and (*c*) the sensuous and the ideal. By the impossible what we mean is what is inconceivable or unimaginable given certain restraints from both a physical and linguistic point of view. Thus, it is impossible that a triangle could be exhibited in a circle or that an irrational number could be expressed as the quotient of two integers, and that is because of the restriction that prevents one figure from exhibiting the features of some other, or any real number from exhibiting what is absurd. With respect to (*b*), then what we are dealing with is the scope or the limit of our understanding, of what could conceivably be but 'is not' and what is and yet could conceivably 'not be'. Thus, it is not inconceivable that there could be a beast with several arms or several heads, but it is perhaps less likely there would be a beast with the ears of an elephant and the tail of a shrew.

So far as it concerns the question of any quiddity, then we may regard this as what is simply undivided in itself— and that we can just as well grasp the meaning of a griffin as one can a tortoise or a hare. That however is not to say there is a universal 'griffin' as there is a universal 'hare'—the concept of a thing should not be confounded with the reality of a thing, whether the thing be in the present, the future or the past. A real zebra is not merely the representation of a zebra or what we place before our minds in some purely arbitrary or capricious way. Therefore, we should not attempt to compare the concrete and the mental in terms of any resemblance between the two, as if there could only ever be a kind of confused image in the mind for what was clear and pellucid in itself. It is sometimes claimed that what we mean by an image is not really a product of the mind, since the mind and the senses are not the same, but that what we are dealing with in the former case must be something that both divides and conjoins any assemblage of parts. The problem with this is that it confounds the meaning of resemblance as a certain *graduated* change with the meaning of resemblance as just an assortment of different parts. Although we might be prepared to countenance universals as the highest *clarity* the mind can attain, we would certainly not do so if there was any kind of vagueness or misdirection that intervened.

This also has implications for the meaning of a bare or perfect universal, that is, a realm of 'platonic essences' that matches or mirrors the world of real things. There are certain considerations we need to attend to here, but most especially between an object that is imaginary and an object that is self-existent. The idea of a unicorn for instance is a product of the mind, but that does not mean it also has an existence that is separable from the mind. It should be clear thus, that there are two things we are dealing with here: either things like griffins and leprechauns that are *mental constructs* or things like humanity and roundness that are *instantiated universals*. As we will later argue, if you consider something such as the quiddity of table, then it is not unreasonable that this will be exhibited in each and every table, but that is not to say that tables cannot exhibit qualities that are peculiar to themselves. It is less appropriate to argue that the whole of 'being a table' is exhibited in each and every table than it is that such a quality is exhibited in many different forms. On the other hand, if there is such a thing as the form of form, then this can only be what is formless, and if formless, then what is vacuous and unintelligible as well.

To consider next a distinction between the sensuous and the ideal, then we need a broader framework and that is the idea of what *must* exist by virtue of being placed before our minds and what *may* exist by virtue of being placed before our minds. Perhaps this can be illustrated if we compare two entirely different things: on the one hand, the figure of a triangle, and on the other, the body of a unicorn. What it is that connects these things is that neither belongs to what could be called our everyday world, that is, the world of tables and chairs, of seashells and sand. It makes no sense to ask *how* many triangles there are any more than it does how many unicorns there are—since we cannot locate these things, neither can we collect or arrange them in such and such a way. But the critical difference consists in this, that in the one case does the object exist by virtue of being placed before our minds, whereas in the other it does not, or to express this a little differently, we cognize the former as a whole and the latter as only what resembles certain parts. The size of a triangle, for instance, is not something that pertains to the meaning of 'being triangular', but there is nothing in the features of a unicorn that is not contained in the concept 'unicornicity'. That is, since no one has ever seen a unicorn, no one would ever know what features it might have that were incidental to what it was in itself. On the other hand, if we attend to the meaning of a triangle or how such a figure is exhibited, then it should be clear it is not something contained in the concept 'triangularity'—it is not something that has been abstracted from a genus or is merely exemplified in such and such a way. What we mean by 'being triangular' is something grounded in the *a priori* nature of space, and to that extent it bears comparison to other concepts such as 'being square', 'being circular', etc. Where on the other hand we have a single representation then this must be regarded as what is complete in itself, not something that is merely one aspect of the more general idea of a three-sided figure. Rather is one specimen of a certain kind just as clear and distinct as any other within the same class or set.

Consider also how we might distinguish between an ideal object and anything of a more substantive or concrete kind. Given two figures in a single plane that are equivalent in their size, in their shape, and the relationship between their parts, then by the act of rotating one through an angle of 180 degrees, it should be clear why we might say they are not just alike but exactly the *same*. Of course, it is true that what this involves is both a mental and a physical act, but that should not dissuade us from the conclusion that such an operation underscores. So far on the other hand as two figures may be said to be different in size but not shape, we might regard these as instances of one and the same form but not of one and the same *space*. Thus, to be of one and the same form means more than just embody a certain set of features, rather does it pertain to a sense of the whole that is embracing of *all* its parts. And this has important implications for the way we might regard the specific quality we call colour. To the extent we might regard colour as partaking of what is sensuous, so would we apprehend it as we do any other quality, only here where there is an absence of properties but not necessarily what we would mean by any richness. Of course, it is true that we cannot rotate a patch of colour such that this would make for any difference, we cannot superimpose two colours or make them into one (unless we mix them), but that should not dissuade us from the view that what we have is something quite distinctive. Pink is not red, crimson is not turquoise, and 'bright' yellow is not the same as 'bright' blue.

Chapter 15

Universals and Particulars II

In renewing our concern with the question of universal being or what is commonly called 'the problem of universals', the issue that arises is whether we are positing something to replace the items of our everyday world or whether we are positing something in addition to the items of our everyday world. How for instance might we regard the relation between the attribute of being human and the existence of different human beings? If we say there is some attribute 'humanity' binding Peter, Paul and John, then the implication is that there is something over and above these different existents. But then does this also imply that if Peter has a left ear and a right arm, then there must also be a quality that we call 'being left eared' or 'being right armed'? Quite clearly then, the problem we are dealing with is how to establish certain limits for where such attribution might begin or end. And so, the way we might approach this is by supposing that a universal is (*a*) merely the mental equivalent that arises in such and such a mind or (*b*) the collectivization of certain things in a way that allows us to use the same word. Thus, we can overcome the need for discursive reasoning by regarding different things as either an aggregate of wholes or an aggregate of parts that any whole might be likely to comprise.

Now let us consider each of these points in turn. How and in what way different concepts may be formed hinges largely on regarding the mind as a kind of 'tabula rasa', so that an idea is merely a reassembled or reconstructed version of what is real. Abstraction therefore is not removal of the purely superfluous or the degree of clarity that might actually be attained, rather just the reverse, since if there are different quantities or different qualities then this must be true of any mental equivalent as well. To adopt the view that we conceive of things quite simply as they are and not as what they might be, suggests there is some paradigm according to which different things can be compared and contrasted, and that presumably is what best fits our specific needs. Whether it is either a word or a concept we are dealing with, this will always be something singular, whereas, it is only in terms of what is expedient there is any more variety to be discerned. As an example, what we call 'food' is the kind of thing we produce in order to nourish ourselves and gratify our senses. What we call 'clothes' are the kinds of thing we produce in order to keep us warm and protect us from the elements.

The counter claim to this is that by making ideas contingent upon some usage, or what we connect with our everyday world, we are really only confusing the relation between the real and apparent with the sensuous and ideal. There is a considerable difference between the unity and coherence of an image, as when we say that something *must* exist by virtue of being placed before our minds, and the prerequisites for something that *may* exist by virtue of being placed before our minds. What distinguishes the idea of a griffin from the reality of a griffin is not simply a confused as distinct from clear impression; otherwise, an eagle's wing and a lion's body would only be obscurely connected as a whole, whereas there would be no such difficulty in the case of an eagle's wing and an eagle's tail. What distinguishes the essence of a griffin from the existence of a griffin is what distinguishes the *real* from the *apparent*—we do not say that a griffin is merely a confused or distorted image, rather it is something chimerical and yet also representational. The mind can represent to itself something imaginary just as readily as it can what is real, and that is because, unlike a hologram, a state of precision is not attained by removing what is obscure, nor is it thrown into confusion by the removal of what is clear and distinct.

As to the second of these points—that universals are merely collections of things and not what *inheres* in these things—then we need to be careful not to confuse a collection of items with what we mean by a collection of *classes*. That is, if we say that 'humanity' is not what pertains to Peter, Paul and John, but rather to the class or species that includes Peter, Paul and John, then we have not solved our dilemma, since it seems there are now classes and sets, as well as the things to which these classes and sets are referable. And this is open to the objection that we are appending the word *universal* to certain things by virtue of their having the same form or figure, rather than any existence separate from just such a form. If for instance you were to divide the species *Homo sapiens* into the subgroups Occidental and Oriental, and then to these add Chinese, Siamese, Frenchmen and Scotsmen, then what you have done is not reduce the number of entities but rather increase them, since we now have classes within other classes and not just classes alongside other classes. And for the sake of economy how is this any better than if we were to just *abstract* 'Scottishness' from all Scotsmen or 'Sudanness' from all Sudanese, that is, if we were to work from the bottom up rather than the top down?

On the other hand, it is not inconceivable we could have arrived at exactly the same result employing an entirely different method, or at least, the method that bases specific identity upon numerical identity. The Schoolmen argued that in incorruptible things there was only one individual for each species, whereas in corruptible things there were many individuals for each species. But of course, this is sheer sophistry, since whatever the status of incorruptible things we should never mix things that are heterogeneous in their kind. The point is, where there is a degree of generalization there must also be an *active mind*, but it does not follow that where there are active minds then there must also be ethereal objects. Neither does it follow that if there are collective nouns then it matters little who applies them, just as long as some connection can be forged between our words and those collections they imply. As we have already indicated, there is no such thing as the form of a form that is real, only the form of a form that is formless.

A further question is whether we should regard universals as intrinsic to the whole of individual being, or whether they should be regarded as what pertains to the parts of individual being. In the first case, we are adopting the view that the individual as a composite or an amalgam is what makes him quite unique—that what he is *specifically* is more important than what he is numerically. In the second case, we are adopting the view that the individual as an amalgam may be either accidental or essential, and that what is universal is what is common, but only common to certain things. And yet from our own perspective neither appears to do much to address the question how existence and essence are related, in the one case because it is too vague and in the other because it is too precise. Consequently, what we are not saying is that there must be either no qualities or two distinct 'qualities' for any particular thing, but rather that there may be several, and that so far as there is a specific nature do we mean what is diagnostic, and that so far as there is a common nature do we mean what is concrete. A 'common nature' therefore should not be added as we ascend from the individual to the species, but rather be taken, since a species may have a certain 'whatness' but not a certain concrete being.

So far in our discussion, we have already suggested that certain qualities that partake of the sensuous may also partake of the ideal, and thus, that there is no reason why there may not be different instances of entirely one and the same thing. Where it concerns the property we call colour, let us address this through a discussion about the relation between intensive and extensive wholes. By *intensive* what we mean is that each part is a whole in itself, and that what is whole is what is constant or what is continuous throughout. By *extensive* what we mean is that each part is unique in itself, and that what is whole may be either regular or irregular throughout. In respect to the former, consider how crimson may be a subset of red or how turquoise may be a subset of blue. In respect to the latter, consider how we might regard colour as either (*a*) a spectrum of different colours (as in a rainbow) or (*b*) a series of waves having such and such a length. In the first case what we have is a change and by perceptible degrees, since it is clear that yellow is not green and green is not blue—all we know is that the colour band is discrete and that there are many ways it could be viewed. On the other hand, if we regard colour as of such and such an amplitude, then we might regard change in a graduated way, that ABC becomes BCD, BCD becomes CDE, CDE becomes DEF, etc.

The point about all this is that in the case of colour what we have is both *descriptive* and *intuitive,* thus not merely sameness in relation to any part but sameness in relation to any whole. By comparison, consider what we mean by the concept or the definition of an aeroplane. Although we may conceive of an aeroplane as something sustained by the upward pressure on its wings, what we are afforded is simply an explanation or description of how this might be achieved. We thus tend to approach this from the viewpoint of a certain prototype and then its different variations, as for instance the Messerschmitt Bf 108 and 109, the Mk and Seafire Spitfire, the B-17 and B-24 bomber. But in the case of colour, not only we do have a broad concept (what it means to be coloured) but also the concept of what each is, in and of itself, that is, not only a certain resemblance but a matrix of relations as well. We do not just say that indigo is more like violet than violet is like blue, rather, that it is indigo that strengthens the distinction between two opposites, and brings out more clearly the distinction 'violet or blue'. And if colours were just imaginary, consider the implications this might have for those depictions in our nightly dreams—not only would they be lacking in order but they would be lacking in texture as well. Are we then to say that colour is not real because the dream is not real, that the dream is not real because the dreamer is not real, and that the dreamer is not real because the world is not real? And so, because we recognize that certain things are and others are not really the case, does not mean the mind can only copy and not be active in and of itself.

Of course, an empiricist might argue that it is really only *this* ball or *that flag* which is red, and not what a ball or a flag has that is common, but the logic of this is perhaps not as persuasive as it might firstly appear. It is true that what we mean by a sensuous object may be regarded as a cluster of properties, as for instance the properties 'shape' 'taste' and 'smell', but it should be clear that this only pertains to a certain range of presentations, not what something *must* be in and of itself. It is true that the sphere we call red must also be the shape we call round, and that the cube we call red must also be the shape we call square, but that does not mean the colour red must be restricted to the shapes we call round and square. The appearance of a red apple is something that adds to the taste of a red apple—we cannot decide that we saw the red apple but did not really eat it, or ate of it but did not know what we were really doing. Hence the quality of our experience depends on the richness of our experiences, not just the knowledge that enables us to separate the taste of what is bitter from the taste of what is sweet. And even if certain experiences could be said to resemble one another, that is not to say there must be exactly the same standard if there is to be anything in common. Whilst it is true we could not perceive an object as being black and white all over, we may nonetheless perceive a meal as being sweet and sour all over, and that is because of the way its different parts are being combined. On the other hand, what we mean by a dappled coat is not exactly what we mean by sweet and sour pork. In the first, there is enough clarity to distinguish between the colours black, grey and white, in the second, we do not have enough precision to distinguish between the tastes of sweet, sour, and something in between. Similarly, when we talk about a 'bitter-sweet' experience, what we are describing is something neither exclusively bitter nor sweet, rather, something that alternates between these different extremes.

Another issue is whether universals should be regarded as outside the constraints of space and time, or at different points in space at altogether one and the same time. To begin our enquiry, let us address what we mean by the *a priori* nature of space and the *a posteriori* nature of time. What we mean by the *a priori* nature of space is something that supplies the ground for all outer intuition, and it does this by placing the parts of space outside one another and then reconstructing them as a whole. Time on the other hand, is not in any sense an *a priori* condition, since we cannot in a similar way say how simultaneity and succession may either be connected or compared. Rather time is open-ended, both with respect to any particular movements and with respect to any particular change. So far as it concerns the relation between time and space, this must also be open-ended, or at least permit of various arrangements depending on how we mark the time. For two objects X and Y and the places a and b, if at t_1 X is in a and Y is in b, and at time t_2 X is in b and Y is in a, then something has occurred and as indicates a change in their overall state. Now size and shape may be relevant factors where it concerns these possible arrangements, but that is only so within this specific framework, not in terms of what we mean by space as it is in itself. In two-dimensional space we can conceive of a square, and in three-dimensional space we can conceive of a cube, but volume as we extrapolate this from from form is not necessarily what we mean by size as any feature of *apriori* space. A geometric figure such as a triangle is something that pertains to the ideal, and what that means is that so far as we take account of its shape we do not also take account of its size. That is not to say it may not have a size, but provided the relation between the parts is the same, there is no reason why any two figures might not be accounted the same. perceived. On the other hand, since colour is something that partakes of the sensuous but not the ideal, not only is its shape but its size of no account whatsoever. It matters little how a colour is exhibited, whether in the shape of a letter box, in the shape of a lizard, or the shape of a tree, it is still one and the same colour, and must be valued accordingly. And so, to the extent that a universal is not something constrained by time and space, neither does it lie outside time and space, rather is it the *a posteriori* nature of time that allows us to distinguish between the 'fleetingly present' and the 'eternally now'.

So far as it concerns our linguistic usage, we need to be clear first of all what it means to be *in* a real thing, and on the other hand, what it means to be *in* a certain state of mind. This is not a question of the difference between the real and the illusory, or being clear-sighted and being delusional, rather does it depend upon the particular viewpoint we might take. A person for instance sitting in a room, might judge that it is either hot or cold, or that it has undergone a change, but that may be because of what his body tells him, not because of any 'objective' assessment that he makes. If we were to place a thermometer in the room and measure these changes in a more clear-cut way, then this would afford a quite different sense of what we mean by 'similar' or exactly the same. That is, it brings into play the idea of a unit of measurement such that things can be judged not only at the extremes but also at any point in between. This however that this does not run counter to any intuitive judgements we might make—we do not say that 'cold' refers to the range from 0 to 10°C and 'hot' from 30 to 40°C, but we do nonetheless form judgements that are 'objectively' based, or at least that are *useful* indicators of when some such a state exists. Neither should there be any hesitation in ascribing something common to what is in our tactile field, perhaps describing *this* stove and *that* anvil as what is hot or *this* icebox and *that* window as what is cold. On the other hand, so far as it concerns what is in the things themselves, on no account would we say that *this stove* and *that anvil* were similar only if they were made of entirely the same constituents. To describe an icebox as 'fairly cold' does not make it any the less a *useful* description, only, it does not tie it in with anything else in a way that would make it more precise. If you compare the temperature 2 degrees and 10 degrees C, then quite clearly they are not the same, but so far as it might cause a person to button up his jacket or take a water bottle to bed, then from a certain perspective (what was comfortable) might they be regarded as essentially just the same.

But where it concerns the question of a universal, then what we need is something a little more determinate in its kind. There are broadly three ways we might regard a linguistic expression. We might say that (*a*) it is informative but not precise, (*b*) it is precise but not informative or (*c*) it is both informative and precise. We have already indicated how the words *hot* and *cold* may be informative but not precise, and the same could be said for certain personal qualities, for qualities such as courage and generosity. No doubt it is relevant whether a person be courageous or cowardly, but that is not to say there are different measurements for courage and cowardice, or that it might be relevant to say that a person had more courage than endurance or less cowardice than indecisiveness. Where it concerns an expression that is precise but not informative, there are several ways we might construe the meaning of superficial. What we might mean is that it is not helpful in enabling us to classify things in a manner that was conformable to our demands or expectations. Consider for instance the property we call 'being red or green'. It is true that we might colour-code a set of traffic lights and that that would be useful, but it would not be useful if we decided to classify all automobiles as being yellow, red or green. In the same way, 'smoothness' or 'coldness' may be useful in the case of an ice rink, but it would not be useful if we tried to ascertain why razor blades were different from knives. However there is a further issue, and that is when we tend to regard 'smoothness' or 'redness' as not simply what is 'in' a thing, but what it is that makes certain things one and all *the same*. For if there are qualities such as 'smoothness' and 'roughness', then something more is required to explain not just what things are smooth and what things are rough, but what distinguishes smoothness from roughness as well. And this in turn requires something further to explain that more perfected but not altogether ultimate state of affairs. The kind of circularity involved here is similar to that we have already encountered in the case of a justified belief, but we can resolve it if we distinguish between any intuition that we know to be precise, and, as in the case of an aeroplane, any approach that is purely descriptive in its kind.

So far as it concerns expressions that are both informative and precise, then in terms of quality and quantity, we need to distinguish between a situation in which (*a*) diversity in number *must* be reflected by diversity in kind and (*b*) diversity in number *may* be reflected by diversity in kind. For all practical purposes, we need to consider only the latter, since there is no reason why any number of things must be reflective of any particular set. Individuals differ only so far as there is some partial difference in their make-up, but if their make-up is the same, then *ipso facto*, they must also be described as one and the same in their kind. We would also tend to take a more probative approach to the question what it means for something to be the whole of any parts, and what it means for something to be the parts of any whole. For two classes to be different, this can only be so if there is a difference in the whole of their content, and of course what that means is the whole of their membership. Consequently, to be able to classify things means also to be able to separate things, and that is why the quality of being human is more descriptive and *precise* than is the quality of being tenacious, since only different men can be tenacious, whereas to be human is to belong to the class called *Homo sapiens,* and that is not the same as what it means to be feline or belong to the class called *Panthera leo.*

Chapter 16

On Personal Identity

In a *Treatise of Human Nature* Hume states that

> For my part, when I enter most intimately into what I call myself, I always stumble on some particular perception or other, of hot or cold, light or shade, love or hatred, pleasure or pain. I never can catch *myself* at any time without a perception, and never can observe anything but the perception.

> (Book I Part IV of Personal Identity)

One wonders why Hume never asked himself whether the same could be said for a table or a dog. Or are we to suppose that it is just the immediate impression he has that is so vexatious and not the fact that it may change from time to time. In *De Corpore* (chapter XI), Hobbes addresses the question of identity in terms of what may undergo a change in its form and what may undergo a change in its matter. The gist of the argument is that some things lend themselves naturally to a consideration of their form (e.g. the development of a child into a man), others to a consideration of their matter (e.g. a lump of wax) and still others to the disposition of an observer (e.g. the ship of Theseus). He points out that in the case of the ship that the Athenians were constantly rebuilding, any change cannot be strictly about the form, otherwise two identical bodies would have to be regarded as numerically the same, assuming we can reconstruct a whole from those parts that were initially discarded.

One way to approach this is to argue that what counts for the same is simply the *best continuation*[4], given that there are a number of factors and that these must be weighed against one another. In the case at hand, what we have are the competing claims of (*a*) sameness with respect to space and time and (*b*) sameness with respect to material constituents. Debate has arisen because it is not immediately obvious which of these is more worthy of our attention. For instance, consider the situation where we have a book club that is composed of twenty members and that it regularly meets at the local town hall. But then a large percentage (say thirteen) decides to move to an adjacent library. If another smaller group then decides to meet in an abandoned tenement, what would you say about this? Is it the 'same' or is it something quite different? Presumably, if there were some members who continued to meet at the original venue then they would be the 'same', but if not, then that honour would pass to the library. We might thus conceive of two extremes, one in which spatio-temporal continuity was not even a factor and one in which it was the only factor. If all the members of the book club moved from the town hall to the library, then there would not be any problem with the question of identity, since we would surely say that those members who meet at the library are the 'same' as those who had previously met at the town hall. On the other hand, if ten members moved to the library and ten members moved to the old tenement, then this would present us with a problem, since although spatio-temporal continuity would be relevant (in distinguishing a library from a tenement), it would not be helpful in the breaking of any deadlock.

However perhaps this misses the point that Hobbes is trying to make— what he wants to know is whether something is the same because it has the same *form* or something is the same because it has the same *matter*.

---

4   Robert Nozick: Philosophical Explanations.

And of course, what we mean by form is not something extrinsic but rather something intrinsic. If we take form to be predominant, then the true heir is the surviving ship, that is, the one that is being constantly repaired. If on the other hand we take matter to be predominant, then the true heir is the reconstructed ship, that is, the one that has been built from the original parts. There is an unspoken assumption however in the case of thinkers such as Locke and Leibniz that we cannot conceive of a change in form as we can of a change in matter, but only that certain things we call 'vital' *must* be composed of elements that are formative as well as elements that are fixed. The oak that is lopped is still the same as the oak that was born from a seed and the horse that is robust is still the same as the colt that was scrawny at birth. The horseshoe that is copper-coated is still the same as the object that was made from iron, but not the same as any *individual*, since for that what we need is a set of particles *vitally* linked to one and the same indispensable form.

On the other hand, we might approach this quite differently, if we consider a situation in which the relation between matter and form is *fluid* and not a situation in which it is *fixed*. For instance, let us say you have two identical jigsaws, then what is meant by 'identical' could concern either their visual representation or the disposition of their quite irregular parts. Thus, we might say that if what they depict is exactly the same then they are substantially the same, or if their parts are the same and are arranged just the same, then they are substantially the same. Suppose one depicted a bullfight and the other a landscape, then certainly we would not say they were the same in their form and yet it would remain an open question if there be any affinity in their parts. If we begin by exchanging one part from one jigsaw with a corresponding part from the other and can repeat this activity, does that not suggest that in some sense they really are the same, or at least if not the same in form, then at least the same in matter? Where however it concerns a situation where the relation between matter and form is *fixed*, we need to distinguish between the sense in which it is form that is prior to matter and matter that is prior to form. In the case of the Athenian ship, we might say that it is form that is prior to matter, since we tend to think of the ship as having a form in the sense of a *function*. In the same way, we might say of an engine that powers a car that it has a definite form in conjunction with an aggregate of parts. Where however it concerns something such as a jar or a vase, this is different yet again, since even though we might describe it as something that is *reparable*, in the same way we would not say it was *reconstitutable*. We may be able to replace all the parts of a ship, but we cannot replace all the parts of a vase, merely restore it in the case it has been damaged or chipped. Or at least, like a work of art, we would tend to think of it as having some enduring or indispensable part.

To begin with, it is important to recognize that what we mean by the durability of the Athenian ship rests entirely on the matching of certain *actions* and not at all on the question whether it occupies the same place or whether it consists in exactly the same parts. It does not matter whether we make old planks into new or replace existing planks with those we have in store; such activity can always be carried on even if there is a change in the workmen. Let us suppose the original ship comprises the parts A,B,C,D,E,F and its derivative ship, the parts U,V,W,X,Y,Z. Now how this has come about could be by the means of exchanging one part for another, perhaps A for Z, B for Y, C for X, etc. Notwithstanding the general impression that any change will be incremental, it is clear that the eventual product bears no resemblance to the original—it is neither numerically the same and specifically distinct, nor the same thing only dismantled and assembled anew. Hence the original whole comprising parts A through F in no way stands comparison to the amended whole U through Z, or at least that is, with respect to its material constituents. What we could say however is that we are building a new ship according to some original plan or design, and from the body or the nucleus of a ship so far as this is not rotting or decayed. On the other hand, suppose that the situation is such that the ship is not at all in need of repair, but that the workers keep rebuilding it nonetheless. In that case, not only would they not be replacing what was old, they would not even be making what was new. The point about this is that no problem arises so long as we have the matching of two *actions*, dismantling and assembling, since we can carry this on for any indefinite time.

The fact therefore that what we require is just the matching of two actions underscores the belief that the relationship between matter and form *must* be flexible and not fixed. In respect to this relationship, it is only an assumption that form can be 'shared' in exactly the same way as can matter. Let us consider this in a little more detail. An object comprising the parts ABCD is not the same as an object comprising the parts EFGH. But that is not to say that under certain circumstances the same part may not also be shared. If we conjoin these objects and then add an additional part 'I' what we have is a composite which also includes this additional part, which might also be regarded as something that is shared. But what we mean by 'shared' in this case is not the same as what we mean by 'shared' in the case of a particular form. When two things share a particular character or type, this means that they partake of a particular form, but this is not a material element, it is a purely mental construct. Hence what we mean by 'change' should be restricted to what is purely natural of its very nature. We might say that a lion does not have the same form as a tiger if looked at from the viewpoint of a *species* but we might if looked at from the viewpoint of a *genus*.

Now let us consider a situation where we may or may not have two sets of matching actions, that is, where the parts are or are not reusable. In the case where the parts are reusable, the possibility might arise that there could be two ships, since the parts that have been replaced could also be used to produce something different. Hence, what we would have here are two ships, the one that is *actually* in use and the one that is *potentially* in use. And which of these is the true and original ship? If looked at strictly in terms of its material constituents then the answer must surely be given as the *latter*. On the other hand, if the parts are not reusable then there is no problem to begin with, since there are not two ships, but simply the one that is being constantly rebuilt.

Or let us consider another scenario. Let us suppose there was a change in the material constituents themselves, that every wooden part was replaced by a metal part. At what point would you say there had been a critical change in the whole? Again however it appears this would be dependent on whichever viewpoint you might choose. If it concerns the purely material whole, then any change will occur when you replace the first part. If it concerns the purely functioning whole, then any change will occur when you replace the last part, since in these terms what you have might not be something functional at all. (Or at least if by 'form' do we mean some quite critical part) In the case of something such as a jigsaw on the other hand, there may well be some intermediate point where the outline of the object was not discernible at all.

In respect to the question of any conscious or living entity, then there are two entirely different ways we might approach it. We could as Hobbes suggests regard the form as permanent but not the matter, since whether he be old or young it is still the same man, but not the same atoms and molecules just grown old and weary. On the other hand, what could equally well be argued is that if we have an active mind and an active memory, then there is really nothing discontinuous whatsoever. If we can remember where we were five minutes ago and if we can remember where we were five years ago, then clearly this must be just one and the same living self. Hence, there may be no discontinuity if we regard ourselves from either a physical or mental point of view.

The next question we need to ask is this: Why is it that the things we call 'vital' cannot be reconstructed as a whole even if they can be produced as a whole? Quite clearly, if there is not a problem with the activities of constructing and unmaking, then it must be with the *processes* of growth and decay. The broad understanding of life as being not only finite but also unlimited has often been stated in terms of the unconditionality of an end, that is, that the emergence of life is really only a return to something already begun, or that it is the transformation of something undergoing renewal. The caterpillar for instance is born anew when it becomes a moth; the tadpole is born anew when it becomes a frog. But in what sense might it be asked is generation simply an increase in the size of a body *that already exists* and death but the involution of certain parts that *can never expire*? Or to frame this question in a more relevant way: Ought growth and decay to be regarded as reciprocal conditions, or is there a sense in which the one is simply an addendum to the other?

To grasp the point at stake here and what is meant by a process that is fluid and a process that is fixed, consider its general purport for the making and dismantling of machines. Let us suppose that growth is akin to the collecting and assembling of certain parts and dissolution to the disjoining and unmaking of certain parts. Now a craftsman, who is an expert in the making and dismantling of a watch, will always ensure that in its resolving no wheel or spring will be lost, otherwise it could never be returned to that original state it was in. His skill and diligence will ensure that the activities of repairing and replacing are in perfect accord, and that no wearer could tell from the finished product whether it was just made or in fact dismantled and assembled anew. On the other hand, in the case of living things it is clear that this goal can never be attained, since it is not 'growing up' that is the end of putrefaction, but putrefaction that is the end of what we mean by growth. And so if the one is not equivalent but rather subordinate to the other, then there must be *less* in the end than there was in the origin, and if less or fewer parts, then quite clearly no ground for a reconstituting of the whole.

This may also have implications for the way we regard the relation between time and space (and for rejecting what we have called the best continuation thesis). For those who would argue that the relation between whole and part can only be construed intensively, then the identity of something concerns its self-sufficiency as an end (Leibniz). For those, on the other hand, who would argue that things can be compared quantitatively and not just qualitatively, then identity must be grounded in time and space, that is, according to the rule that the same thing cannot have two beginnings nor two things occupy one and the same *place* (Locke). To supporters of the former, the fact that two things cannot have the same history is evidence that they cannot also be qualitatively the same (given that time and space are relational not absolute). To supporters of the latter, since there is no way of establishing whether two things are or are not qualitatively the same, the only recourse we can have is to how they compare on the score of space and time (Given that time and space are the absolute determinants for those things which concern them). Of course, we may need to qualify this a little, since it only makes sense if we suppose time to be an adjunct to space, that is, if we have a coordinated approach that matches different times to different places. In the case of objects that are constantly at rest, then all we really have is the simple assumption that the same thing cannot have two beginnings, and however logical that may seem, it in no way accounts for what may or may not be the case. That is, it is a purely *provisory* question about the relation between time and space.

A more serious objection is that we tend to regard space not so much as an addendum to time but rather time as an addendum to space. (Einstein) For instance, if there were two railway cars on adjoining tracks and two passengers looking across at each another, then what this indicates may be the same as if there were two trains that just happened to be moving at exactly the same speed. As we will see later (Ch.19), what relativity tells us is that simultaneity may concern no more than what we perceive or simply believe to be at rest. A self-initiated action on the other hand does not consist of points or anything that could be divided into infinitely many parts, rather a finite number of parts that are just *those* parts that have actually been traversed. Consider a child playing a game such as hopscotch—what we have are not only certain distinctive movements in conjunction with some end but also either one movement or some movements or all these different movements combined. In the sense of duration as we normally experience this, perhaps a better analogy would be not to a train that is moving at uniform speed but one that is constantly speeding up and slowing down. Time has its own 'inner' metric; it is not like the parts of space that can be placed side by side and then reassembled as a whole. If we attend to certain objects within our visual field then we would not expect to see them contracting and expanding, or receding and coming closer without any logical explanation. But this is exactly the way we experience time; it is not like the flat prairies or the deserts, but rather like the valleys and the snowy mountain peaks. That is why we have a memory for what is recent and something more selective for our long and distant past; that is why we fidget in a waiting room or are constantly looking at our watch.

However, if it suits us to regard time as being in some sense uniform, so does it suit us to regard it as being in some sense discontinuous. The present moment we believe is the only thing that is real because the present ego is the only thing that is real. If we have any knowledge of the past, then this can only be through those memories that bring it back to life. If we have any knowledge of the future, this can only be through those hunches and those outcomes that we hope for. On the other hand, this is not how it might be regarded if looked at from the viewpoint of who and what we have *become*. A crash survivor for instance is someone who synthesizes his experiences such that this will colour all his judgements about the past. A trainee doctor is someone who synthesizes his experiences such that this will colour all his judgements about the future. But a crash survivor is someone who must also learn to retain certain feelings at the same time as relinquishing certain others. In the same way, a trainee doctor is someone who must learn to disabuse himself of certain habits if he wishes to acquire a good repute. What makes someone a better person will thus depend not on his anxiety about the future or any wallowing in the past, rather on the kind of person that he actively chooses to *become*.

But to return to the Athenian ship, let us suppose we introduce the idea of an inoperative part to mimic the process of mouldering. What we have would then be a heterogeneous whole, that is, essentially a combination of two things—operative and inoperative parts. We would not say thus that A,B,C,D,E,F becomes U,V,W,X,Y,Z, but that the whole is potentially composed of either sort of part. If we then view growth and decay as the kind of processes that involve a change in quality but not quantity, what his means is that initially there will be six operative and zero inoperative parts, at the midpoint three operative and three inoperative parts (let us say A,B,C,X,Y,Z) and at the end six inoperative and zero operative parts. On the other hand, if we adopt the view that growth and decay involve change that is quantitative but not qualitative, then initially there will be six operative and zero inoperative parts, at the midpoint six operative and six inoperative parts and at the end six inoperative and zero operative parts. But no matter how we approach it there is still a problem, since the relation in question is being handled in a purely mechanical and not versatile way. That is, either what we are saying is that (*a*) different degrees of growth can be matched by different degrees of decay or (*b*) the addition of certain parts can be matched by the removal of certain others.

Heterogeneity therefore must surely mean something different when we say that growth and decay are heterogeneous than when we say that the parts of any whole are heterogeneous. What it must mean is that there will be a certain incompatibility between the essence or effectiveness of any part and the essence or effectiveness of any whole, not that the specific 'use' of any part must be different from the specific 'use' of any other. *Function* in the sense of purpose is very different from *use* in the sense of exertion. Looked at in terms of a differentiation of function, the parts will always be subordinate to the whole in the sense that a part can only be effective when it supports the organism *as a whole*. In growth and development, the parts achieve a certain order that enables them to proceed from a state in which there is less clarity to a state in which there is more. On the other hand, looked at in terms of a differentiation of use, this is precisely what we mean when we say that the obsolescence of any part is connected with the durability of any whole, or that the obsolescence of any whole is connected with the durability of any part.

Suppose you were given a number of pieces that belonged to a jigsaw puzzle and you began to assemble them just as you found them. The individual steps of growth could thus be construed as the dismantling and reassembling of just such a whole. But let us say that each time you reassembled it, what you found was that an extra part had been added. Eventually when there are no new parts to add you will have reached the point called *maximum growth*. Now let us suppose you have a whole that is composed of differently coloured parts, some of which are active (green) and some of which are inactive (red). By embarking on the same process of dismantling and reassembling, what you find is that at every step there is an extra red part, but no change in the overall number of parts. And that is what we mean by decay, a change in the character of the whole but not a change in the magnitude of the whole. We may well infer that if something has increased in size, then this has been by the addition of something new, but we should not infer that if something has decreased in size, then this has been by the expulsion of something old, rather only a modicum of shrinkage in conjunction with any *qualitative* change that occurs. Hence, in our original model what perhaps we *should* have said is that initially there will be six operative and zero inoperative parts, at the mid-point six operative and six inoperative parts, and at the end twelve inoperative and zero operative parts.

Chapter 17

On Topology

Before embarking on a discussion of the topic at hand, let us ask a general question that has implications for the way we might regard space. Would you say that the ratios 1:2 and 2:4 were exactly the same, that is *identical*, or would you say they were exactly alike, that is *isomorphic*? Would you say that the relation that holds for two things applies equally to both things or is it rather something that lies outside them? By arguing that the relation between A and B is not something you *abstract* from A and B but rather something which is *in* A and B, what you are saying is that A and B cannot be viewed absolutely or according to any independent gauge. That is, if you were given a single whole and then proceeded to divide this into nine equal parts, then you would not say that the ratio 1:2 and 2:4 were the same, but rather, in the same proportion to the whole (i.e. 3:6). On the other hand, if you were given two wholes of the same magnitude, and then divided them into three and six equal parts, then you might say that the ratios 1:2 and 2:4 were exactly alike. (This more or less follows the approach that is taken by Leibniz)

Where however it concerns the question of any actual distance or any actual interval between two bodies, it is very much to the point whether we regard this interval as appended to the bodies, or what is outside them or beside them in any given *place*. Of course, where there are exactly two such bodies, we cannot abstract something that we call their 'common space', since what constitutes the relation we call betweenness is unequivocal, or at least, only ambiguous in the sense that we might choose one system of measurement and not another (say centimetres rather than inches or kilometres rather than miles). We could equally well say body A is six kilometres from body B or body B is six kilometres from body A, such being an 'accidental' property of either A or B. We might also discount betweenness in terms of the kind of geometry that is being applied (or at least the system of geometry that is being applied).

If, however, we are dealing with at least three bodies, then there will always be ground for some equivalence or inequality as well. Suppose that there were three collinear points A,B,C and we arranged these so that A was to the left of B and B was to the left of C. Now so far as it concerns the relation between AB and BC, we can certainly express this in comparative terms, that is, the relation that holds between the one by comparison with the relation that holds between the other. It becomes a little more complicated however when we also consider the relation between A and C, since this is not something we *observe* to be such and such, but rather only *deduce* to be such and such. (Although as we have elsewhere argued, this need not preclude it from counting as a relation.) If for instance the distance between A and B is twice the distance between B and C, then it follows logically that the distance between A and C must be three times the distance between B and C. Of course, this is not to say that if the distance between A and B is the same as the distance between B and C, then such must be some fixed interval, but it nonetheless remains the case that what we are dealing with is something deductive rather than inductive in its kind.

On the other hand, what could also be argued is that if the relation between A and B was isomorphic with the relation between B and C, then no conclusion could be drawn about A and C other than what was isomorphic to some other relation, say perhaps between C and D. (We will assume that there is a fourth collinear point.) That is, we may change the order of coexistents that are 'in' space and in a way that is both observable and testable, but what we mean by the actual 'places' within space are in no way discernible or provable—we merely *assume* that they exist as a sum. We might imagine that there is an actual distance separating Bristol from Stoke, but that is different from the 'real' relation that holds between Birmingham and Stoke and Birmingham and Bristol. We may well compare the distance from Bristol to Birmingham and Birmingham to Stoke, but we cannot compare these in order to ascertain the distances between two purely imaginary sets of points. Of course, this does not address the broader issue of what we mean by the monadic in terms of what is conjunctive and the modemic in terms of what is disjunctive. For instance, the relation between AB and AD in conjunction with AB and AC might be said to engender a whole which comprises AB, AC and AD. On the other hand, if we compare just AB and AC, then this might be regarded as disjunctive, since if some whole has a unique lack or possession status different from that of both AB and AC, then this will surely be AB *minus* AC rather than AB *plus* AC.

What however might be a strength in the case of one theory could also be regarded as a weakness in the case of some other. Since the meaning of a 'spatial' part contains nothing more than the meaning of any concrete part, there is no need to compare what is 'empty' with any part that may actually be 'filled'. On the other hand, if we regard space as incorporating its own metric, then the question might be asked how any such comparison is, or in fact should, really be made. Are we to say that a cubic centimetre of 'filled' space corresponds to a cubic centimetre of 'empty' space, and if so, is it the same standard that is being applied? Consider this extract from the work of a famous pedagogue:

> Space and time are *quanta continua* because no part of
> them can be presented that is not enclosed within limits
> (points and moments), and therefore each part of space
> is itself a space, each part of time is itself a time. Space
> consists of spaces; time of times. Points and moments
> are but limits, that is, mere places of limitation in space

and time, and as such always presuppose the perceptions which they are to limit and determine.

(Kant: Transcendental Analytic Critique of PR)

The problem with this is that it seems to confound what is *intensive* in the sense of what has a boundary or a limit, with what is *extensive* in the sense of what has a border or an edge. So far as we might support an *a priori* conception of space, what we are dealing with is also a question about limits, but not necessarily of what is being delimited and what is doing the delimiting. If you draw a line on a piece of paper then this is merely the representation of a line, and since any line consists of an infinite number of points, we cannot distinguish between that whole which is being delimited and those parts that are doing the delimiting. On the other hand, where it concerns the question of a simple percept, we may well be able to distinguish between the stimulus and the ground. The hound that is baying in the moonlight has certain distinctive features—but what brings it to our attention is the way it appears within the setting that is given. Hence there is one set of characteristics for what it is, that is its shape, and something altogether different for any contrast that this brings out. But if the container theory has a weakness in at least this respect, then in what might one ask lies its strength? In order to address this, we must distinguish between an integrated whole and not just a whole that is the sum or the combination of its parts.

To begin with, we need to distinguish between the kind of changes that an object may undergo, which could be called *dimension free* and the kind of changes that could be called *dimension specific*. Reflection and rotation are good examples of the former; that is, we might regard these as different kinds of congruence. In reflection what we have is a one-to-one correspondence between the points of two figures and in conjunction with a line that is equidistant from them both. In rotation, what we have are two consecutive reflections but through a pair of intersecting lines (not through the same line since this we call translation). Of course, if our understanding of 'being congruent' includes a continuous movement and that through a rigid plane, then it is natural to regard this as what pertains to any closed figure of a specifically two-dimensional kind. Such however may not always be the case, since 'being congruent' may not only mean having the same orientation, but also emanating from the same point, as in the case of a pair of clock hands rotating at a different rate, or when one figure is simply the 'upside down' version of another.

And in a similar vein, if you compare a concrete object such as table with its mirror image, then you could do so with respect to all the parts or only some, say perhaps the simple plane represented by its surface or its top. So far however as it concerns a change that is dimension specific, we need to approach this through two different types of rotation—in the one case movement in a single plane, and in the other movement through two intersecting planes. The first of these, which could be called an inverting or a turning around, accords with our original description, the second of these, which could be called a turning over or a turning inside out, does not accord with our original description or at least not what we understand by reflection. From this perspective, it is easy enough to appreciate how a pair of hands might be regarded as incongruent, given a fourth dimension, or how a pair of triangles might be regarded as incongruent, given a third dimension.

How we handle this however is really only a matter of convention— we could for instance regard a pair of hands or a pair of triangles as congruent in the strictly Euclidean sense, if we attend only to the ordering or arrangement of their purely external parts. And of course, this also raises questions about the orientability of space, although we need to attend to the difference in the way one dimension may being used to acquire knowledge about another, and the topological properties of space, assuming that this does not concern what is dimension specific. Perhaps this can be illustrated in the following way. Although it is true that an asymmetrical object and its mirror image do not have the same orientation, and thus, could well be described as being 'incongruent', that is only because of our assumption there is a different *space* that could make them congruent. On the other hand, what we mean by the orientation of an object *in* space is not necessarily what we mean by the orientability *of* space, understood as an end in itself.

Suppose you were given two differently shaped figures, the one a 'T' and the other an 'L' shape. Now if you were to press the T shape against a pane of glass, then no matter from what side you observed it, it would not undergo any change in how it appears. On the other hand, if you did the same thing with the L shape, then it would certainly appear quite differently from one side than it would from the other. That is, it would undergo a change in its appearance consistent with a change in its orientation. But what we mean by 'orientation' here is not some property that it has in and of itself, merely that particular impression supplied by an observer. To an observer, the T shape may appear to acquire a certain orientation if it is rotated through ninety degrees, and the image — is certainly different from the image —, but that does not alter the fact that what we are dealing with is a shape having entirely the same *intrinsic* properties. Hence, it is important not to confuse what we mean by 'local' when this concerns the broader makeup of space and 'local' when this concerns simply a dimension *within* space.

This may also be relevant where it concerns the following line of reasoning. A pair of triangles may be said to be incongruent if a further dimension is needed to turn them over and make them congruent (from the previous convention). In non-orientable space however, such a triangle does not need a further dimension in order to transform itself into its original analogue. Our conclusion therefore is that in the first instance what we are dealing with is something enantiomorphic whilst in the second what we are dealing with is something homeomorphic. However the issue with this is that (*a*) it is not entirely clear in what sense one thing is being mapped upon another since the figure is only undergoing a change in its *appearance* and (*b*) it seems to confound the meaning of orientability in terms of what is free from any dimension with the meaning of orientability in terms of what is dependent upon any dimension. An aberrant or one-sided space is clearly in breach of the general rule that any closed curve in a plane divides the plane into exactly two regions (Jordan Curve Theorem). And what is true for two dimensions is essentially no different from what is true for three. The Möbius strip and the Klein bottle are exceptions to the rule, since in the case of the former what we have is only one side or one surface and in the case of the latter what is self-intersecting within some three-dimensional space.

The important point however is that in the sense in which it is a different kind of space we are dealing with, this is not necessarily what we mean by a different *dimension* within the boundaries of space itself. If you think of a closed asymmetrical figure that is moving around the surface of a Möbius strip, then it is true that it will undergo a change in its *appearance*, but that does not necessarily mean any quintessential change—it is still skewed rather than regular, in the actual thing that it is. Quite clearly, the figure is not 'flipping itself over'; it is not *becoming* homoeomorphic, rather, it is simply mirroring or exhibiting the quality of that space which is being traversed. We do not need to invoke any rule that it will undergo a change in its own region of space or that it will move 'out' and back 'into' that region. Even if moving around the strip twice is indistinguishable from the result you obtain when there are two half-twists and not one, that is not to say these states are indistinguishable rather than topologically distinct. As is also well known, the Möbius strip has certain peculiar features, as that when it is cut down the middle it remains as an undivided strip. For something having two twists however, what results will be two bands with two twists which are linked as a chain. The outcome in the case of the former could be called *modemic* because this is not at all what we would expect; the outcome in the case of the latter could be called *monadic* because this is entirely what we would expect.

What we mean by the topological properties of space raises some quite complicated issues, but essentially it has to do with what remains the same throughout the bending or stretching of certain geometric shapes, given that there may also be continuous mapping and no deformation at all. Let us begin with the idea of connectivity and what might be suggestive in just this regard. For starters we might take this to mean it has a boundary, a side or an edge. A figure that is fully enclosed and continuous throughout has only one boundary and thus connectivity number 1 (a bounded disc). For polyhedra, this can be applied to the number of sides or the number of faces. A tetrahedron, for instance, has connectivity number 4, a cube has connectivity number 6, a dodecahedron has connectivity number 12, etc. On the other hand, for something such as torus or a sphere, although these are closed surfaces there are also unbroken surfaces, and so in this case they have connectivity number 0. It may also be necessary to distinguish between a surface that is open and a surface that is closed, since there are both open and closed surfaces that are bounded and open and closed surfaces that are not. A Euclidean plane for instance is a surface that is open and unbounded, since it is homoeomorphic with a punctured sphere or a disc without its boundary. In dealing with three-dimensional figures, it is also necessary to stipulate whether they are solid or cavernous. Quite clearly, if we have a solid sphere then removing some part of it will not make it any the less solid, just as, a cut through a solid torus will not change it in any quite critical way.

Having addressed the issue of connectivity, we now need to consider the meaning of a *genus*. In the main, and so far as it concerns any surface without a boundary, we might define this as the largest number of non-intersecting closed curves that can be drawn without dividing the surface. A sphere, for instance, has genus zero, since by the Jordan Curve Theorem it will always have an 'inside' and an 'outside' no matter what we do with it. On the other hand, this is not the case for a torus, since if we make a cross-sectional cut then this will deform it, but it will not also divide it; that is, it may become cylindrical, but it nonetheless will remain complete. It will thus have genus number 1. And if from this were we to construct a twofold torus (much like a steering wheel that has a cross-sectional arm) then it will have genus number 2, etc. For any closed and bounded surface, including polyhedra, the genus becomes what is known as the *Betti number*.

In the case of a polygon, this is the number of edges that can be removed without affecting any vertex, number 3 for instance, in the case of a tetrahedron. For a circular disc on the other hand, this will be the number of punctures that might be made on it. A single-hole disc will have Betti number 1, a double-hole disc will have Betti number 2, etc. So far on the other hand as we are dealing with just closed planar figures, the meaning of a cut may also be used to signify a single arc that joins a point on the boundary with any other point on the boundary. This we might call a simple cross-cut. And so, if we have two cross-cuts formed by a single closed surface through two segments of the same boundary, then a different relation will hold between the Betti number and the genus (we will retain the idea of a genus for a simple cut). That is, the genus will be half the Betti number, or in the case of an odd number, either what is the same or what is one less (i.e. it will be the same for a single cross-cut).

So far as it concerns the relation between the Betti number (b) and the connectivity number, this will always be encompassed in the simple formula $b + 1$. A disc for instance that has one hole has also two boundaries and so a Betti number one, that is, two boundaries less one puncture. An application may be found for converting what is multiply connected into what is simply connected through an appropriate number of cuts, together with the drawing of a closed curve through any two boundaries. Where it concerns the relevance of this for polyhedra, a 'cut' means simply the removal of an edge so that the Betti number will always be one less than the total number of surfaces or sides. For something without a boundary such as a sphere, the Betti number may have a certain application, given the existence of at least the genus one, but not the genus zero. A sphere for instance can have no Betti number, since it has no genus—if you puncture it and stretch it out what it becomes is a simple disc. In the case of a torus however, a cross-sectional cut in addition to a cut around the centre may produce the number 2, although of course the cut around the centre will have to be construed as a simple cross-cut, even though the figure does not have any edge. What we can also say is that there is a model that is homeomorphic for all ordinary closed surfaces without a boundary, and that this is a sphere that is connected to a handle or an annulus. Hence, an unbounded surface with genus n will be homeomorphic with any sphere connected to n number of handles.

If we wish to express a relationship between the vertices, edges and faces of a simple polyhedron, then we can do this by means of Euler characteristic, and since a geometric shape can be deformed into a sphere, this applies equally to the vertices, arcs and regions of a map on any curved surface. Let us say you have a closed map that comprises eight non-intersecting arcs in conjunction with five regions (four inner and one outer) and five vertices (this will be similar in appearance to a kite). And let us say you have a smaller closed map that comprises four non-intersecting arcs in conjunction with two regions and four vertices. If you were to superimpose the smaller one on the larger one and in a lattice-like fashion, then what this would do is create four new vertices for a total of nine. It would also give you four new arcs and four new regions. Imagine however that the original map is modified by the addition of four new vertices but not four new arcs, and likewise where there is no change in the number of regions.

To summarize the situation, what we have in the case of (*a*) is five vertices, eight arcs and five regions; in the case of (*b*), four vertices, four arcs and two regions; in the case of (*c*), nine vertices, sixteen arcs and nine regions; and in the case of (*d*), nine vertices, twelve arcs and five regions. To express therefore a relation between the vertices (V), the arcs (E) and the regions (F), in the form of V - E + F, then will this always produce the same result, the number 2. This is called Euler's formula and it is invariant for any surface x and anything that is homeomorphic with any such surface. To say however that it is invariant does not mean it is the same for every surface, but rather for what pertains to such and such a *genus*. Consider a torus that includes three crosswise arcs and one arc around the centre. In this case, there will be three vertices, six arcs and three regions. Hence it will have a characteristic that is number 0, not number 2.

This also raises questions about the relation between a genus and such and such a 'characteristic'—is it just the case that there is a different characteristic for each genus, or are they linked in some quite fundamental and irreducible way? To begin with, consider the implications if one were to remove a disc from a sphere when the disc was either (*a*) part of any region or (*b*) the whole of any region. In the first case, it would be like adding a single arc but not a bounded surface, and in the second case, it would be like removing a given region but retaining all the boundaries. In both cases however, the Euler characteristic will be reduced by one. If we were to remove two discs, then there would be a further reduction, and since an open cylinder can be deformed into a torus, this would seem to be a perfectly appropriate result. Consider now the prospect of attaching a handle to these newly created openings, then, as we have already stated, any unbounded surface with genus *n* will be homeomorphic with any sphere connected to *n* number of handles.

What we mean by 'attaching a handle' however, may not be quite as simple as it sounds, since strictly speaking if we were to begin with a torus then we would need only to remove some closed curves to achieve the result that we want. Under these circumstances, the surface of the sphere will be continuous with the surface of the torus (much as the ears are continuous with the head). On the other hand, if we consider this attachment as what occurs at two entirely different *points*, then the ends of the handles must be matched with the ends that they join (much as a handle is attached to a briefcase). In order therefore to ensure that it is the handle that is attached to the sphere and not the sphere that is continuous with the handle, we need not only a cylindrical attachment but also an arc running lengthwise along and beyond its extent. The explanation here is that in order to preserve the regional nature of the surface, it is important to ensure that each region is not doubly connected, as may occur when we add a handle to a map (of course such a consideration is irrelevant if there is no mapping of the surface).

But now suppose we were to add a vertex to one end of each handle and then detach this end to create a protrusion, or what might be called a tube. If the total number of vertices added to the map is v, then the increase in the total number of arcs will be $2v$ and there will be a v increase in the total number of regions. That is, the new vertex will double the number of arcs and add to the number of regions. When the handles are detached at one end, the arcs and vertices on the boundaries will also be duplicated, making a total of F + 2v vertices, E + 3v arcs and F + v regions. In order to make this homeomorphic with a sphere it will be necessary to fill in the boundaries with a disc, the number needed being 2g (one for the tube and one for the sphere). Since we also know that the Euler characteristic for a sphere is two, the full equation becomes (V +2v) - (E + 3v) + (F + v + 2g) = 2. From this we can deduce that the relation between the Euler characteristic and the genus will always be 2 - 2g.

Chapter 18

Nature and Art

The relation between nature and art can be addressed either through a comparison of origins and ends or through a comparison of means and ends. In the first case, the broad question that presents itself is as follows: Is the origin contained in the end in the sense that the origin is refined in the end or is the end contained in the origin in the sense that there is a perfect alignment of *all* origins and ends? In the case of the second, the question that presents itself is as follows: Are the means subservient to the end in the way the parts are subservient to the whole or is the end subservient to the means in the way the whole is subservient to the parts? An architectonic view of nature could be described as one in which (*a*) the whole must comprise more than the sum of its parts and (*b*) the function of the whole must reflect not just some but all its indispensable parts. Thus, in artistic impulse what we have is the fitting of such and such a means to the attainment of such and such an end, since the artist cannot work unless he has some materials at hand, if there is not something that can be moulded and in such and such a way. The sculptor imposes his ideal on a piece of marble; he uses a chisel and a hammer just as a painter uses a canvas and a brush. Where on the other hand it concerns any natural teleology, then the relation between whole and part will be even more closely aligned, since in the words of Aristotle "Nature does nothing in vain"

Not only that, but since the meaning of the whole must reflect the very meaning of all its parts, then every part must be productive and not just instrumental to what is good. Thus, what the progenitor does is harness a force for the expression of a particular ideal, that being the preservation of the species, but the end is not given in the means, rather, it is the the means that must be given in the origin. And of course, this is entirely in keeping with the view that things that differ specifically must differ numerically, but that things that differ numerically may or may not differ specifically. That is, there must be at least one member for every species since it is the latter that supersedes the former, not minute changes that produce anything of a more lasting or durable kind. And so, if we regard the preservation of the species as our ultimate aim, and individual striving as a mere accessory to this, then a distinction will arise between selfishness and self-sacrifice, between any effort directed towards one's own good and that which is preservative of the whole. The individual can only preserve itself at the expense of the species, just as the species can only preserve itself if it is indifferent towards any self. Nature will be indifferent to the weal and woe of the agent - she will be indifferent to that cast of actors just as they appear and leave the stage. (Schopenhauer).

From our own perspective however, it seems that what we mean by altruism is the awareness of a possible disjunction between the selfish and the self-surviving on the one hand, and the dutiful and the self-denying on the other. In other words, the individual may be symbolic of the group so far as it concerns either its origin or its end, but the group is only symbolic of the individual so far as there is a perfect alignment of *all* their interests and aims. A system that is mutually supportive or destructive can only be gauged with respect to the interests of all its members, and whether this supports or runs counter to such an end. In order for such conduct to be perfectly self-consistent, the individual will be supportive of himself so far as he is supportive of the group, and destructive of the group so far as he is destructive of himself. Thus, what we have is blind or delusional egoism on the one hand and a more constructive form of egoism on the other. Where the latter is concerned, there may be a further ground for eliciting true egoism and not just feigned altruism, given the purely formal distinction between public and private ends. A person may believe that it is reasonable to pursue his own good so long as this does not encroach upon others, or he may believe that it is requisite to pursue a more disinterested aim, but in any event, all we really have is a confounding of means and not a contrariety of ends.

True altruism can only be grasped in terms of a relationship that puts more focus on the individual and less focus on the species, which regards the latter not as a guiding principle, but the former as the outer appearance of some inner but not necessarily orderly drive. There can be no agreement if we compare the will to self-destruct with the will to stay alive, but there may be, if we compare the individual to either the end or the origin of the species, understood as a single founder or a last survivor. Consider what would happen if you introduced an altruist to a group of selfish individuals, then the altruist would be converted to their ways, he would become just as selfish and greedy as all the rest. Or consider what would happen if a selfish individual were introduced to a group of altruists, then presumably it is the group that would undergo some change. What we have here is absorption and conversion where it concerns two entirely different types, the one domineering and the other submissive. Consider however a situation somewhat different from this, when it is not the group that is mediating through the individual, but the individual that is mediating through the group. This we commonly observe in a colony of ants or bees. In this case, what we have is not the conversion from an altruistic to an egoistic type, rather, a self-sacrificing spirit for the sake of its continued survival. In the way we might draw such a comparison, what we have on the one hand is both selfish and self-destroying, on the other both altruistic and self-surviving. What this represents is a balanced relationship between whole and part, such that there is room for both the development of the individual and the survival of the group.

To pursue our enquiries, let us consider the relation between the form and function of a living thing understood as either an origin or an end, and the general conditions that give rise to it, in conjunction with any methodology we might employ. Perhaps there are two areas in which we would say there is some pre-established form, and they are (*a*) where it concerns the rationale for how we behave and (*b*) where it concerns the expression of artistic desire. Certainly, in the case of the latter, there is no doubt form will always be superior to matter, since the composer will always be more important than the orchestra, and the painter will always be more important than the brush. So far as it concerns the former, then although there may at times be a certain equivocation, it is clear on the whole that our plans and designs will necessitate a means that can be fitted to such an end. If you were to ask a person why he chooses to swim or to jump from a plane, then the answer could be either because he enjoys the water or he enjoys the air, but also, because he has learnt the backstroke or he can open a parachute.

On the other hand, we need to be careful when we describe a cause as that *from* which something has come to be, rather than that which is doing the forming, in conjunction with that which is undergoing the change. A teacher may have a role in imparting the elements of music and a pupil may be the recipient of such a skill, but it is not a cello or a flute that is the *cause* of being musical, any more than it is a textbook or a podium that is the *cause* of being learned. We need therefore to distinguish between a cause in the sense of something that is strictly antecedent, and the kind of condition that facilitates such and such a change. If you ask a person why he has become a teetotaler, his answer might be because drinking is ruinous to his health. If you ask a person why he has taken up jogging, then his answer might be because he is trying to lose weight. And of course, these may be equally sound reasons, but that is not the same as the act of raising a fork to one's mouth, or the method one has for concealing a bottle of scotch. It also raises the question in what sense it is not the form or function that precedes the means, but the means that are effective in and of themselves.

Or to take another example, consider the making of an urn in relation to the use of such a vessel, or the making of a house in relation to the use of such an edifice. In what sense does something later in time pertain to something that is prior in its nature or essence? Certainly, we might describe the purpose of an urn as the containment of a person's ashes, but then, in what sense is its production really *contingent* upon this intention or aim? Might it not just as readily be used to store our valuables or to decorate our kitchen or our hearth? Likewise, in what sense could the occupant of a house or the rent that is owed ever be deemed prior to its assembling or making as such? Were we to argue in such a way then this would only be to confound the meaning of potentiality and actuality, or at least, the potential for occupation with the reality of being inhabited. We would no more say of any building that it is occupied only when it is *potentially* so, than we would of any tenant, that his existence is conditional upon the *potential* for any rent. Here, what we mean by the purpose or the function of the whole should never be deemed prior to the materials or those conditions for its creation.

And perhaps this also has its corollary in the products of nature. Let us consider a traditional account of causality based on a distinction between organic and inorganic matter, such that in the former case it is the *final* and in the latter case the *proximate* causes that are more easily discernible. It could be argued for instance, that there is a certain beauty and sublimity in nature if we are viewing it from afar, but that at closer range, it is only the efficient causes that capture our attention. Thus, the Appalachian Mountains may affect us quite profoundly; they may fill us with joy and delight at one instant, but horror and dismay at the next. And yet for all that it might still be asked, 'Is this beauty really in the object or only in a certain point of view?' A final cause therefore ought not to be inferred from any feelings we might have, and if there is a simpler or more sparing explanation, then there is really no need of anything more intricate or complicated in its kind. If a geologist were asked to account for a crater or a canyon then he might reply that this was the result of a giant meteorite, but it would hardly be appropriate if we asked *why* it fell in just this locale, or *why* it came from just this asteroid belt.

Much in the same way, it is not difficult to connect a silo with the storage of wheat or a greenhouse with the cultivation of plants, and that is because we have a discernible intelligence, and hence, no need of any fancy or whim. Where organic matter is concerned, the argument that is frequently adduced is that it is the final causes that are most striking and the efficient causes that are more obscure. Thus, it is the storage of acorns that affords a reason for the woodpecker's bill, the shape of a termite nest that affords a reason for the anteater's jaw, nocturnal sounds that afford a reason for the canine ear. The problem with this is that it confounds what is strictly deductive with what is only vaguely or inadvertently so—it is a little like saying that the existence of a jaw is contingent upon the existence of an ant, the existence of a bill is contingent upon the existence of an acorn or the existence of a bee is contingent upon the existence of a pollen grain. Quite clearly, no one with a grasp of aetiology would argue from something later in time to something prior in time, and this applies no less to the workings of nature than it does to anything else.

Perhaps we can approach the question of aetiology on two fronts, first, where it concerns the question of what is useful, and secondly, where it concerns the question of what is useless. As we have already stated, there is a difference between the sense in which an end is contained in an origin so far as it is *conceived* in an origin, and an origin is contained in an end to far as it is *refined* in an end. In this respect, we might adopt as our example something such as the long-term evolution of the mammalian ear. There are a number of structural changes that have occurred here, but essentially, the malleus may be attributed to the bone in fishes and reptiles that joins the upper to the lower jaw, the incus to a bone that connects the skull (quadrate) and the stapes to those bones that were originally the instruments for biting. As to the second of these, the principle of disuse, we can observe this in the case of consumption and decay, as when material intended for the limbs of certain lizards is hived off and taken over by the trunk. There is also the existence of an obsolete organ such as the legs in the belly of a whale—this underscores the meaning of what is 'dormant' or 'functionless' rather than what is active or beneficial.

So far as there is any difficulty in supposing that a living part might be 'useless' rather than 'useful', what this stems from is a prejudice concerning the relation between actuality and potentiality. That is, we tend to regard the actuality of a living organ as what pertains to its functionality rather than its material constituents, and thus as, having a potential use which is based on some pre-existent but in no way self-evident design. Let us consider the relation between potentiality and actuality within the following framework. So far as the construction of an artefact is concerned, we might discern the following stages: (*a*) there is the art of building and the knowledge of structure and design, (*b*) there is the process or the technique of building and (*c*) there is the product of building or the object itself. And from this, we might consider that (*a*) there is the activity of building so far as there is the builder and the materials to build from and (*b*) there is the actuality of building so far as there is the art and the act of building. Furthermore, there is actuality in the art or the knowledge of design *qua the product* and there is potentiality in the conceiving and striving for an end *qua the materials*. Thus, potentiality concerns only the end of the act whereas actuality concerns both its origin and its end.

Where however it concerns change of a more protean kind, we might treat of this as follows: (*a*) The function of the whole must be prior to the function of the part, (*b*) there may be a change of state in which the presence of the one is discernible through the absence of the other (e.g. sickness and health) and (*c*) the power or efficiency of any part must be prior to the use or application of any part. This also ties in with the idea that the drive or capability of a living thing must originate from *within* and the drive or capability of any artefact must originate from *without*. We can in a sense incorporate the use of an eye within the function of the eye, just as we can the use of a hand within the purpose of the hand, but we cannot join the art of building with the end of building or artistic design with the object of art. We tend to think that a watch for instance, will continue to work so long as there is a battery to sustain it or that a computer will work so long as it has an electronic chip, but that in the case of any living entity, this must originate from within. And yet the question is, if there is some internal source of growth for the things that are living, why might there not also be some internal source of decay for the things that are dying? Let us say for instance you were in possession of a watch and you took it to a jeweller for repair. Presumably what would happen is that certain parts would be removed and others fitted in their place. But let us suppose you were to return to the same person, only this time asking him to dismantle and reassemble the device just as it was first of all. No doubt the trusty jeweller would be somewhat bemused, and yet that is not to say he would not be equal to such a task. Hence what we mean by an *external means* so far as restoration is concerned could well be matched by an *internal means* so far as reconstruction is concerned. And is this not the very pith of our argument—that the living thing may well have an external means so far as restoration is concerned, but no internal means so far as reconstruction is concerned?

To pursue our enquiries, let us again address the question of means and ends in terms of (*a*) what is intrinsic or what originates from within and (*b*) what is extrinsic or what originates from without. There are two kinds of causality that need to be distinguished here: what on the one hand could be called *immanent* and what on the other hand could be called *efficient*. Immanent causality embraces two fundamental ideas: (*a*) that it is the model or specimen that constitutes the ground for any duplication and (*b*) that it is a purpose or directive that constitutes the ground for any action. Thus, what we have firstly is *form*, or that prototype on which all other existents are based, and secondly *function* or that assemblage which is the most economical overall. Efficient causality on the other hand embraces the ideas that (*a*) there is an element or ingredient from which something comes to be, as the statue comes from bronze or the rapier comes from steel and (*b*) there is a primary source of change originating from without, as the potter constructs a vase or the milliner makes a hat.

So far as it concerns this latter there is no ambiguity to be discerned, since we can just as readily recognize a producer as we can any particular product, and we can just as readily recognize a set of ingredients as we can any particular shape. But where it concerns the question of immanent causality what we make of it will depend entirely on our point of view. That is, so far as it concerns the relation between nature and art, we might proceed on the assumption of (*a*) a perfect agreement that lends a certain weight to the former or (*b*) a perfect disjunction that lends a certain weight to the latter. Let us examine the kind of claim that the making or replacing of a part in purely *mechanical* terms can be matched by the making or reconstituting of a whole in purely *organic* terms. It seems that an organism is more capable or competent than any mechanism, firstly, because it can reproduce itself as a whole, and secondly, because its parts can be grafted or replaced in a manner that is not detrimental overall. Thus, the kind of causality that collects the parts to produce what is complex, is not the same as the underlying or incipient force that creates the conditions for that which is whole, or at least, what preserves the whole from beginning to end.

On the other hand, we might obtain an entirely different result if we assume no compatibility between the products of art and the products of nature. To begin with, let us address the question what is the value of a beautiful object such as a sculpture, a painting or a piece of music. Quite clearly, these things are of no practical use in everyday terms, but let us say their purpose is to inspire or give pleasure to any audience or any viewers. Where it concerns the relation between whole and part there is nothing irregular to be discerned, since what we mean by 'good form' is precisely just *this* arrangement, just *this* harmonizing of all the parts. At another level, and where it concerns the meaning of any manufactured whole, the issues that arise are of an entirely different sort. Since a part must always be regarded as what is subservient to the whole, there must be some general relevance in the way these parts are combined. And more specifically where it concerns the function or the meaning of the whole, there must be some basis for connecting this with the use of any part. We might say for instance that the function of a spring is to prevent stress, that the function of a piston is to impart motion, and that the function of a strut is to bear weight. We could well imagine the whole as being otherwise than what it is, as sustaining more or less than what it does, and that is because what makes it what it is depends upon the *instrumental* value of each and every part.

To proceed to a living organism however is this relationship quite different yet again. Quite clearly, living things have not been created with any overall purpose in mind, but that is not to say the question of use is altogether without purport, as it might for instance be Van Gogh's *Sunflowers*, only, we should not approach this in any fixed or predetermined way. We might approach this by asking ourselves the general question: In what sense is it true that the whole is dependent upon the parts and in what sense is it true that the parts are dependent upon the whole? There is a tendency to suppose that since the eye is imbued with the power of sight and the ear with the power of hearing, if you were to remove these powers then most assuredly would you anything that is connected in their immediate environs. And yet it must surely be admitted that there is a difference if we say that the efficiency of the whole is exhibited through the activity of *all* its parts or that it is only *some* of the parts that are active in the main. For is it not the case that there may still be life despite a loss of power, that the paralyzed may yet have the use of their arms, that the blind may yet have the use of their legs, that the deaf may yet have the use of their tongue? In order to address the meaning of purpose in this context, what should be clear is that the word *useful* no more connotes the idea of what is ample, sparing or handsome, than its opposite does needful, wasteful, or ugly. The use that an instrument has may be as variable as its size or its shape, and so it should not be confounded with specific qualities such as clumsiness or dexterity, deformity or regularity.

Not only that, but in terms of the relation between nature and art we may also discern this difference, that in the latter is it elegance and in the former versatility which is at the heart of what they body forth. From a certain perspective we might consider Beethoven's *Ninth symphony* or Milton's *Paradise Lost* as a great achievement, but to treat of this in terms of the products of nature we need not just inventive minds but inventive *means*. Consider the following as an example from the handbook of nature. It is well known that certain insects of a particular noxious kind are also brightly coloured as a warning and a signal to their foes. Bees and wasps, for example, whose stings may be lethal, have very familiar black and yellow stripes. In many instances, animals with such striking colouration are imitated by others in such a way as to give them an adaptive edge. One of the most intriguing cases concerns that of the swallowtail butterfly known as *Papilio dardanus*. Throughout tropical Africa, females of the species are very different from their male counterparts, mainly on account of their wings lacking the customary tails and their presence in a wide variety of colours. It has been thought that at some stage in central Africa when there was an abundance of a more noxious species, a certain recessive trait appeared that was passed on to a small number of offspring. Since this trait was modelled on that of the more menacing species these offspring were able to avoid predation, and their characteristics were strengthened in the general population. In due course, once this mimicry had been perfected further modifications appeared which permitted imitations of an even more specialized kind.

So far as it concerns the relation between causality and procreation then in no way should these be run together, although we do quite casually say that one person is the cause of another's being, that in human reproduction is there both an object and an agent, and that a living thing is both the product of such and such an act and the object of such and such a *will*. What thus arises is the distinction between a 'free' and 'necessitated' cause or something creative that is matched by something purely instinctive. In sexual intercourse it should be clear we have nothing more than a basic urge in conjunction with a *specific occasion*, not any unconscious means that corresponds to a more deliberative end, an 'immanent' will in conjunction with a 'rational' desire. However, not only is it a mistake if we connect causality with what is simply inadvertent, but to a lesser degree, if we connect what is created with what is simply reproduced. Of course it can hardly be denied that we use the expression 'human reproduction' without the least hesitation—that we do at times describe a child as the 'spitting image' of its mum or ad, but a little reflection on the richness and diversity of life should disabuse of the habit we have in thinking in quite this way.

There are several things that may be meant by reproduction—by natural means, as in the regrowth of a claw, by artificial means, as in the transfer of a cell, by mechanical means as in the copy of a voice. But now let us address the difference between sexual and asexual reproduction. In the case of the latter, what we have is the creation of something through fissure or budding and where it is perfectly clear from whence this is derived. In the case of the former, what we have is the creation of something through different donors but where it is not so clear how this has been achieved. That is, although 'reproduction' may be perfectly appropriate where it concerns any particular offspring, it is not nearly so clear where it concerns any particular agent, that is, what it means to 'reproduce' in the case of either the mother or the father. And so if we cannot be sure about the meaning of any original agent, there must also be doubts about the meaning of any original species—apart from the forces that may be at work in the *shaping* of any particular species.

Where on the other hand it concerns the question of what is generable and what can be remade, then what we need to keep in mind is the more fundamental distinction between renewability and non-renewability per se. A reproduction is something we take to be a copy or facsimile of the original—and it is true we also say this of the offspring of living things. But what it means to be renewable in the strict sense—this is something that needs investigation, not something we can simply take for granted. Does it mean to be generable though such and such a means or does it mean to be *reformable* as such and such an end? Let us pursue this through a treatment of the whole-part relation which accounts the part as necessary but the whole as not. Consider a simple amusement such as a jigsaw puzzle. There is no difficulty in assembling the parts of a jigsaw or any reason for departing from some original plan or design.

We can assemble and reassemble it just as often as we like, provided there is nothing lost at any new stage we are in. What this suggests therefore in purely mechanical terms is the idea of *immanent* causality, or what is durable and timeless in the context of a reproducible whole. You might also take this to the next level where it concerns an engine or watch; only here, where the desire to achieve a certain result must be matched by the *knowledge* that you have concerning such and such a means. But where on the other hand it concerns what is generable, there is something altogether different to be discerned, since here there is no continuous movement in the sense that what is lost can always be exchanged or replaced. The best we can hope for is what is partly restorable, since you may be able to replace a kidney or a heart but not necessarily a spinal column or the brain.

And this underscores the difference between a whole which is strictly homogeneous, and a whole which is strictly heterogeneous. In the case of the ship of Theseus, what we have is a whole which is homogeneous, but that does not mean there is any true variation. On the other hand, where it concerns a living thing we might approach this rather differently. Given that there is both a coming-to-be and a passing-away, it seems reasonable to suppose there must be at least two parts, or at least two types of parts, those that are functioning and those that are not. The next question that needs to be asks is as follows: Are these parts also convertible or simply immutable? For this what we need is the following thought experiment. Let us suppose we have something such as set of blocks that comprise the parts A,B,C,D,E. Let us then join B to A, C to AB, D to ABC and E to ABCD. Proceeding in the other direction let us remove E from ABCD, D from ABC, C from AB, and B from A. The question then is: Does this activity mimic what we mean by the processes of growth and decay? Quite clearly it does not, since what we mean by the ageing process does not mean to revert to what one was as a child. (Or at least if anything, only mentally). Hence, so far as there is any change in the ageing process, this can only be what is qualitative and not quantitative in its kind. And what can that mean otherwise than that parts that were functioning have become what is functionless?

And this seems to be in keeping with what we have argued for in a previous chapter. To return to the Athenian ship, what we argued for there is that the removal of the first part will make a change in the material whole, and the removal of the last part will make a change in the functioning whole. But this changes when we consider what is meant by a heterogenous whole. A heterogeneous whole is one in which there are both functioning and functionless parts. Hence, removing the first part will not just make a difference to the material whole, it may also make a difference to what is functional *as a whole*. That is, if we assume there is some threshold or a critical number of "working" or "functioning" parts, then the removal of a certain part may or may not disturb what is functional overall. That is, if the first part you remove is something functionless then of course this will have no effect whatsoever, but it could be otherwise if it were functioning, since that could make a critical difference to any general efficiency. In other words, the part that went missing may also be the part that was needed.

The next thing we need to consider is the idea of convertibility. Let us consider a number of instances where two things would appear to be interchangeable. A mutation is an error that occurs in the DNA sequence and there is not an exact copy from one level to the next. However, the question is, should this be described as what was functionless or rather just dysfunctional? It appears we would have to settle for the latter, since in one case, cancer, it is certainly quite harmful, and yet in another case, sickle cell anaemia, it may actually be quite helpful. We might also approach this in terms of what we mean by parasitism. A parasite is something which lives on or in an organism of another species, and from which it obtains nutriment. However, we would not on this account describes it as simply functionless, since it may have an altogether different role in terms of what we mean by the whole-part relationship. When the parasite is in a sole relationship with its host, then this relationship may become more benign, since its reproductive capacity will be enhanced by the durability or longevity of its host. On the other hand, when the parasite is not in a sole relationship, then competition will cause it to become more aggressive and the forces of evolution will cause it to reproduce more rapidly. In this case, it needs to reproduce more quickly in order to fend of any rival. Convertibility in this case also means a kind of compensation, since if there are no counter forces this will be favourable to the host, whereas if there are, this will be prejudicial to the host. In other words, if parasites are in competition with one another they will also be in competition with the host, but if there is no competition, then the host may also become reliant upon its guest.

Where it concerns the functioning and functionless parts, we may be able to address this through a couple of examples. Autotomy is the behaviour where an animal discards one or more of its appendages, either to elude a predator's grasp or simply to distract it. Some lizards such as salamanders are quite adept at shedding part of the tail, and in many instances the tail will continue to wiggle even after it has been shed. It may also be possible to regenerate such a part, although in this instance when it is more cartilage than bone. Here what we have is something manifestly useful, what is useful in itself and as a means of self-defence. Now let us look at this from the other side. Moulting is a natural process experienced by animals with an exoskeleton. That is, as the animal grows, the outer carapace must be discarded for something newer. Initially this will be softer but then harden over time. In the case of certain arachnids (e.g. the tarantula) this may also have its pitfalls, since it may become trapped and eventually die. Although a little counterintuitive (in respect to its timing), this could be said to constitute what we mean by a purposeless or functionless part.

Chapter 19

Time and Space

Space and time have frequently been described as the formal condition for all outer experience, but we need to be clear how and in what way there is some real agreement and how or in what way there is not. As we have already seen in our treatment of intensive and extensive wholes, there is a fundamental difference if we conceive of unity through the division of any whole, or unity in the assembly of any parts, since in the one case there is a thorough and in the other a purely incremental kind of change. This in turn can be used to express a difference in the meaning of a spatial or a temporal part, or a difference between the objects and events that occupy the parts of space and time. What we mean by a spatial interval is one that does not contain any discrete parts but rather can be divided into infinitely many parts. The part that forms the boundary of this interval we call an end point, just as, the part that forms the boundary of any time span we call an instant. Time however, unlike space, has only one real boundary and that we call the present, although we may also distinguish between the parts that are coincident in the present instant and the parts that are successive in the future and the past. Essentially however, we can only conceive of time within a framework that permits of either a single point or a constant recurrence of one and the same thing.

Where on the other hand it concerns any interval or any distance in space, then what we are dealing with is the externality of all the parts such that it is the *point* that will place a limit on any line, the *line* that will place a limit on any plane and the *plane* that will place a limit on any occupant. However, the minimum 'quantity' we are dealing with here can only be conveyed in the concept of a line—it is something bounded by end points and having an infinite number of points in between. Just as we can discern a difference between succession and simultaneity, so can we discern a difference between the contiguous and the interjacent, as when we survey the squares of a chessboard and discern that the black squares are next to the white squares but that the white squares are not next to themselves. So far however as it concerns the meaning of a 'place' we should approach this with a little more caution—there is no relation implicit in space which is some sense external to space, otherwise any continuum might be said to comprise an assignable number of just such 'relations'. A relation *within* space can only be gauged through the externality *of* space as we lay bare its parts and that is only what is closer or further from any particular point. Since there is nothing that corresponds to what is synchronous or simultaneous, neither is there any 'place' that persists throughout any discernible change.

However, to argue that there is no such thing as a place that is determinate, does not commit us to the view that a place is merely the order of co-existents within space, given of course that this latter is not something real but rather ideal. Certainly we would agree that if there is a relation between the bodies A,B,C,D such that the relation between B,C,D remains fixed whilst A, say, is replaced by X, then X does not occupy the same 'place' as A. But that is only because 'place' is not a clear or determinate thing, not because the order XBCD is one description of space and ABCD yet another. To return to our example of the chessboard, suppose that we had pieces that we arranged in the usual fashion, such that the rook was in the corner, then alongside that the knight, and further in the bishop, queen, etc. Now if we were to remove the rook and replace it with a pawn, then indeed there may be some question as to whether it did or did not occupy the same 'place', but what should not be inferred is that we can conceive of space no otherwise than in terms of the way any objects may be arrayed. That is, that a pawn and a knight constitute one relation, that a rook and a knight constitute another, that a pawn and a rook constitute another, etc. We might for example exchange the white and the black squares occupied by the queen and the bishop without disturbing the actual order of the pieces—and would this not give us a slightly different understanding of a 'place', or at least, in terms of what we call 'being wider' or 'being narrower'?

Thus the problem with the relational view is that it seems to distinguish between the space that is occupied by a body and the space that is mediated by a body, such that we can add and subtract in the one case but by no means in the case of the other. If for instance we place two identical bodies side by side, then it seems reasonable to suppose they would occupy twice as much space as they would if considered solely and with respect to themselves. On the other hand, if we compare two things based on the distance between them, then it seems one body must be said to constitute one relation and the other something altogether different. Thus, if we say that the distance between Birmingham and Sheffield is two-thirds the distance between Birmingham and Hull, then this is not altogether meaningful, since there must be a one-to-one relation between Sheffield and Hull just as there is a one-to-one relation between Birmingham and Sheffield. The problem with this is that if you are going to describe space as an *intensive* whole, then number would have to be interpreted as what was purely extensive in its kind. And so, although you might be able to add things how could you really divide them?

On the other hand, so far as it concerns an *a priori* conception of space, it is equally true that certain objections could be raised to this approach, especially where it concerns the question of how something can be divided into infinitely many parts. When we compare two lines that are in close proximity and discover that there is a discernible difference between them, then it may seem reasonable to suppose there must be a precise method for deciding which is longer or which is shorter and by how much. That is, if we can see that two things are different it must be possible to quantify this through something such as a tape measure. On the other hand, when we are dealing with the question of division in purely abstract terms, it is equally clear that this could be carried on *ad infinitum* and that there must be any number of fractions between the numbers 0 and 1. And so how do we reconcile these different viewpoints, or the meaning of a whole that can be reconstituted with the meaning of a whole that cannot? We can assemble and reassemble any object consisting of three equal parts without in any way affecting its appearance, but we would not say this of the three indivisible parts that make up the number 1, the fractions 1/3, 1/2 and 2/3. In this case, what these fractions are when we divide a whole is different from what they are when we construct a whole, since one is certainly not the same as one and one half.

Perhaps we might approach this through a clearer explication of the indivisible or what it is that is binding on some whole rather than any of its quite manifold parts. It might be easier to understand for instance how the abstract line can be made up of infinitely many parts, if we bear in mind that it is the 'indivisible' element that is its real sine qua non. Although it may be true that a finite whole could be said to comprise just a finite number of parts it is not necessarily the case that there is anything 'indivisible' in all this, only an interrupted aggregate in conjunction with the appearance of that which is not. As we have already suggested in an earlier remark, if body AB becomes ABC, and this in turn ABCD, ACD, CD, then clearly the more and the less can be compared, but that is not to say that what results is anything that has actually changed. (Or at least not quantitatively). On the other hand, if you consider a line of such and such a length and then divide it into two, not only you have retained a proper sense of what is 'whole', you have also created two points on the inner terminus of each segment and so something 'more' than was there from the beginning. Or you might approach this in terms of what we have already said about the difference between the reductive and the conjunctive. To say that AB and BC becomes ABC involves a mental act, as it does to deduce that ABC may also become AB and BC. But of course, this is different from the operation of producing the colour purple, since in this instance, once you have achieved it there is no way you can separate the colours red and blue.

Now let us consider the question of a change in location in conjunction with a change in duration, such that a body is either at rest or in motion over time. It has sometimes been argued that the 'identity' of a body is based on its location in time and space, as when it is said one thing cannot have two beginnings nor two things one, that nothing can occupy different places at the same time, nor two bodies be in the same place at the same time. However, what this rests on is a purely *logical* connection that we form in our minds; since it is by no means clear what demonstrable sense there is in being 'in the same place' or 'at the same time'. What we should really begin with is the distinction between (*a*) different bodies that are at rest and not in motion and (*b*) a body that is in motion and not at rest. In the first, what we are dealing with is the relation between a place and any occupant, in the second, the relation that anything has to what it is in and of itself. Furthermore, what we need to recognize is that when we define the motion of the *same* body as what is in different places at different times, then this is not what it means if it is different bodies that are so disposed - otherwise, we are confounding the absoluteness of a change in place with the absoluteness of a change in time. That is, if two bodies are oscillating or merely swapping places then this is not the same as describing a motion that is unique to each, it is purely conditional so far as it concerns the relation between time and space. We might illustrate this in the following way. If for two objects X and Y, and the places a and b, then if at t_1 X is in a and Y is in b, and if at t_2 X is in b and Y is in a, then a change in location does not specify what is different about each, but only that such and such is not descriptive of X and that such and such is not descriptive of Y. If however, we wish to make a claim that is at all meaningful, then we need to express this in the following way, that given two objects X and Y and the places 'a,b,c', then if at t_1, X is in a and Y is in c, and if at t_2, X is in b and Y is in a, then what this evinces could be said to be a true relation, or a relation that not only specifies what something is but discriminates between what it is and is not.

So far however as it concerns the relation between time and motion, we need to be careful in our assumptions, since the general disposition that a body has to behave in such and such a way is not necessarily equivalent to the space that it traverses over such and such a time. That is, it is true that motion connects the parts of time and space and that it underscores the continuity of space and time, but by that what we mean is a place and an instant not a point and an instant. We are familiar with the following expressions: (*a*) different bodies cannot occupy one and the same place at the same time and (*b*) one and the same body cannot occupy different places at the same time, but this does not assume a relation between a point and an instant, it only stipulates what is *impossible* for the same body at rest, not what may be *possible* for different bodies in motion. Of course, that is not to say there may not be a purely mathematical account of motion, but that is a little like putting the cart before the horse or the theory before the facts.

Let us consider the kind of objections that might be raised to the view that space and time are isomorphic or that what can be said of the one can always be said of the other. First, it could be argued what we mean by the space that is traversed cannot be compared to any quality or any disposition prior to being in motion or at rest. That is, the condition from which spontaneous motion begins and ends is not in any sense like the boundaries that join any continuous line, since the one (that is motion) could be just as simple and unvariegated as is the other (that is rest). Secondly, although we might concede that a spatial interval is something necessarily comprising an infinite number of parts, this is not necessarily so obvious with respect to time, since there is only one indivisible 'now' and it is unclear whether we should treat this as infinite or what is only instantaneous. When we say that any line or any segment is infinitely divisible, what this encompasses are the following ideas: (*a*) that we can divide the whole into an indeterminate number of parts and (*b*) that a smaller part must be included within the meaning of any larger one, that is, there are end points as well as intermediaries. When on the other hand we say of any spontaneous movement that it is divisible into parts, what this implies is that (*a*) acceleration and deceleration may be perfectly matched so far as it concerns any total effect and (*b*) a larger part must be included within the meaning of something smaller. We have already addressed the first of these in terms of the way we experience time, the fact that we are sometimes busy and we are sometimes bored, but it could also be construed in the sense that getting somewhere may proceed by "fits and starts". So far as it concerns the second, then not treating time in a purely mechanical way means that to know *that* something has started is not necessarily to know how it might end. What this evinces is a difference between time and space so far as it concerns any collection or assemblage of parts, since if we cannot decompose any movement then neither can we reconstruct it, and what the whole is in this sense is only what *potentially* is contained in any adumbration of its parts.

And so, if we are not at ease with a conception of time which makes it a mere appendage to space or its simple mirror image, then how should it be viewed, as discontinuous and yet complete, as a metaphor for what is 'filled' but in way for what is vacuous? We might approach this through an examination of the kind of problems that were raised by the Greeks, and especially one Zeno of Elea, who argued that time cannot be real since it comprises neither indivisible units nor a whole divisible into infinitely many parts. In 'The Stadium', we have three rows of objects A,B,C such that B (comprising three objects) is above A and C below it. Now if B and C are moving in different directions and at a uniform speed, then B_1 would have moved from C_1 to C_3 in successive instants without passing through C_2. What this demonstrates thus is that half the time taken must be equal to twice the time taken. In order to resolve this matter, let us consider two rows of objects as follows:

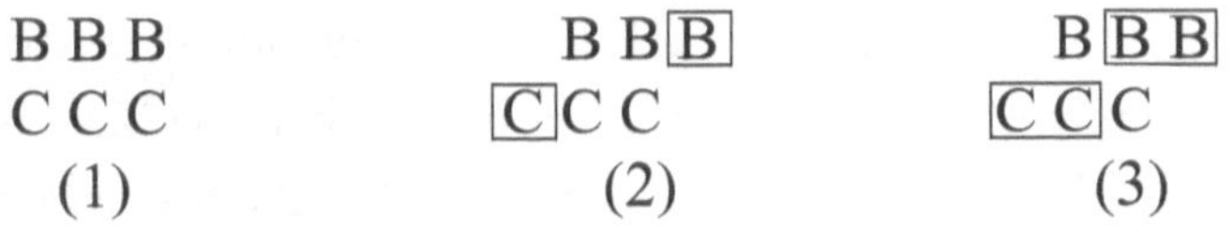

B B B	B B B]	B B] B
C C C	[C C C	[C C] C
(1)	(2)	(3)

Now in terms of the relative change in these states, we tend to think of (3) as potentially 'contained' in (2), that is, that a larger movement is contained in a smaller one. And in a similar manner, we might suppose it is a smaller space that is contained in a larger one. The problem here however is that what we mean by the first of these conjectures is entirely out of keeping with the second. When we say that a larger movement is 'contained' in a smaller one what we are *not* saying is that it must be composed of smaller and smaller parts, rather that it can simply be characterized or described in such and such a way. There may well be a difference between 'uniform' 'accelerated' and 'decelerated' motion, but that is more on account of what is qualitative rather than quantitative in its kind. Where space is concerned there is a problem with this idea of containment, since a smaller space is not additional to any larger one, rather does any determinate space comprise exactly the parts that are its. And of course, this only begs the question what is meant by an 'indivisible' part of space, since in no way is this comparable to what we mean by an 'indivisible' movement as such. Certainly, if you look at the extended parts of (2) and (3), then the former may appear to be more 'atomic' than the latter, but for all practical purposes is the one just as indivisible as the other. And so in the case of this paradox, when we are asked to believe it is a smaller space that is contained within a larger one, this gives no indication where the limit should be set for the largest and the smallest overall.

And the tenor of these remarks will be essentially the same when we address the paradox that is called 'the arrow'. What is argued for here is that an arrow in flight is really at rest, since in any given instant it occupies a space that is equal to itself, and if it could move in this instant, then what would be necessary is a space larger than itself. Now there are two ways we might approach this: (*a*) in terms of the question of a movement that is instantaneous and (*b*) in terms of the question of a movement that occurs throughout different points of time. With respect to the first of these, it must be admitted that no object is capable of moving within an instant since that would make it everlasting, but it may be a different question altogether where it concerns movement *between* different points of time. If what is being argued for is that we can compare an 'indivisible' element of time, that is, the time it takes a body to travel its own length with an 'indivisible' element of space, that is the length itself, then it raises more questions than we can ever hope to address. Are we to say that an arrow takes as much time to travel half as it does the whole of its length, or are we to say it cannot do this at all? Are we to say that the basic constituents of space are different for an elephant than they are for an ant, since if their sizes are different so must be the 'indivisible' part they traverse? We cannot even begin to resolve these issues if we consider that the space a body occupies can in some sense 'constrain' any movement that it makes, or that there is an 'indivisible' quantum of time that limits any action that may be shorter than what this is.

The last paradox is the one that is best known, and that is called 'Achilles and the tortoise'. We can imagine a race between the fastest of all runners Achilles and the slowest of all runners the tortoise, such that, given a head start, the latter could never be overtaken, since by the time Achilles has come to this point the other will have advanced a little further, and similarly, any other point along the way. On the other hand, if we were to give Achilles a headstart then similarly he could never be overtaken, only in this case because it would be impossible for the other to ever match his speed. And so, the question arises: 'How can we bridge the gap between what seems to be logically impossible on the one hand, and yet not physically impossible on the other?' In order to address this issue what we need to keep in mind is that the velocity of any object involves the compounding, and not the resolving, of times and distances, nor the subtraction of time from any distance. Suppose that we had a course that was marked out by metre posts from A to Q and we were to place the tortoise (T) at the start and Achilles (A) at the end. Let us suppose that T has been given a two-metre start and is proceeding at the rate of 1 m/sec whilst A is proceeding at the rate of 2 m/sec. By a simple calculation, we can deduce that their paths will cross somewhere along the interval GH. And likewise, if we were to give A this start, we could deduce that their paths would cross somewhere between E and F. Hence, there is no problem in establishing under what circumstances the one will overtake the othe,r and that is because we are compounding the times and distances not deducting a time from any distance or a distance from any time. On the other hand, in the situation where they are both at the same end and it is Achilles that has been given the head start, then we need to distinguish between each 'indivisible' movement and the speed or the rate or its change.

In the way we have treated of time in this regard, it is also important to distinguish between the sense in which a movement may be spontaneous and the sense in which it may be uncaused. That is, to act spontaneously is only what it means to act in the *absence* of such and such a cause, not in some Kantian sense to be accorded the status of an 'end-in-itself'. Gravitation for instance is a cause that is constantly at work, and no matter what its inner urgings no physical being without the requisite means (e.g. a pair of wings) can lift itself through the simple exercise of its will. But to say that time cannot be assimilated to space in the case of Zeno, does not mean this cannot be achieved at all, since this is to approach the question in terms of what is self-reflective and not in terms of what is strictly verifiable. To consider how this is possible, let us in the first place distinguish between absolute and relative motion, in conjunction with the meaning of absolute and relative rest. When we say that motion is 'absolute', then this could mean a wide variety of things. It could mean (*a*) that the difference between motion and rest is absolute so that there is a qualitative difference between a body that is in motion and a body that is at rest. It could mean (*b*) that space is absolute and thus that there are strict and determinate points through and from which any motion must proceed. (That is, it does not imply a mere change in the order of co-existents, but a change in their station as well.) Or it could mean (*c*) that the frame of reference we are using is absolute and not relative, so that our idea of absolute motion is underpinned by our idea of absolute rest. Of these three options, it goes without saying that the third is the most important, since it leads on to questions about the absoluteness of rest and the relativity of motion, and those different reference frames in which we regard something as in motion or at rest.

The usual sense that we give to the idea of 'relative' motion is when there is some fixed point and there are different things to which it may apply. The fixity of the stars for instance, constitutes a reference point for the movement of the earth, just as the fixity of the earth constitutes a reference point for those bodies that are moving on its surface. The argument in favour of absolute rest however, is one that has been largely ignored, firstly, because there are many different systems that have an equal claim to being called 'inertial', and secondly, because there is at least one observable phenomenon, the speed of light, that is indifferent to both the speed of its source and the disposition of any observer. A car for instance that is moving at uniform velocity, is just as much an 'inertial' reference frame as the signposts at either end of a street, since we could just as well be drinking a soda in the back seat as we could standing in our kitchen or our living room. And if the speed of light is indifferent to any other motion in its vicinity, then there is certainly no fixed or stationary point from which we might discern any change. In addition to this, certain questions have been raised about the meaning of simultaneity, as what might be discerned from any succession or sequence of events. (The Einsteinian view)

Consider the kinds of observations that might be made to ascertain whether two distant events were or were not occurring at precisely one and the same time. Let us suppose we supply two observers with identical clocks and ask them to record data at different locations. One person, standing outside Buckingham Palace, notices that the changing of the guard takes place at exactly two o'clock. The other person standing by the river Thames, notices that a drawbridge is being raised at precisely two o'clock. What we might conclude therefore is that both these events are occurring at precisely the same time. Now imagine a person standing halfway between two lamp posts in a darkened alleyway. If the light from both lamp posts reaches him at exactly the same time, then of course it is perfectly sensible to conclude that they have been turned on at exactly the same time. The only problem with this is that although the claim that both events are occurring at the *same* time is incompatible with the claim that both events are occurring at *successive* times, it is not altogether clear how this could be verified as such. That is, we are only dealing with a certain logical connectedness, not what is demonstratively true. Of course, it could well be argued that simultaneous events are acausal whereas causal events are successive, but this is not altogether to the point, since it only proves that different successive events may or may not be causally linked—it does not rule out causality for what is coincident as such. In the case at hand, no attempt has been made to compare and contrast the meaning of succession and simultaneity—in the one case we are merely using a fixed mechanical time and in the other a fixed distance to ascertain the 'fixity' of different events.

Similarly, when we say that different bodies cannot be in the same place at the same time, or that the same body cannot be in different places at the same time, what we are doing is using the 'fixity' of any place to underscore the 'fixity' of any time. This however does not address the question what is successively possible for the same or for different bodies, rather is the latter just as uncertain as the former is perfectly clear. To pursue this a little further, consider the case of a person who is in fixed position relative to what is moving and a person who is moving but only relative to that system in which he is housed. In a moving railway car for instance, suppose a waiter was standing halfway between two table lamps and the light from both lamps reached him at exactly the same time, then as we have argued before, it would not be unreasonable to surmise they had been switched on at exactly the same time. But to someone on the railway tracks and looking in the situation will be somewhat different, since there will be a slight pause between the first event and the second. And this has its corollary in the fact that different events in the same place will be viewed by different observers along different *parts* of the track, so that there is relativity with respect to both a time and a place.

The important point however is since we are dealing with the relativity of different systems it is not so much the existence of a given place we are denying as the existence of a given *time*. That is, the event that takes places in a railway car, say perhaps one person vacating his seat and another sitting down, may be witnessed by different observers in different locations, but it is still the same place or the same part of the car in which this occurs. On the other hand, where the issue is whether different events are or are not occurring at the same time then this is much more open, since we may not be able to decide *whose* viewpoint is correct, whether the events are simultaneous given the waiter's account, or the events are sequential given the bystander's account. It leaves us with little option but to reject the former and so affirm a single continuum, that consisting of successive times in conjunction with successive and concomitant places.

Chapter 20

Space and Matter

Although, as we have already argued, it is by no means easy to elucidate the meaning of a 'place' as distinct from what we mean by space, let us pursue this and along the following lines. It seems that the problem we have encountered revolves around the following points: (*a*) whether there be such a thing as a place, which is separable from any body and (*b*) whether a place that is not separable concerns either the form or the matter of any object. With respect to the first of these this has only aroused our suspicions, since the notion of a shared space as what is common to different 'places' or what is occupiable by different bodies, cannot really be sustained otherwise than in terms of some implicit distinction, which may be purely grammatical in its kind. That is, what we mean by a 'shared space' is only the result of a certain act of intellection—there is no way of demonstrating that the air in the kettle is in the same place as the water that *was* there, but that does not prevent us from supposing it may be, provided the kettle has not shifted. Of course, in common parlance a 'place' such as a park or a mall is something with quite discernible features, but not something we would normally describe as mobile.

So far as the second point is concerned, it might seem reasonable to suppose that if the place of a body is its limit, then its place must be both its size and its shape, since only in these terms could it be said to be precisely the thing that it is. However, if we consider this a little more closely then perhaps it is not so obvious why the form of a thing should be deemed prior to any matter, nor the matter be deemed prior to any form. In the case of a work of art such as a statue, then undoubtedly there is a certain shaping or moulding irrespective of the materials, but such is not necessarily the case if one considers the activity of a creature such as an ant or a bee. Certainly, there is a formative aspect to this behaviour, but there is also the collecting and assembling of parts to ensure there is sufficiency in that result it obtains. Hence, it seems we have a different perspective when it is size (or volume) that is important, than when it is shape that is important. If the statue of David had been a little smaller it would have made no difference to how it struck the eye, but a beehive would not be nearly so useful if it was only half complete.

Hence if it is neither size, shape, nor the combination of size and the shape, then what this leaves us with as the meaning of a place is the surface that surrounds a body or more precisely, the surface that is shared by any body and any host. This also helps in the case of our kettle—what constitutes a place that is 'inside' must be different from what constitutes a place that is 'outside'. It is certainly true that for anything to be deemed a body, it must have such and such a length, such and such a breadth, and such and such a depth, or, under certain circumstances, at least such and such a shape. The vase that is presently sitting on this desk must have such and such a shape and such and such a weight—to this degree it has a boundary that it shares with other things. Of course it is true that two vases could have exactly the same dimensions, that they could have exactly the same size and weight, but that is not to say we would describe them as having entirely the same place, since in whatever sense they may be qualitatively the same, they are not yet numerically the same. And as we have previously argued, the place that is 'potentially' occupiable is an utterly elusive place, firstly, because there is no such thing as a discernible unit of space, and secondly, because it is unclear whether we are describing a thing as having a relation to other things, or merely what is commensurate with itself.

Now let us address the meaning of 'intrinsic' in terms of what is (*a*) common or generic and (*b*) immanent or all-encompassing. To consider the first of these, it has sometimes been argued that there is both the 'place' occupied by a body and the 'space' that encloses all bodies. As we have already seen however (Principle of Individuation), a problem may arise if we regard space as what is logically prior to matter rather than space and matter as being altogether different in their kind. The statement 'No two things can occupy the same place at the same time' may appear to convey something meaningful, but in fact be only what is grammatically *correct*. To restate our position, what we mean by 'essence' is that set of characteristics that distinguishes one class from any other and yet binds *this* species to just *this* genus. What we mean by 'existence' on the other hand is necessarily inclusive of everything to which it pertains, but we do not treat the existence of the group just as we would the existence of any member. And it is for precisely this reason that we should not confound the meaning of what is specific with the meaning of what is unique. To take the species *Homo sapiens*, we may divide this into the subgroups Occidental and Oriental and these further into Englishmen, Scotsmen, Chinese, etc. Now so far as it concerns the question of 'essence', what is proper to the genus must be proper to the species, just as what is proper to the species must be proper to any specimen, but we do not say that what is incidental to the individual must be proper to the species or that what is incidental to the species must be proper to the genus. We would not say that if there were 1,000 Englishmen and 1,000 Scotsmen, then we could add these to the number of Occidentals, rather, just as we distinguish the class of all men from the class of all Occidentals, so also, do we distinguish all Liverpudlians from the class of all Englishmen. And in a similar vein, when we say that a particular existent occupies a particular place, we are not entitled to add to this the place of all existents; otherwise we are confusing what makes something the whole as *any class* with what makes something the whole as *any part*.

With respect to the second point, we need to consider how or in what sense it is matter that is the measure of space and not space that is the 'container' of matter. Space is often envisaged as the kind of grid you might find in any street directory, only it is not a network of streets and thoroughfares but some immovable and limitless sheath. On the other hand, what would you say of a jug, that it was half-filled with water or that it was half-filled with air? Surely not the latter, since what we mean by water is something unequivocally *inside* the jug, whereas what we mean by air is something either inside or out (as we have previously described 'the place' that may be inside or outside a kettle). It is only language that permits us to say that something is 'half-filled' or 'half-empty', since for any real container it can only be full, empty, or partially filled, not 'half-empty', since this is not a true description but perhaps more reflective of a certain state of mind. There is therefore no such thing as an intrinsic place that we can simply add to or subtract from—either a body of air is something that occupies its own place or anything that occupies a place must be deducted from its surrounding milieu (that is, what is inside any surface must be deducted from what is outside any surface).

Furthermore, it is important to be clear that what we mean by the fullness of any body is altogether different from what we mean by the emptiness of any space. In respect to our initial question whether there be a place which is separable from any object, it is much easier if we deal with this by comparing what is sensible with what is purely intellective. Any tangible body, understanding that in a purely physical sense, can be divided into a finite number of parts and ultimately that means the atoms out of which it is made; an interval of space on the other hand is something that is divisible into infinitely many parts. If there is any confusion here, that is because we tend to associate the matter that occupies a space with that space itself, on the assumption that just as there is a body, so must there be a space, that comprises such and such a number of assignable parts. This however is entirely without foundation, since there can be no qualitative comparison between a space that is empty and a space that is filled. This also follows from the assumption that perception pertains to the imagination but not to the intellect, and that whilst we can conceive of something being divided into an infinite number of parts this should never be the true aim of our enquiry.

This may also have relevance for the motion of a body in space, as the following demonstration should bring out. Since the speed of a body through any medium is influenced by the density of that medium, then in order to compare the speeds of different bodies, it may be necessary to compare their different mediums as well. For example, if sand has a greater resistance than water, then a moving bullet will take longer to traverse a particular distance in the case of the former than it will in the case of the latter. And of course, the thinking here is by no means unsound; it only becomes problematic when we attempt to connect it with something that is empty rather than something that is filled. That is, since there is no way of ascertaining the relative density of a plenum and a void, the speed of an object through the latter must be either instantaneous or not at all. However, the fact is, we cannot really compare an 'empty' with a 'filled' space, and this is a little like the mistake that we uncovered in 'Achilles and the Tortoise'. Where it concerns any true magnitude, you cannot subtract one part from any other without arriving at something that is at least infinitesimally small. On the other hand, there are an infinite number of fractions between the numbers 0 and 1/3 or 0 and 2/3, and that surely proves that zero must be included in any series if we are to describe this as what is dense. In no way should an interval of space be compared to what is discontinuous as such, otherwise there would be a magnitude without any part or an interval without any *limit*.

Of course, for all practical purposes it is true we do have a clear conception of what it means for a space to become empty or to be emptied, but what we mean is something separable, not what is qualitatively comparable in and of itself. If for instance, you were sipping a soda through a straw and then placed your finger on the top, the liquid would hold fast, and if like the Ancients, you did not know better, you *might* think this was to prevent the creation of a vacuum. And in a similar way, when we place a sponge in water, we do not say it has mysteriously increased in size, rather, that the interstices that were empty have become filled, but not that it is empty space that has in some sense become 'filled'. In the first instance, what we are doing is comparing one kind of pressure with another, not one kind space with another. In the second instance, if we were to squeeze the sponge it would become smaller, and that is because we are comparing different quantities of matter (i.e. the water and the sponge) but certainly not different quantities of space. (i.e. what is empty and filled)

In order to grasp more fully what we mean by a vacuum or a void, we need to divest ourselves of those assumptions we might have, but most especially when we regard space as an adjunct to matter and not matter as an adjunct to space. When we say that matter can be made to mediate between a plenum and a void, what we mean is that there can be more matter, but only in conjunction with the removal of more space, and less matter, but only in conjunction with the annexing of more space. So far however as the question of any *agency* is concerned, by no means are these statements interchangeable, since space cannot act to produce less matter, although matter may act to produce less space. Or at least this we would suggest, this is the orthodox point of view. Given some theoretical state of equilibrium, from that point will adding more matter eventually issued in a plenum and removing more matter eventually issued in a void. For the container theory of space, the difference between a plenum and a void reflects the difference between the infinite and the finite, so that there can be a void if we take that to mean something infinite in extent. On the other hand, looked at from the viewpoint of the relational theory, a void is purely an imaginary construct; you cannot subtract one quantity from another and arrive at something that is not commensurate with either. That is, however far you take this activity there will always be a remainder even if that be what is infinitesimally small.

This however is a rather simplistic way of regarding the relation between matter and space, since it is possible to envisage how there could be an increase in the one without a decrease in the other, as for instance, when the internal part of a body becomes more and more compressed. We do not necessarily need to 'add' or 'subtract' matter, merely deform it in such a way as to produce an opening or fissure that was previously not there. Likewise, where it concerns the question or an increase or decrease in the amount of space, this is not really as clear-cut as it might firstly appear. For instance, taking as our model the expanding universe, and leaving aside the question of any local deformations or the rate of expansion, then in theory if it is expanding evenly, this will be from every point of view. For any inhabitant on the planet x however the impression may be given that everything is moving away from him, when of course this is not really so. (Bearing in mind what we earlier said about a fixed reference point). What we might conclude therefore is that (*a*) the creation of space may well be the result of a certain deformation (that is, matter contracting or pulling back on itself) and (*b*) what we mean by 'contracting' space can just as well be connected with a fixed rather than variable amount of matter, assuming of course that the universe has a fixed amount of matter that is neither being created nor destroyed. It should be clear however that in neither case is there any true indication of what it actually means to 'create' a space, rather than 'make' a space by some purely artificial means.

What we mean by the *creation* of space can perhaps be illustrated by the following schematization. Consider in the first place what it means for a certain cavity to be made either smaller or larger. With respect to the first of these, let us say we have two holes that are being gradually fused or aligned.

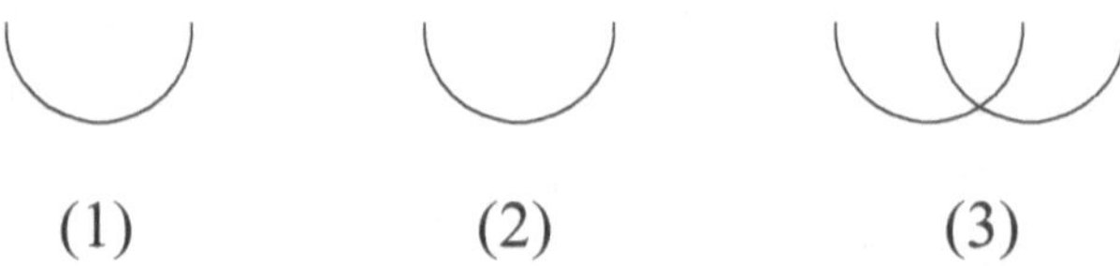

(1)   (2)   (3)

If you consider how much matter will be required to fill the larger hole (3), then it is certainly less than that for the combined total of (1) and (2). Thus, where it concerns the question how we might make a hole smaller, we need to approach this through the removal of fewer and fewer material parts. Now let us consider under what circumstances it may be possible to make a hole larger. Of course, what could be argued is that a larger hole is merely the development of a smaller one so that in the case below (4) becomes (5), which becomes (6) etc...

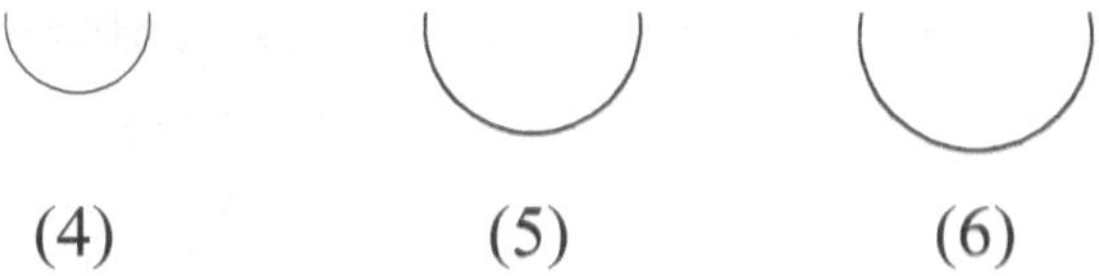

On the other hand, we might adopt the view that there are a series of pair wise holes with interstices and that each pair or 'tube' is a little larger than the last. Thus, what we have might be as follows:

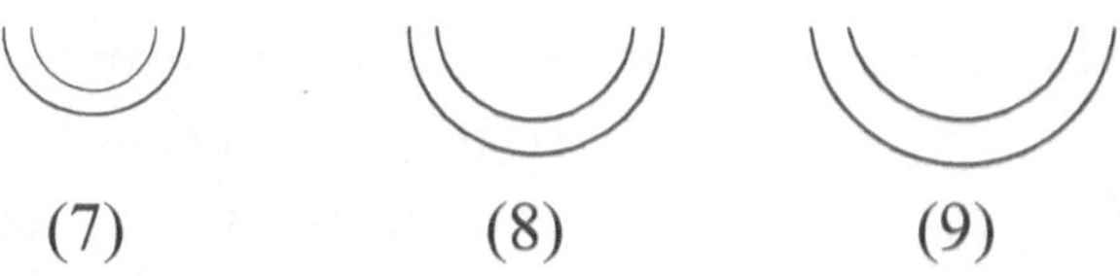

Here it is quite clearly the case that (7) does not become (8), but rather that each cavernous part must be added to all the previous parts in order to make the hole larger. And so, making the hole larger must be taken in conjunction with more and more cavernous parts. What this enables us to do is free our conception of space from its dependency on matter and give it a certain meaning that is peculiarly its own. We might then approach the general question of change by distinguishing between (*a*) a change in magnitude (extensive), (*b*) a change in degree (intensive) and (*c*) a change that is both intensive and extensive. When we think of a body that expands, we think of it as becoming *more rarefied*; when we think of a body that contracts, we think of it as becoming *more condensed*. This, however, is only change of an extensive kind; it concerns the disposition of certain material parts but nothing more. What we mean by intensive change, on the other hand, is what is strictly qualitative and in no way quantitative in its kind. For instance, in the case of the expanding universe, the meaning of 'expansion' concerns the skin that surrounds the moving parts—we regard the 'skin' as what is changing and only incidentally how anything may be changing in itself.

And this also underscores the meaning of expansion in connection with a void and contraction in connection with a plenum. We must however distinguish between the kind of change that is (*a*) absolute, and the kind of change that is (*b*) periodic. So far as it concerns (*a*), we need to approach this by connecting expansion with a change in degree and contraction with a change in both its magnitude and degree. So far as it concerns (b), and given a certain nexus between matter and space, then for matter expansion will always follow upon contraction where a plenum is concerned, and for space contraction will always follow upon expansion where a void is concerned. (Think of how a change occurs between end points that are asymmetric and between end points that have an intermediary.) What then constitutes a purely qualitative relation between matter and space could be summarized as follows: (1) Less space will create less matter where the reality of an object is concerned and (2) more space will create more matter where the appearance of an object is concerned.

Let us address each of these points in its turn. If space is the measure of matter, then it is not *more* matter that will create less space but rather less space that will create less matter, since the implication of a void is that there is surely not enough space that can be filled by any object. In this connection, think of the basic condition that needs to prevail when (*a*) we assemble a jigsaw puzzle and (*b*) we reassemble a jigsaw puzzle. In the case of the latter, there needs to be a sufficient number of parts by comparison with what we began, and in the case of the former a sufficient amount of space by comparison with what we began. And yet what one might ask do we mean by a 'sufficient' amount of space? Suppose you were presented with a situation where you had two jigsaws that were identical in shape and in the arrangement of their parts, but that one was twice the size of the other, then of course there would be no problem with swapping *places,* but what would happen if we did this piece by piece? Again, there would be no problem if you started with the smaller version and replaced a larger piece, but how, starting from the larger version, could you conceivably replace a smaller piece?

With respect to the second of these points—that more space will create more matter—we need to approach this from the perspective of comparing more and less matter or at least the addition and subtraction of more and more material parts. To return to our example of the jigsaw, if you begin your task with a few pieces and keep adding to them, the result can be no otherwise than an increase in its overall size. But to remove the pieces from a jigsaw could be done in a variety of different ways. If the pieces in question have been systematically removed from the margin, then of course, what result will be an overall reduction in its size. But what if they have been removed from the middle, will the result we obtain be exactly the same? Quite clearly, so far as it concerns any general appearance, we might view this as the removal of more matter *or* the addition of more space, since what results is not just a change in its quantity but in its *character* as well.

Of course, it is true that the ideas of expansion and contraction are much easier to understand than are the ideas of contracting and expanding space, but we need to approach this from the viewpoint of what is both ordered and what is disordered as an end. The idea of a space that is getting smaller is something quite repugnant to our minds, since although when dividing a piece of matter we are also in some sense dividing its space, we cannot divide a space and at the same time divide its matter, or at least shrink it to fill a space that has been newly created. However, if it is not the whole but just a part of space that is contracting, then we might be able to countenance this in terms of what is effectual or ineffectual as an end. For instance, if you were asked to assemble a jigsaw but were given only half the pieces, then it would make a considerable difference by what method these had been removed. If the pieces were taken from the margin then you could recommence without much fuss, but if the pieces were taken in a quite random manner it might be a more pressing issue given the absence of certain intermediate links. Or let us say you were asked to construct a chessboard from exactly 128 squares, half of which were white and half of which were black. Ideally, you might proceed by pairing the differently coloured squares, but if you were given just sixty-four randomly chosen, it is highly unlikely you would be able to achieve the result that you want. (Not impossible of course, if thirty-two just happened to be the colour white).

Consider also the sorts of examples that are found in perceptual psychology. If you sketch two lines of equal length and place them side by side, then to one affix outwardly splayed ends and to the other inwardly splayed ends, the impression may be given that the former is a little longer than the latter (Muller-Lyer illusion). The explanation for this is that there is both an implicit cue for distance and an implicit cue for shape. The shortened figure appears like the outside of a corner building, just as the longer figure appears like the inside of a room, thus creating the impression that the former is getting closer whilst the latter is moving away. A simpler explanation is that it is impossible to estimate the lengths of the lines independently of the whole figure, and hence, our judgement is based on what appears to be more elongated or more condensed. What this assumes however is that matter is the measure of space, but does not address the question what we are really being deceived about—since that is surely not the way we regard space. And how can we be sure that this 'elastic' property is not something indispensable in itself?

Another such illusion consists of a circle with equidistant lines originating from its centre and ending at its circumference. A smaller circle is then drawn to the immediate right or left of the centre. If you concentrate on the smaller circle, it will appear to be 'flattened' on one side but perfectly regular on the other (Orbison illusion). The explanation for this is that we tend to see the radiating lines as continuous, but the smaller figure as only a series of parts that intersect with these lines. For any number of lines, the area they delimit as they enter the figure is very different from what it is when they exit it. Hence it is not difficult to grasp why the portion of the figure that is closer to the centre will appear to contain 'less' space than that which is closer to the circumference. Such however is altogether different from the phenomenon of a bent stick in a glass of water, where the diffraction of light gives a full and final account of what it is, we are actually witnessing with our eyes.

And then of course there is something such as a reversible figure, one of the most common being a vase or a bird bath on a black background. As we focus on this, it may change and assume the appearance of two opposing faces. To what degree however this is really 'reversible', hinges more on a relationship in the size of the parts than it does on any mental disposition we might have. That is, since the lines that form the top and bottom of the bird bath are continuous with the sides, to reduce the size of the stimulus will be to focus on this and bring it out more clearly. On the other hand, were we to increase it to such a degree that it was touching the outer edges of any framework, then the facial images would be that much easier to discern. Hence, the way we manipulate space may also be used as a kind of organizational tool—rather than confusing us it helps dispel the illusion there is anything deceptive at all.

Turning now to the question of the visualization of space, then this is an area in which there may be any number possibilities. By adopting an approach that is purely discursive, we have convinced ourselves that we can proceed from within to what lies entirely outside, and not at all through the intervention of our senses. That is, if we begin with the barest entity, a point, then from this we can construct a line, from a line a plane, and from a plane all the things that could conceivably occupy our everyday world. And this also ties in with the belief that although we might be able to step outside any two-dimensional world, we cannot step outside any three-dimensional world to ascertain what that may be in and of itself. (Otherwise than if we consider time as a fourth dimension) Looked at entirely differently however, it may only be an assumption that how we construct our world from zero or plus one dimensions must also have implications for what it means to be plus two or plus three. Consider for instance the different meanings that a point might have if you lived on a torus or a sphere. In the case of the latter, you could certainly experience contraction or what was contracting to a point, but that would be ambiguous, since every point would have its equivalent on the other side of the sphere. In the case of the former, there would be no such thing as a fixed or determinate point since everything would be relative to one's direction of movement and that might vary for any time or any place. Consequently, if the world we inhabit possesses certain qualities it may also be lacking in certain others, that it may be undulating or it may be flat, it may be open or it may be closed, that it may be symmetrical or it may be skewed. The axioms of geometry are a reflection of the fact that certain limitations *must* apply comprehensively, and that if the senses cannot be given free reign then neither can our intellect. (Or at least, that there is both a rational and sensuous whole)

The question that might then be asked is this: If there is no privileged geometry, then in what sense could there be a more or less 'objective' assessment of the actual space which we occupy? In order to address this issue, what we need to keep in mind is that there are two senses for the 'objectivity' of what it is that is in space, in the first case, for what we take to be mensurable, and in the second case, for what we take to be its measure. If space itself contains no absolute metric, then a definition of congruence can only be given if we are satisfied with the accuracy of our tools, so that any change in their *place* will not be accompanied by any change in their size. Assuming however that there is no problem with our tools, it still remains an open question what we mean by space itself, whether after all it might not be just a concretion, a synthesis, a loose amalgam of ends.

To pursue this a little further, let us suppose there is a quantity of space so small that no meaningful description could be given of anything that was actually smaller—not however a fixed quantity such as the

Planck length but an actual atom of space. And what do we mean by a quantity such as this? Suppose we have fifty-five units of matter and fifty-five units of space, but that the basic quantity of space conforms to the principle x, and the basic quantity of matter to the principle x/y. If we were to divide the space into five basic elements, the result will be $1^2 + 2^2 + 3^2 + 4^2 + 5^2$. Matter on the other hand will be divided into five equal elements, according to the formula 55/5. Now if you think how you might add or subtract the parts of matter, then the notion of the smallest element becomes quite important, since any particular 'joining' will be between two different parts of space, and so, will prevent us from achieving that result which we want. That is, one 'part' of matter will always be between the 'third' and 'fourth' parts of space.

So far as it concerns the actual behaviour of a space atom, then we need to consider this against the backdrop of how we ordinarily conceive the behaviour of matter. Take for instance the meaning of a charged particle or how matter behaves in the vicinity of electric and magnetic fields. Most bodies can be induced to receive a charge from other bodies and we might view this in terms of (*a*) a movement of free electrons from the one to the other, (*b*) a concentration of electrons and a separation of the forces and (*c*) a change from attraction to repulsion or repulsion to attraction. In all this however, there is neither the creation nor destruction of a force, only the alignment of forces that are complementary and the dispersal of forces that are not. The notion of a force that is repulsive is consistent with the notion of a force that is attractive, since (*a*) a concentration of charges is consistent with a scattering of charges so far as any total effect is concerned and (*b*) an alignment of charges having the same signature is consistent with an alignment of charges having the very opposite.

On the other hand, were we to adopt the view that it is only space that is effective then of course our approach would be different yet again. The notion of a space atom would be something without any analogue; it would be solitary, isolated, incapable of any connection. We would therefore describe the force that it exerts as something altogether repulsive, something that it initiates in order to prevent any encroachment on its privacy. And so under these circumstances, the way that space interacts with matter would be (*a*) where the motion of a particle was directly in the path of such an atom and (2) where the motion of a particle was susceptible of different influences, depending upon the 'pull' or pressure that was exerted on it. In the case of (*a*), given that the force of any space atom would be extremely difficult to detect, an element or particle that entered its domain would not be repelled but only deflected and that presumably according to the size and speed of such a particle. (The question of direction would be one of simple probability.) In the case of (*b*), what we are dealing with is a net effect or a product of forces, since repulsion is never the counterforce to attraction but rather attraction a mere addendum to repulsion. If for instance a particle of matter was equidistant between two space atoms (and they the same in size), then the net effect on it would be zero. On the other hand, if it were nearer to one than the other, then to this extent it would be drawn to the atom at a greater distance or away from the one that was nearer at hand. And similarly, if one atom were twice the size of another and any particle twice the distance from it, then again, the net effect would be zero. Consequently, the total force exerted would be the result of (*a*) the size of the atom and (*b*) an inverse relation between size and distance where two atoms were concerned. What however could be said for a single particle is not necessarily what could be said for a stream of such particles. That is, an interference pattern for a stream of particles is not necessarily what results from the interference of just single particles. Quite clearly, there would be no discernible result if we consider space atoms of the same size and the same distance apart, since what results would be merely the swapping of different places. On the other hand, if the atoms were equidistant but varied in their size so that a larger was interspersed with a smaller one, then the amount of deflection in the one case would be different from that which it was in the other. And so, what this might do is produce an interference pattern, given that smaller deflections when added to larger deflections would produce a 'filled' locale and smaller deflections when subtracted from larger deflections would produce an 'empty' locale.

Chapter 21

Creation, Destruction and Formation

How or in what way we might conceive of a *continuous* creation hinges very largely on our ability to conceive of purpose otherwise than what is strictly verifiable, that is, in terms not only of *how* things have come to be, but also of *how* they must end. Thus, it is universality that must override particularity, constancy that must override changefulness and form that must override matter. In the sense in which it is form that predominates, not only do we tend to think of this as a kind of substratum but what is incessant as well. That which originates from within is one kind of form (intelligent or creative design)—that which originates from without is another kind of form (mechanical or artistic design). The implicit idea here is that the set of causes that explains how things have arisen must also explain how they will end—it joins the meaning to the mechanism of our lives. In the human arts, there is the imposition of form upon a ground that is entirely indifferent, as for instance the skill of the sculptor which may be applied equally to bronze or stone, the skill of the healer which may be applied equally to the neck or the spine, the skill of the artisan which may be applied equally to wood or clay. Here the underlying matter has a meaning that is afforded by such and such a form in conjunction with such and such a mind.

As to its corollary in the natural world what we have is the idea of an enduring form, since the parts no less than the whole, must be regarded as efficacious in and of themselves. And of course, this ties in with the belief that the forces that tend to the preservation of the whole must always supersede those that tend to its destruction or impairment. What we mean by inertia in this context is not resistance to motion or any change in motion, but the mere adjunct to a force that imparts motion in a complete and uninterrupted way. This idea of persistence can also be understood in the context of the preservation of the species, or the simple union between the sexes. Consider if you will the way the individual endeavours not only to duplicate itself through its offspring, but also to ensure the continuity of the species. The preservation of such and such a form must thus be regarded as the end or purpose of every act of generation, even though by comparison, the lives of individuals are like footprints washed away in the sands of time.

And yet despite these comforting surmisings the question still remains: How far and to what degree do the workings of nature evince any overarching plan or design? To what extent are we entitled to infer anything truly unific at the heart of all we see? Certainly, it would seem a rather odd assertion that in the case of marriage for instance, sexual intercourse is not merely the expression of an animal urge but something quite transcendent—an equally *rational* desire, the working through of some preordained design. We surely accord greater worth to artistic achievement than we do to the basic urges of men, and so why should the author of *Paradise Lost* be regarded as any the less worthy than what is able to reproduce itself or its kind? Not only that, but if we regard the act of procreation as what is truly 'creative', this will not help us escape the circle that encloses all acts and effects, since if the father begets the son then the son begets the father, and it is by no means clear when and where this activity has arisen or when and how it might end.

In terms of the relation between existence and essence, what adds meaning to a continuous creation is the dependence of the one upon the other, and the assumption that 'being in itself' precedes 'doing in itself', that a cause that is the cause of 'what is' precedes a cause that is the cause of 'what does'. When we join reality to immanent causality at one extreme what we have is a perfectly *necessary being*, whilst at the other extreme, when we separate a cause from what in any sense is conceivable what we have is a perfectly *chimerical being*. The basis for *contingent being* thus arises from a situation in which there is no genuine conflict between the idea and the reality of a thing, but no good ground for their connection withal. Hence what is contingent might also be thought of as what is inadequate or at least not adequate to connect any origin to any end.

On the other hand, what this fails to do is explain what we mean by a cause as the precondition for any end, and a cause as the instrument for the attainment any end. In the final analysis, what we are doing is arguing for the precedence of essence over existence, and although this may be a good way of explaining what we mean by unity, not for what is conjunctive or disjunctive in itself. The distinction between the necessary, the possible and the impossible must thus be seen to rest on the distinction between what *must* have a cause of its being, what *cannot* have a cause of its being and what *may* have a cause of its being, but only where it is the latter for which there is any real or demonstrable proof. In terms of what we mean by creation, it is a mere *petitio principii* if we begin with the assumption of an 'immanent cause' and yet can summon nothing positive to support it. When we say that the cause of an event has not yet been fully explained, then there may be some sense to this if we are able to follow our enquiries, but that is not to say it is 'unknowable' unless we can adopt some entirely different point of view. We may not know how or in what way the pyramids were built just as surely as we do the Hoover Dam, but that is not because the latter is just as 'clear' and 'distinct' as the former is 'vague' and 'obscure'.

Some confusion may easily arise here, since if we assume that what is more recent is also more pellucid and so is easier to explain, this may lead to the conclusion there were 'darker forces' at work in the case of the Egyptians or the Greeks. This is similar to the view that the genus is more 'distinct' than the species, that the species is more 'distinct' than the individual and that the individual is more 'distinct' than its parts. But whatever the thinking, this does not support any 'hierarchy of causes' such that genera are created *prior* to species or species are created *prior* to individuals. Quite clearly, it is not essence that is prior to existence, but rather a representation of the whole that is afforded through a *demonstration* of all its parts, just as we might trace the rise and fall of a species through the rise and fall of all its members. We do not say that the idea of a dinosaur must precede the existence of a dinosaur, otherwise, just as the idea of dinosaur is as clear to us today as it ever has been in the past, so must we be able to catalogue all the dinosaurs from their beginning right through to their end.

The idea that there are both internal and external forces at work in creation, that we can gain a better understanding of the world if we examine not just the physical but immanent causes as well, would seem to rest entirely on the assumption that there could never be more energy needed to preserve things than there is to create them. And hence, that what we mean by destruction is entirely illusory—that it is only the destruction of some form that we are witnessing, not the removal of any quintessential being. Whether however such a connection exists between the nothing into which something has passed and the nothing from which something has come, is very much a matter for debate. Consider the following quite pivotal kinds of change: (*a*) Change of something into something, (*b*) change of something into nothing, (*c*) change of nothing into something and (*d*) change of nothing into nothing. Now assuming that in (*a*) there is a clear case of permutation and in (*d*) no change at all, then in what sense must (*b*) and (*c*) be said to involve unqualified change but no real contrariety as such? The answer quite routinely given is that since there can be no change of something before or after its existence, then neither can there be any real difference in how these conditions might be elucidated as well. In general terms, change from something into nothing or nothing into something is equally possible or impossible, given that what they represent are two entirely agreeable and not incompatible states of affairs. But if we regard this in purely phenomenal terms, then it should be clear there must also be some change in our outlook, since (*c*) implies only *qualitative* change, whereas (*b*) implies something that is both *qualitative* and *quantitative* in its kind. That is, it is possible to express transience in terms of how a thing becomes smaller at such and such a rate of change, and how a thing becomes larger but at a different rate of change. Existence on the other hand must always be viewed separately from non-existence, assuming that the latter is antecedent to the former.

And that is why we might argue that the true opposite of destruction is not creation but rather reconstruction, since what the latter represents is mediation of one sort whereas what the former represents is mediation of something altogether different. Opposites may thus pertain to the idea of a *just limitation*, but that is not what we mean by opposites in the sense of what we observe throughout any series of changes. It should thus be clear that we cannot connect creation and destruction in any factual or phenomenal way, only in the manner in which we *think* of this connection, and that may be no different from the way that Euclid conceived of space. Consider the following passage from a work by Spinoza:

> Hence it follows that God is the cause not only of the coming into existence of things but also of their continuing in existence, or, to use a scholastic term, God is the cause of the being of things (essendi rerum) For whether things exist or do not exist, in reflecting on their essence we realize that this essence involves neither existence nor duration. So it is not their essence which can be the cause of either their existence or their duration, but only God, to whose nature alone existence pertains . . .

> (Ethics 1, Cor. to Prop. XXIV)

There seem to be two major assumptions that underlie this kind of errant thinking, and they are, first, that creation and destruction are in some sense comparable, or at least that the kind of causality that informs the one must also inform the other, and secondly, that preservation and destruction are antipathetic, but that creation and formation are in general accord. As concerns the first point, what we need to ask ourselves is whether the influences that begird the beginning of our lives are the same as those that begird their cessation. We might say of a man for instance that he died of pneumonia or that he died of a heart attack, or we might include the broader circumstances by saying that he died in his sleep, that he died in an earthquake or that he died of a shark bite. But by comparison, how might we describe the conditions that are relevant to a person's being born? Would we say it is becoming that is the cause of birth, craving that is the cause of birth or sorrow that is the cause of birth? The grounds for creation we would hold are as impenetrable as the driven snow, and since we do not know why things have arisen or why they exhibit the qualities they do, how can we entertain any prospect of causality otherwise than what is non-descriptive in its kind?

As concerns the second point, let us address this by asking what the difference is between a renewable or recoverable and a perishable or irretrievable state of affairs. If you consider an artifice or a machine that has been put together in such and such a way and then dismantled and reassembled, would you not say it has undergone some *modification* in its being? On the other hand, if you were to remove and then dispose of all the parts, would you not say the whole has become *irretrievable* or not reclaimable to even the least degree? Consequently, it is not formation and destruction but rather destruction and reconstruction, that are more properly in a state of disaccord. And in the same vein, since it can hardly be denied that destruction is a necessary prerequisite for re-creation, then it is these two, rather than creation and formation, that might more fittingly be said to constitute a distinction of the reason.

But to return to the question whether there could ever be *more* needed to preserve things than was needed to create them, then what this hinges on is whether a thing can be changed not only in the act of creation but also in the act of its impairment. The Ancients believed that in the case of arising or originating, this must also involve a certain nexus between matter and form, different types or categories of being, the real arising from the potential, vitality arising from what is lifeless, change in quantitative terms for what is the same, to change in qualitative terms for those accidents that were originally just the same. And yet the question still remains, whether by giving or acquiring form have we truly proved or only presupposed the existence of some more primordial condition or state of being. That is, whether by 'coming to be' have we demonstrated or only presupposed a creative essence that must be imparted, in order to ensure the fulfilment of such and such an end. If we say that the same thing may both be and be done to, looked at the same or in different respects, then it may still be asked whether *doing* or *being done to* underlies this in any truly quintessential way. From our own perspective, it seems there is a fundamental difference between 'acting' and 'being acted upon', which cannot be bridged over by any appeal to the supposed intrinsic connection between matter and form.

And that is why we might define creation as the act of *being creative* and destruction as the ultimate condition of *being destroyed*. The one is present, the other is past, the one is active, the other is passive. That something '*is*' means that something is active but not that something is compelled to be; that something '*is not*' means that something has been acted on, but not that it is destructive in and of itself. The assertion on the other hand, that by 'being creative' we do mean modification of any particular kind, does not, despite appearances, afford any real basis for change but only for a sense of what *has* been changed, since we can always ask who created the creator or what is that mobilizes any initial force. If what has been made or created can never be increased or diminished (as we commonly understand by growth and decay), then there is neither more nor less activity in the end than there was from the beginning. And if no *more* activity, then no more likelihood it is a divine presence that contrives certain ends and prevents certain others. The idea therefore that in creation is there anything more than the act of creating, or some disguised effect exhorting things to the attainment of such and such a good, is a patent nonsense cooked up by the kind of minds that refuse to recognize that certain things may in fact be tending towards their own destruction, and thus that if such be deemed a legitimate end, then *more* will be needed to preserve them than was needed from the outset. And it is precisely this that we mean by efficient causality: something which ensures that on certain occasions *more* will be needed to preserve things than is needed to destroy them and on other occasions *less* will be needed to preserve them than will be needed to destroy them. (That is, we are not saying that everything is tending to its own destruction, but only that certain things *may* be.)

Broadly speaking, what we might say is that creation involves a *qualitative* leap, a change in either intensity or degree, but destruction a change also in the *quantity* or the *kind* of being. Perhaps we can illustrate this a little more clearly if we draw on certain developments in the field of atomic theory. It has been well documented that if you expose matter to electromagnetic radiation, then this will issue in the creation of an electron pair, one with a negative charge and the other with a positive charge. This process can also be reversed to produce photons, just as it is photons that were active in the first place. This occurs when a positron encounters an electron with a negative charge and they annihilate one another, in turn producing energy as a substitute for their collective mass. Thus, what we appear to have is something entirely commutative in its kind, a conversion of energy into mass and mass into energy or a conversion of photons into electrons and electrons into photons. If, however we examine this a little more closely, then perhaps the situation is not exactly as we have herein described. Certainly, when a positron is annihilated then what results is a real transformation in its character or its category of being. Not only that but it may also undergo a change in its magnitude, since we can discern a numerical difference when two particles become three, as will sometimes occur. Thus, what we would say of the resultant is that it has been *recreated* but not *created*, just as we would say of any means that it has been *destroyed* but not *remade*.

By contrast, what is truly created will be either the loss of energy or a conversion into mass, but on no account, what is open-ended or commutative in its kind. It is irrelevant whether it be lively photons or anything else that supplies the energy in question, since we can only characterize this as a change in quality but not a change in magnitude or in the character of its being. It should be clear that there is only potentiality where creation is concerned and yet strict antecedence where destruction is concerned, or at least between destruction and recreation, since what is created may or may not be destroyed, whereas *ipso facto* what is recreated must result from something metamorphic in its kind. Where it concerns the ideas of unmaking and remaking or destroying and recreating, what we observe is a strict antecedence, since you cannot remake something that is not already made, and you cannot recreate something if it has not in some sense already been destroyed. But so far as it concerns the link between unmaking and destroying then there is this further observation, that in the former is there retention of both a whole and its parts, whereas in the latter only the whole (energy) but not its parts (mass).

Having pursued our enquiries up to this point, it is clear that what we mean by a 'constant creating' rests on two assumptions: first, that there is a substratum for every single action or event, and secondly, that what is the cause of itself or a 'thing-in-itself' (Kant) also has the capacity to impart this quality to others. We might however take an altogether different approach, by asking ourselves in the first place not only what it means to create or to shape a particular event, but what it means to duplicate or reproduce it as a whole. Consider the effect of arranging billiard balls on a table and then striking them with the end of a cue. So far as it concerns the means and the actual event as it unfolds, there is no difficulty to be discerned, but could you imagine what might happen if you were then asked to duplicate exactly the same result? Not even the most accomplished player could hope to split the balls and bring them to rest just *exactly* as he had done first of all. Or consider the case of a ball that leaves a person's hand and then shatters a pane of glass. If you had a film of this incident and were able to reverse it, what you would see are the splinters rising up, the pane miraculously repairing itself and the ball lodging in the offender's hand. In practice such a scenario would certainly be quite absurd, but how and in what way might one attempt to repeat such a series of events? Perhaps you might think to pick the pieces up and with due care return them to their original state. Or perhaps you might repeat this experiment and hope the pane broke in precisely the same way, although of course the chance of this would be vanishingly small.

What this demonstrates is that there are certain events that could be described as asymmetric in their kind, since there seems to be a natural progression from order to disorder rather than disorder to order. Certainly, you might be able reassemble the fragments of glass as far as their *proximate* order was concerned, but you could not repeat this as far as their *temporal* order was concerned. And what this also does is raise further questions about the relation time and space, since with the former can we get chaos out of order, whereas with the latter is this entirely unpredictable. (That is, space may serve an end that is either ordered or disordered). It is clear in this instance that what we mean by the means for creation is very different from what we mean by the means for replication, and hence, that there is a discernible difference between creation and formation per se. In a similar vein, we might compare and contrast the ideas of destruction and reproduction, only here adopting as our model what is fluid or interchangeable in its parts. In the case of an amusement such as a jigsaw puzzle, we can imagine both assembling and dismantling it in its entirety, since here it is equally order that prevails in the absence of chaos or chaos that prevails in the absence of order. So long as the pieces remain intact, there will always be the potential to dismantle it just as there is to assemble it, and there is no reason why this should be halted merely on account of the rigours of time. On the other hand, if some of the pieces became lost or misplaced then this would run counter to such an end, if not in the short term then at least in the long term. Consequently, it is not difficult to see how destruction might be opposed to any kind of reconstruction and not simply production per se.

Since we must conclude therefore that destruction can no more be allied to formation than formation to creation, let us consider how or in what respect it may be possible to reach some consensus of ideas. To begin with, we might compare the activity of making something with the activity of reproducing it. Looked at from the viewpoint of form, then it is clear that no matter how many the number of articles or copies that are created, these will always evince entirely the same shape, entirely the same character, entirely the same design. We have seen this in the case of a jigsaw puzzle, but it could also apply to any template or even cookies that are sitting in a baking tray. What we mean by reproduction therefore can only be the accentuation of such and such a shape, what has the *appearance* of a bird as distinct from a fish or what has the *appearance* of a tree as distinct from a rock. And of course, since we can never dissolve or destroy a particular prototype neither can we recompose it, only draw comparisons with what it is more or less similar or dissimilar in its kind.

Looked at from the viewpoint of matter on the other hand, diversity may be represented in either of the following ways: (*a*) so far as it concerns a spatial ordering of the parts, then these may or may not be uniform in their kind and (2) so far as it concerns a temporal ordering of the parts, then these may or may not be invariable in their kind. Consider again the quite casual means we employ in the assembly of a jigsaw. How and in what manner *might* we undertake such a task—would we begin with the overall pattern and work back to a location for each and every part, or would we begin by connecting a small number of parts and then to these add more until we attained our goal? Or let us extend this to the activity of reassembling. Must we always proceed in exactly the same way, or is it possible to envisage a quite different *causality* as well? In this case there is good reason to believe it is matter that antecedes form and not form that antecedes matter—otherwise we could never deviate from our original plan or adopt an approach that was something less 'perfected' in its kind.

Having established a connection between making and reassembling, let us now proceed to a more general discussion about the meaning of creation, destruction and formation. So far as it concerns the first two, there are essentially three ways we might approach this: (*a*) on purely dialectical grounds, by taking them to be antithetical but in some sense comparable as well. Thus, from a logical perspective and for any terms A and B, although A ≠ B and B ≠ A may be regarded as essentially the same, we would surely not say this of A = B and B ≠ A. (That is, we would not say there is something that connects what is with what is not.) Or (*b*) by distinguishing between object and act such that it is creation that precedes destruction, just as it is the motive that precedes the agent or the cause that precedes the effect. (That is, we would not say the state of being changeful was also the state of being destructive.) Or (*c*) so far as it concerns our general approach to change, where quality and quantity may or may not be aligned. (That is, we would not say that the rate of change is something that must always be fixed.)

So far as it concerns the question of becoming or formation, there are essentially two ways that 'coming to be' and 'passing away' may be connected. First, we could argue that there is an underlying essence that is impervious to change and that 'coming to be' and 'passing away' represent a kind of just limitation on what could or could conceivably not be. That is, where there is a limit at one extreme, which we call the *necessary*, and a limit at the other extreme, which we call the *impossible*. So far however as it concerns what *is*, then growth and decay will take us from birth at one extreme to death at the other. Or we might adopt a slightly different approach by suggesting that it is not growth and decay that are subordinate to being and not being, but being and not being that are subordinate to growth and decay - understood as two entirely compatible states. We could do this by introducing the idea of an imperceptible change. What we mean by generation is really only a certain kind of growth, just as what we mean by death is really only a certain kind of diminution, only, we do not recognize this because it is not evident to our senses. Death may appear to be complete cessation, but what it really is, is only a kind of involution, that is, the involution of certain quite critical and indispensable parts.

Now let us consider these points and in a little more detail. Even if we grant that there must be *some* magnitude if an organism is to grow, does it also follow that there must be *some* magnitude after the thing has decayed? So far it might be argued that 'coming to be' and 'passing away' are indeed reciprocal conditions, this could be proved by analogy and in the following way. When water is converted into steam, we do not say that there is 'growth' because the volume has increased, rather, that there is simply the eduction of one thing and the disappearance of quite another. And this is not unreasonable, since steam may in turn become water, so that if the one is potentially the other, then no matter the present circumstance is it surely just the same, only under a different order or species of being. On the other hand, although this may well be the case for certain phenomena, where growth is concerned there is an additional element, and that is the direction of movement taking us from one position to the next. For if considered quite closely, what waxes must be waxing from some point to another, just as what wanes must be waning from some point to another, and so, what connects them must be what distinguishes them, just as what distinguishes them must be what connects them. And from which we might conclude that either (*a*) it is birth that is coincident with growth but not diminution with what is 'ceasing to be' or (*b*) it is diminution that is coincident with death but not growth with what is 'coming to be'.

So far as we adopt the view that growth involves the appending of certain parts and decay the removal of certain parts, the comeliness of this arrangement may well suggest a certain interplay with or without any supervening power. That is, it might be conjectured that in the end of decay is there the prospect for growth, just as in the end of growth is there the prospect for decay. However, the problem with this is that although we may well accede to the second part of this deduction, we cannot accede to the first. For if growth were continuous with decay just as decay is continuous with growth, then all we would have is the basis for *remaking* something that was already there. The idea of birth and death as unfolding and enfolding is clearly underscored in this remark by Leibniz that . . .

. . . since generation is merely the growth of a changed and developed animal, death will be nothing but the diminution of a changed and developed animal . . . but the animal itself will always remain throughout such transformations . . . (Reflections on the Doctrine of a Universal Spirit 1702)

The assumption here is that nothing can be destroyed but that everything that exists must be created anew. And thus, what we mean by destruction is either (*a*) a seeming limitation but not an ineluctable truth or (*b*) a simple illusion brought about by a change in appearance but not a change in what is essentially real. This is a good example of the kind of unbounded optimism that flourished in the 17th century. And yet as we would steadfastly maintain, it is not change from something into nothing but nothing into something that is truly problematic, and it is not death and decay but death and rebirth that is at the heart of our general distrust.

Chapter 22

On the Meaning of a Universal Spirit

How and in what way we might conceive of a universal spirit raises certain questions about the relation between the microcosmic and and the macrocosmic, but also how and in what way such an idea can be realized as what is distinctive in and of itself. That is, on what grounds we might regard the universal as what is non-specific or non-particular, not simply the product of a number of isolated and unrelated ideas. Although, as we have already argued, the relation between form and matter is not such that the one is strictly antecedent to the other, so far as there is any genuine convergence this can only be accomplished by regarding the latter as what is 'real' and the former as what is 'ideal'. If form is potentiality and matter is actuality, then not only is there a certain formlessness as the precondition for what has being, there is also an understanding that what has the *potential* to be is not really in the thing but only in the *cause* of any change. Whether it concerns the relation between the artist and his canvas or the builder and his tools, there is here no true synthesis but only the capacity to realize something dormant or elucidate something that lies hidden. Form thus means the 'forming' of such and such a particular end.

On the other hand, so far as we might regard the form as what is real and the matter as what is not, what this implies is that there is some self-sustaining force, the existence of a power that lies deep within and not merely in any agency or its capacity to undergo such and such a change. And of course, this is exactly what we mean by the spirit or the animus, something that raises lifeless matter from a state of potentiality to actuality and infuses it with a degree of potency as well. There is a soul therefore in even the most rudimentary forms of life, although as we ascend the tree of life there will be a fuller and more explicit recognition of precisely what this is. Less completeness in the whole will be matched by more diversity in the parts, more completeness in the whole by more efficiency in the parts. Thus, the various powers may be classified as to whether they are dependent upon (a) the body or (b) a synthesis of both the body and soul. In the case of the former what we have is something common to all sentient beings, instinct and nutrition, in the case of the latter acts by means of corporeal organs such as sight, smell and touch.

However so far as we might wish to acquire a truly adequate conception of the soul, we must do so not only with respect to its origin but also with respect to its end. That is, although we may indeed regard the living organism as a composite of body and soul, that does not explain in what sense the one remains over once the other has left the stage, that is, not only how the body may be connected with the soul but how the soul may be effective in and of itself. Certainly, if we regard the soul as a tension between two poles, then it is difficult to see how, or why, it might survive the dissolution of all the parts. Would you say for instance that a filament outlasts the existence of a globe, that an escapement outlasts the existence of a typewriter or that a thermostat outlasts the existence of an engine? On the other hand, if what we are saying is that it is the means by which something reaches its pinnacle, as a certain training is the means by which someone becomes an engineer, then again it would be difficult to say how the latter might outlast the former, or how a scholar for instance might outlast the subject in which he is versed.

Such a difficulty cannot be resolved by regarding the soul as the driving force *behind* the body, so that there must always be a certain incipient stirring before anything can attain the full perfection of its being. If there were nothing more to it than this, then it seems that in old age a person would still have the full flush of youth, all his faculties intact, and that any loss would be merely provisional, not a full and final close. If on the other hand, we attempt to link the origin with the end, then again, we must fail, since what we mean by a 'purpose' is not any immanent tendency, only the use that may be made of something at any given time and place. An implement such as a drill or a skrewdriver may have a purpose or design, but this is not a precondition for its being— only what makes it effective as an end. Likewise, where it concerns a living organ by no means is its use a precondition for its being, no more than the eye is the precondition for the making of a mole, or a limb the precondition for the making of a snake.

Let us now investigate a particular conception of the soul based on the existence of a supersensible realm in which individual things have only a tentative share, together with the claim that knowledge is a kind of reminiscence, and that what we acquire through the senses is really nothing new but the return to something ancient or primordial. In this case, although there may be adequacy with respect to any end, there is certainly no adequacy with respect to any origin. So far as it concerns the first, we may lay bare its intention through a distinction between the essential and accidental make-up of anything. What we mean by the essence of a thing is that in which it participates, but not necessarily the whole of what it is. A fire for instance may be warm, but that does not mean it is the embodiment of warmth; a wheel may be circular, but that does not mean it is the embodiment of circularity, the universe may be vast, but that does not mean it is the embodiment of what is limitless. Much in the same way, when we are dealing with things that have opposing properties then it is the properties that cannot co-exist, not the things that contain them, since if we withdraw the softness from a pillow, then it will become less like a pillow, and if we withdraw the hardness from an anvil, then it will become less like an anvil, but that is not to say we have destroyed their very meaning in the process.

The question that might then be asked is as follows: Given that there are certain distinctive forms, do sensible things receive as their share the whole of any form or do they receive only the part of any form?

Or to return to our original example (the warmth contained in a fire): Would you say that the fire participates in the warmth in the sense that it expresses essentially what *is* warm, or would you say that the fire exhibits such a such a property, but not in any critical or quintessential way? And of these we would certainly be more inclined towards the latter. Since the quality of being warm or exuding warmth may express itself in many different ways, i.e. there may be warmth in the air, warmth in a spa, warmth in a pipe—it is not a quality that is peculiar to solidity or combustibility per se, rather, what is solid or combustible *may* exhibit this given such and such an opportunity or such and such a circumstance. And the tenor of these remarks will apply equally in the case of artefacts or the products of art, since to the degree there is any participation must this be perfunctory at best.

Or perhaps we might also approach this in the following way. If you consider what is meant by the 'essence' of a table, then it is not unreasonable this will be exhibited in each and every table. But since specific tables also have certain characteristics that are peculiarly their own, it is much less appropriate to argue that the whole of 'being a table' is exhibited in each and every table, rather the whole plus any accidents that may also be evident. Quite clearly, we can always have the concept of a table whether or not there are any such things in existence, but what is in and of itself an existent, is not thereby in and of itself a conception (as for instance in the case of a person who we designate with such and such a particular name). Thus, despite some scepticism regarding ideal forms, we may at least concede a certain 'sharing in' of quintessential being. On the other hand, so far as what we are dealing with is a true *organic* being, we may well be more receptive to the idea that there can be something singular through and in conjunction with a range or diversity of *means*. That is, that what each individual incorporates is not just the meaning of any part but also the meaning of any whole. If you attend to the activity exhibited in a school of fishes, or that which is present in a flock of starlings, then it is perhaps not so difficult to imagine how the whole might be expressed through a diversity of parts—how there might not only be an amassment of bodies, but also a 'jostling and communing of souls'.

So far however as it concerns the second of these points, that knowledge is merely a kind of reminiscence, on no account would we admit this, nor that our senses can only serve to return us to a state that existed before we were born. According to this theory, that is, the theory of transcendental forms, it is only from the idea of equality we can *know* what may or may not be diverse, it is only from the idea of beauty we can *know* what may or may not be deformed, it is only from the idea of eternity we can *know* what may or may not be fugacious. And unless we are completely oblivious to any information we may have received, 'to know' means simply to retrieve and not dismiss what was there from the moment we were born. And yet if we examine this with the carefulness that it deserves, then perhaps it is not the ignorant who are the same as the forgetful, or the forgetful who are the same as the intractable, rather, the ignorant who are the same as the intractable and the forgetful who are the same as the *reforming*. That is, there is a difference between 'coming to know' when this concerns something factual and 'coming to know' when this concerns something implicit in the very structure of our thought.

In the case of empirical or scientific knowledge, what we have as an activity involves both a gaining and a losing, a gaining of the future through a reinventing of the past. Where on the other hand it concerns the 'coming to know' of any absolute truth, then of course, there cannot be any losing as such or at least not any willful abandonment of what we have already acquired. We would not say of Pythagoras theorem for instance, that it was more or less 'true' in the past than it is in the present, but we *might* say of the Ptolemaic system that it is 'less true' in the present than it was in the past (or at least that it is, a less satisfactory account of the workings of the solar system). And so, what we are dealing with here are two distinct forms of knowledge, not the sense in which the one is only amenable through and in conjunction with the other. If it were true that the only genuine truth was that of the discursive kind, then there would be no prospect for advancement or the shedding of outmoded ideas. On the other hand, if there was no point to our capacity for reasoning, then we would be driven by instinct, and unable to organize such data as we might scrupulously acquire. In the same way, so far as we may argue for a present that is real and a past that is not, or that our memories are the only means for acquiring any knowledge, what this overlooks is the difference between a *collective* past which is the domain of all, and a private past to which others may or may not have due access. Although there are certain experiences we may accept or repress (as in Freudian terms), what we mean by a 'collective past' is not a recoverable past but something we all share as the legacy of who and what we have *become*. Thus, we may have access to the past so far as we have a collective responsibility for what *is* in the past, but we do not always have access to the leavings and the fragments of ourselves as these may change from day to day. This may also have implications for what we mean by collective guilt, since in the way we take responsibility for our acts, we are not acquiring new knowledge but rather coming to a fuller awareness of how and in what way we have erred.

Let us now address the question of change or transformation along the following lines: (*a*) where it concerns the transformation of both a body and a soul, that is, their permanent synthesis through and in conjunction with certain incipient parts, (*b*) where it concerns the passage of souls from one body to another, that is the transformation of a body but not the transformation of a soul (metempsychosis) and (*c*) where it concerns the relation between the single and collective, where there is change from either the former to the latter or the latter to the former. In the first of these what we have is the permanent conjunction of a body and a soul, not their joining and loosing, rather their simple attuning in connection with certain indissoluble parts. 'What is' exists not only in miniature *before* it is born, but also beyond death, as a kind of enfolding or closing of certain basic parts. Growth and development at one extreme are matched by flexure and involution at the other. With respect to the second of these points, what we are dealing with is something more transcendent in its kind, the expiation of sin through a cycle of lives until the soul is purged and free of its bodily captor. This is what is commonly called transmigration—the shedding of one skin and the putting on of another. The soul in this case is conscious of a struggle between good and evil, and that the body is the battleground for just this struggle; what it hopes to do is escape all corruption and achieve a more worthy or commendable state of being. So far as it concerns the third, what we have is a difference between the local and the global, a soul that is contained within the body at the microcosmic level and a soul that is contained within the body at the macrocosmic level. A transformation may occur in either direction, since just as there is something that connects two individuals (the need for expiation), so must there be a return to something that is higher or that is purer in its aim.

One might think of the drops that collect in a pool of water, the rapid wind that rustles through a tree or a swarm of ants that collects around its prey. In all these instances there is one as distinct from many, a 'collective soul' that distinguishes itself from all its members, which is identical to none and yet is vital to them all. However, what we mean by a collective spirit in this sense should not be confounded with what is universal, since what we mean by the latter is what is distinctive in itself, whereas, there is a certain ambiguity when the transformation that occurs may do so with respect to either the origin *or* the end. That is, we might regard the matter in such a way that it is the single soul that enters the collective or the collective that enters the single, but in any event, there is no specific direction of change and hence nothing univocal as such. We cannot say the drops are not there because the pool of water is not there, only that there has been a dispersion of the whole and thus *not* what is universal in and of itself.

In order to grasp the meaning of a universal spirit, and this in its most relevant sense, we need to eschew all prospect of it in any cooperative guise; otherwise it would not be distinctive or unique as precisely the concept it is. And of course, this is why we might take issue with some more orthodox accounts, since the general aim has been to reach some middle ground that connects the large and the small, or the eternal and the evanescent. There is for instance the belief that what is universal is what is common to the human and divine, that we can ascend from the former to the latter or return from there to our more humdrum and modest way of life. The soul in this case is not something contained in the body but rather encompassing of the body, be it active or supine. It is therefore an interior force if looked at from the viewpoint of any object and an exterior force if looked at from the viewpoint of the universe as a whole (pantheism). Not only that, but what we mean by the universe is a living entity, not something that has arisen in any purely ad hoc way, rather, through an act of generation, so that there is preformation in the case of members as well as maturation in the course of time. (Bruno)

The kind of duality implied in such a model however is by no means coherent or clear, since there is a considerable difference between any 'mother spirit' to which there might be a return, and that tendency which all things have to divide and self-destruct. In the one case what we mean by divine unity is something inherently simple, the wish of any individual to be stripped of its physical accoutrements. In the case of the other, and where it is matter not form that is the superintendent agent, there will always be a tendency for things to sunder and fall apart and hence to dissolve and come to rest. But if there is a 'natural' order of things and this is rooted in our senses, then there will always be a mixing and a mingling of opposites, of the light and the shade, of the painful and the pleasurable, of the bitter and the sweet. In order to be embracing and not dismissive of this fact we must always fit the object to the means, the means of being joyful to the end of being mournful, the means of being venturesome to the end of being cautious and the means of being excitable to the end of being insouciant. The intermediary between the most spirited of beings and the most malevolent of beings is not something that is absent but rather present in them both. Therefore, to achieve greater mastery is not to abandon but rather embrace what is degrading in oneself, just as, to become saintlier is to embrace and not abandon what is devilish in oneself.

Such a position however is very much at odds with that conception of virtue which is strictly a *mean* between two extremes (Aristotle). Courage for instance may be regarded as a mean between timidity and recklessness because it avoids these two extremes, temperance is a mean between insensibility and promiscuity because it is neither insensible nor promiscuous, reasonable self-love is neither humble nor boastful. The kind of ethic we are dealing with here is certainly more austere and more demanding, the individual is admonished not to give in to purely corporeal desires but to stick to his ideals, to practice self-denial and self-control no matter what the consequences this may incur.

To return however to the question how the parts of a living universe could be said to be mirrored in the parts of any body, be it living or be it dead, then this is very much a matter for debate. Of course, it is true as we have already argued, that there may be a certain association in the context of what is simply mimetic (e.g. a flock of starlings), but this is much easier to envisage than when what we are dealing with is *both* a separated part and an integrated whole. The problem that we have here is as follows. It is easy enough to grasp how a part that is simple may reflect what is homogeneous as a whole, but it is not nearly so easy to grasp how a whole that is complex may reflect what is both qualitatively and quantitatively quite diverse. In other words, however we view the universe, either it is susceptible of certain descriptions in the form of the one or the form of the other, but it cannot be both. Not only that, but by creating a different order for the divine will the soul may be encouraged to throw off all bodily ties, to free itself from injury and disease, and yet at another level, cling to what is carnal and any means that may be supportive of just this end.

The question that might then well be asked is this: How can we conceive of a universal spirit if we do not suppose that it has something specific or unific as its end? Perhaps we might suggest that it is either specific or non-specific, but only the latter when it is a question of its origin and the former when it is a question of its end. In the first place, let us consider what it is that is binding on all men, what is common to our species or what is meant by a collective sense of being. The fact that the dreams of all men and the cultures of all times are replete with general themes (Jung), that there are common elements in both our legends and our myths, that so much of our divining is centered around the stars—all this points to a common store of symbols, to a shared inheritance, and no matter what the time or place. What therefore we mean by 'the unconscious' is not a dumping ground for all our unwanted fears, rather, it is a *collective past* that connects us with a living present and heightens the sense of who and what we are. There is therefore a basic or pre-psychic form to which our everyday experiences can attest, an instinctive mechanism that exists at all levels, from the most rudimentary to the most complete and perfected. How and in what way the Galapagos turtle returns to its breeding ground, how and in what way the bee signals danger, and how and in what way the peacock raises its tail—all this evinces a high degree of efficiency and what is tending to the conservation of the whole

What we might mean by a collective unconscious however is very different from what we might mean by the unconscious in its normal acceptation, since the former has none of those negative connotations so often connected with the latter. At the supra personal level, there is no such thing as a 'forfeiture' of the past or a 'forgetting' of the past, no such distinction with respect to a practised forgetting (repression) and a clinical forgetting (amnesia). Rather, there is only the most enormous store of images and ideas, everything from the most commodious to the most dysfunctional, from the most hallowed to the most profane, from the most venerated to the most despised. And yet despite the absence of any real forgetting, there is nonetheless a double aspect to this, or at least, so far as there is both a source of change that impacts positively and a source of change that impacts negatively on our lives. This we have touched one elsewhere in the comparison of a good and bad effect; the problem of good and better effects is the necessity of greater and more everlasting gains, and the problem of bad and worse effects is the necessity of greater and more everlasting guilt. The former concerns that transformative power that exists in each and every one of our living symbols and which enables us to reinterpret the past in the light of our present demands. So far however as there is a 'taking on' of the past must there also be a reckoning *for* what is past, that is, a willingness not only to accept credit for our achievements but to take responsibility for our own mistakes. In the one case our response consists in a certain use or availing of the past, and in the other a certain respect and fidelity towards the past. What is requisite therefore is an adjustment between two things—between the debt that is owing our forebears for the good that has been ceded us, and an engagement with the past so far as this may be useful to our present set of needs.

As for the meaning of universality as what is specific to such and such an end, we need to approach this through a comparison of two quite specialized forms: what we have called a monad on the one hand and a modeme on the other. There are several key features that distinguish a monad from a modeme, but they are basically (*a*) the sense in which the latter is the *cause* of its own activity whereas the former is not and (*b*) the sense in which the latter is in communion with the past but the former, only pregnant with the future. Let us consider this in a little more detail. A monad is something that has a degree of spontaneity, but this is not complete spontaneity, since although it is free in itself, it must yet conform to any force that is imposed from without. That is, it obeys its own laws, the laws of good and evil, but this is not to say it is indifferent to the general laws that govern the behaviour of all things. So far as there is a point of agreement for these immanent and efficient causes, this concerns only their *origin* and not their end, since the end of the latter (efficiency) is simply the conservation of force (the principle of conservation), just as the end of the former (wisdom) is simply the conservation of justice (the principle of equity). They are nonetheless as one in their origin and that is the kind of development that governs them both (not however the kind of moral development that concerns a collective unconscious). The soul may exhibit a certain spontaneity in its appetites and in its stirrings, but that is not to say it is the source of its own activity, otherwise, as a simple representation, it must also be *productive* of everything that exists in the aggregate. The soul however can only anticipate certain changes, it cannot *create* them—ultimately does this redound to the cause and the author of our being. A modeme on the other hand is something that contains the very source of its own activity, since it is unregulated but nonetheless inventive as a means. (That is, not unregulated with respect to an origin but unregulated with respect to an end, the *neutral* outcome thus being the conservation of opposing forces.) This we have already dealt with in comparing what is 'ordered' and what is 'disordered', what is 'functioning' and what is 'functionless' (Chapters 3 & 4).

With respect to the other major point, consider the implication of the idea that any change in the microcosm must be matched by a change in the macrocosm, or that if there is a certain 'natural' development within the whole this must be matched by any development within the parts. If there is a certain 'natural' transition from the present to the future but not the present to the past, then what else can this mean if not that the present is *implicit* in the past, just as the future is *implicit* in the present. On the other hand, when we say that the present is *big* with the past, then what this means is something altogether different, not a 'natural' unfurling or unravelling of the past but a constant interaction and collaboration *with* the past. A psyche that is selective and yet not censorial is a psyche that is at one with itself—it is able to take us from a reformation of the past to a recreation of the past, and from a sense of shame at our own misdemeanours to a sense of contentment and thankfulness for precisely that which is ours.